Lives with Autism

Edited by Dr Steve Mee

Other books from M&K include

Valuing People with a Learning Disability
ISBN: 9781905539666

The Occupational Therapy Handbook: Practice Education
ISBN: 9781905539758

The Primary Care Guide to Mental Health
ISBN: 9781905539109

Lives with Autism

Edited by Dr Steve Mee

Lives with Autism

Steve Mee

ISBN: 9781905539-84-0

First published 2014

British Library Catalogue in Publication Data
A catalogue record for this book is available from the British Library

Notice

Clinical practice and medical knowledge constantly evolve. Standard safety precautions must be followed, but, as knowledge is broadened by research, changes in practice, treatment and drug therapy may become necessary or appropriate. Readers must check the most current product information provided by the manufacturer of each drug to be administered and verify the dosages and correct administration, as well as contraindications. It is the responsibility of the practitioner, utilising the experience and knowledge of the patient, to determine dosages and the best treatment for each individual patient. Any brands mentioned in this book are as examples only and are not endorsed by the Publisher. Neither the publisher nor the authors assume any liability for any injury and/or damage to persons or property arising from this publication.

Disclaimer

M&K Publishing cannot accept responsibility for the contents of any linked website or online resource. The existence of a link does not imply any endorsement or recommendation of the organisation or the information or views which may be expressed in any linked website or online resource. We cannot guarantee that these links will operate consistently and we have no control over the availability of linked pages.

The Publisher

To contact M&K Publishing write to:
M&K Update Ltd · The Old Bakery · St. John's Street · Keswick · Cumbria CA12 5AS
Tel: 01768 773030 · Fax: 01768 781099
publishing@mkupdate.co.uk
www.mkupdate.co.uk

Designed and typeset by Mary Blood
Printed in England by H&H Reeds Printers, Penrith

Contents

Acknowledgements

To the people with autism who have opened my eyes to the possibility of there being another way to be.

To all the authors in this book, who have so generously given their stories, often at considerable cost to themselves. Some of them found sharing their stories a traumatic experience and yet they willingly took part.

To Kate Mee for interviewing for and co-writing two chapters.

To the people who told me a story of their experiences which was truly shocking. We are not able to include this chapter for legal reasons.

To the National Autistic Society for 14 years of partnership delivering our joint module, and for help in creating the environment in which many of these chapters were first written. Many individuals have made contributions, including Luke Beardon, Chris Barson, Steve Owens, Lynn Tidmarsh, Lorraine McCallister and Mandy Rutter. My apologies to anyone who has been inadvertently omitted.

The University of Cumbria continues to support staff by giving scholarly time. I could not have edited this book without that support.

To Mike Roberts (M&K Update Publishing) for commissioning the book, Kelly Davis for copy-editing, Mary Blood for her work on the design and Fliss Watts for proofreading.

To Hazel for her patience and willing ear.

Dedicated to Hazel and Kate

Introduction

"The thing about autism, if you suffer from it, is that you can't tell the difference between yourself and someone who doesn't. You can't think any other way. You only have one perspective, and from your perspective you can't tell that anything's wrong. Other people say you've got it. You're different. There's something wrong with you. They give you this label. There's nothing you can do about it. It doesn't matter what your perceptions about yourself are; it's other people who define you. I wouldn't know I was autistic if people didn't tell me I was. So it's not what *I* think that's important; it's what other people think. No matter how much you hate it, no matter how much you try to change yourself, it doesn't go away. It's like the scars left by a hot iron brand; you can't run and you can't hide. You're autistic and there is absolutely nothing you can do. You have no idea how soul crushing that is."

This is how an 18-year-old A-level student, Christopher, sees his autism (his full account is in Chapter 7 of this book). There is something stark about the way he compares the 'autism label' to 'the scars left by a hot iron'. He feels that being labelled in this way is like being branded and left with a lifelong scar. In the town where I live, convicted prisoners used to be branded so that they could be easily identified in the future. Likewise, slaves were branded to denote ownership. Christopher says this label has given him a lasting mark, from which he can't run or hide.

He suggests that autism is not something he recognises in himself; rather it is something visited on him. Someone else has identified him as something he does not recognise. It is always there. He thinks there is nothing he can do about it. Other people determine what will be, and he feels helpless. It is not the autism that is a problem – it is the professionals who apply the label. It is not his own perception of self that defines him; it is the perceptions others have of him. He thinks he 'suffers' from autism and yet he does not think that there is anything 'wrong'; he is just himself. This is a powerful description of alienation from self and others. This is Christopher's story.

What is *my* story, as the person who has gathered together the personal accounts in this book? I am a neurotypical; nothing special, just another example of the majority of the population. We neurotypical professionals are trained to identify the ways in which those we label 'autistic' are pathologically different. We supposedly become 'experts' and receive a professional salary in return. Most of us try to do our best for our 'clients'. Yet assessment, the procedure we are paid to carry out, feels like a scar from a hot iron to Christopher. It hurts him and perhaps others like him. Our actions have contributed to a deep sense of alienation. None of us have set out to have this effect, and yet it seems to have been the consequence of our actions – at least sometimes. On the other hand, all the parents who have written in this book say that getting the label for their child was a positive step. It is like negotiating a minefield. What are we to do?

As the Autism Programme Leader at the University of Cumbria, I have been engaged with autism for the past 13 years. During this time, there has been a rapid increase in the number of books and articles on the subject, reflecting a rapid growth in knowledge about autism. Yet, despite being familiar with the literature, I find that personal testimonies such as Christopher's provide a different, more profound, understanding of what it really means. Academic literature can define autism in a way that is often clinical and pathology-orientated, whereas personal testimony can tell us, in vivid colours, what it is *like*. It can also give us an insight into how our interventions make people *feel*. This book offers a collection of narratives from people whose lives are touched by autism. The challenge for the practitioner is to listen deeply to what is being said.

All the chapters in this book contain personal accounts from people touched by autism. The stories are mostly told 'straight', with little added analysis. Three chapters offer reflections from professionals but for the rest it is for you, the reader, to carry out your own reflection and analysis. For me, these stories offer the chance to think and learn in a 'slow-burn' way.

Many of the authors describe professional practice that is damaging and misses the mark entirely. It might be argued that the narrative created by a professional is very different from, and sometimes even counter to, the narrative of a person living with autism. The accounts in this book offer readers the opportunity to engage with the viewpoints of people with experience of autism and reflexively incorporate them into their professional narratives. There is no intention here to develop a discussion on narrative processes but, for those who are interested, a good account can be found in Frank (1995).

This approach might feel alien to many professionals who are used to reading academic and professional guidance literature. For example, this book has a fairly short bibliography because there are not that many references to list. It is all about personal narratives from people whose lives are directly touched by the day-to-day realities of autism. The contributions are not from academic experts – they are from people whose expertise comes from experience.

A personal narrative

During my time as Autism Programme Leader, I have met, and befriended, many people with autism and their families. Through listening to their stories, I have had many moments of profound challenge and insight. Some of these insights are described in the following pages, as a book about narrative should also include some of the editor's narrative. It would be dishonest to claim that my role is entirely neutral. I chose the stories in the book and this selection was partly influenced by how each person's story resonated with me.

Before sharing some personal insights, I will briefly explain my use of language. The term 'on the autism spectrum' is commonly used by professionals and authors but I know few people who use it when discussing themselves or family members. The author of one chapter refers to himself as having an 'autistic spectrum condition'. Christopher, in the quotation at the start of this chapter, calls himself 'autistic'.

Two other authors in this book choose this term unprompted. One author is very clear about asserting that this is what he prefers to be called. He sees himself as categorically different from neurotypicals – in fact a different species. This is not, of course, biologically accurate, but it gives a good sense of how he sees himself. He states that he is offended if people say he 'has' autism and that it is like being called 'coloured' rather than 'black', or like being described as 'having gayness' rather than 'being gay'. He thinks that autism is the thing that sets him apart and biologically defines him.

Three of the authors use the term 'Aspergian' to define themselves. This is a term that tends to evoke a negative response from some professionals. It might be interesting to explore why this is the case, but – whatever the reason – neurotypical professionals seem to retain control over labels. This may come as no surprise while we continue to pathologise autism and so apply diagnostic labels. Perhaps the phenomenon of people with autism using arguably derogatory labels is similar to that of gay people appropriating words such as 'queer' and 'dyke' or black groups appropriating the 'N' word (as a white man, I do not have authority to write the actual word). I have attempted to limit my own reference to the label but where necessary I have used the phrase 'has autism'.

We neurotypicals describe people with autism as having a triad of impairments, which most people reading this book will probably have learned off by heart. I have assumed that most readers will be able to understand and define the main terms used when discussing autism. Anyone not sure about the more 'technical' aspects of autism will need to look elsewhere. There are many excellent textbooks available, and the National Autistic Society website is a good source of authoritative information.

The triad of impairment is the basis of autism diagnosis. One aspect of this well-known triad is impairment of imagination. Yet the quotation at the start of this introduction seems to demonstrate that Christopher, a man labelled as being on the autism spectrum, has a rich imagination. Seeing a label as a scar from a branding iron is, after all, a very powerful mental image.

On the contrary, perhaps it is neurotypicality that can sometimes be a barrier to truly perceiving the world. As a neurotypical, I never really 'got' the enormity of this issue before reading Christopher's account; so it appears that it was *me* who had the impaired imagination. Another author in this book agrees with this point, arguing that it is indeed the neurotypicals who have impairment of imagination. He describes having to use his imagination every day to attempt to fit into a neurotypical world, most of which is not suited to his needs or worldview. He believes that neurotypicals seldom use imagination when attempting to understand *his* world. This book is an attempt to help generate such understanding.

A second aspect of the triad of impairments involves communication. In assessing and labelling people, we decide that some individuals have impairment in communication. Yet one author has told me that when he is with other autistic (his term) people, he never experiences problems in communication. It is only when he tries to communicate with neurotypicals that he struggles. He and others who have contributed to this book find the way neurotypical people express themselves very vague and imprecise. Apparently the neurotypical impairment is in precise communication. As one person with autism said to me, 'Why can't you bloody neurotypicals ever say what you mean? What is wrong with you?'

As we all know, half of communication is listening. People with autism have told me on numerous occasions that neurotypicals often do not listen; we have an impairment in this area too. One of the authors in this book gave me an accolade that meant a lot: she described me as 'an honorary aspi', adding that 'for a neurotypical, you are not too bad at listening'. Perhaps we can all learn to listen, but not always as 'professionals', with our tendency to interpret and analyse. We can listen in an open-minded way, to truly hear and attempt to understand. I hope this is how readers will approach this book. Christine Mayer, a woman with a learning disability, explains how she wants us to listen:

If you are going to work with me, you have to listen to me.

And you can't just listen with your ears, because it will go to your head too fast. If you listen slow, with your whole body, some of what I say will enter your heart.
(Quoted in O'Brien *et al.* 1998, p.71)

We can try to read in a subjective way, rather than the objective way that becomes the 'default setting' for so many of us who are engaged in professional practice. Perhaps by reflecting on our default professional responses we can give ourselves a chance to develop empathy. Rather than reading through a 'how can I intervene?' lens, we might look through a 'how might this feel?' lens. If we attempt to understand as fellow human beings, we might avoid some of the common neurotypical pitfalls. Understanding what it is like to live with autism, in all its nuanced detail, seems to me to be essential for practitioners. Perhaps the most important point is to understand how our interventions and interactions can impact on the people we claim to support.

One of the contributors to this book makes two observations about the triad of impairments. Firstly, he states that the notion of 'impairment' is wrong in this context. He believes that 'difference' is a more appropriate idea, that neurotypicals and autistics (his preferred term) are, to all practical purposes, essentially different species. This difference only becomes impairment when the neurotypical majority make no attempt to accommodate that difference. Those readers who know about the social model of disability will be familiar with this concept. In other words, it makes no sense to him that people on the autism spectrum are said to have an impairment in imagination, when his experience is that most neurotypicals appear unable to comprehend what his life is like. The only times in his life when he has been harmed have been when he has been in contact with a neurotypical. He says that, on these occasions, the perpetrators appeared to have little idea of what they had done.

I have reflected on these points and considered the views sometimes expressed by people on our autism course or in practice and think that I understand what this contributor means. I have come across many examples of course participants who have demonstrated an impairment of understanding when describing their practice. One teacher thought a pupil having a meltdown was 'being attention-seeking'. A support worker thought the person they supported would 'get used to' the noise in the supermarket. One social worker thought a family 'enjoyed complaining'. A psychologist stereotyped according to the label she had given, and pathologised an individual's love of twiddling paper. A consultant said he was sometimes reluctant to give a diagnosis to desperate parents because he thought 'autism was a trend'.

These are just a few examples – there are many more. Each of these individuals appears to be imposing their own neurotypical perspective on the world of the person with autism in their life. Some of the stories in this book describe times when professional responses like these have caused serious problems for people with autism and their families.

The use of stories

This book is based upon the assumption that, as professionals, we can learn from stories and modify our practice accordingly. This might be challenging for some readers who adhere to the current orthodoxy of evidence-based practice. Can stories ever be perceived as 'evidence'?

As Autism Programme Leader, I have been in the remarkably privileged position of reading hundreds of assignments describing professional practice and life with autism from all over the country. The struggle of professionals attempting to do their best in difficult circumstances produces, for me, a real sense of practice community. A popular feature of the course is the sharing of accounts from practice. These narratives appear to offer the potential for deep cognitive learning. A particular example of learning and fundamental change in practice as a result of narrative is illustrated by the following story (first described in Mee 2012).

Spiderman

John is a boy who is on the autism spectrum. One day John's mother was talking on the telephone to a friend. She told her friend that a story had recently appeared in the newspapers, saying that since the tragedy of 9/11 the makers of *Spiderman 1* had removed the World Trade Centre towers from the film, using computer technology. John overheard his mother and was very upset when she hung up.

He asked his mother why she had lied. Mum assured him that it was true. He insisted it was not and took her to the TV and put the *Spiderman 1* video on. He fast-forwarded the film to the exact point at which Spiderman emerges from the underground and scans the streets. The shot shows a close-up of his face and, for a fleeting moment, there is a reflection of the skyline in the black eyes on his mask. In that moment the twin towers can be seen in the reflection; the film-makers had missed it. John had found it immediately. It should be noted that he did not watch *Spiderman* in an obsessive way; it was just one of the films he had which he watched from time to time.

This is an account of an everyday experience that is typical for many people with autism. John experiences the world in a way that is incomprehensible to others. Tiny details that would typically go unnoticed by a neurotypical can overwhelm people who are on the spectrum. In this case, the boy had noticed something apparently unremarkable and was able to recall that detail easily.

This story was told on the autism course and led to a significant change in the support offered to Sarah, a woman with a learning disability, diagnosed with autism. She was thought to need three care staff most of the time because of her extremely challenging behaviour. The care plan included input from a range of specialists. The situation had remained static for a long time and the manager of this service felt 'stuck'.

Then she heard the 'Spiderman' story and was struck by it. She already knew the facts about hypersensitivity but the story helped her to realise the all-pervading nature of this difference, and how it applied all day, every day, every minute, to every sense, and every detail. Sensory overload is not just overwhelming; it means being drowned in detail, with no escape and no means of switching off. Some of that detail might cause overwhelming nausea, pain or some other unpleasant sensation. She wondered whether the woman she was supporting was experiencing the world in this way.

The manager decided to sit in the woman's chair for several hours, and try to imagine herself into her world, to see the world as she might. The manager reported that it was difficult to remain in this mindset, a different sort of 'discipline' to that usually suggested by research literature. It was like seeing a new world. She noticed the noise of outside traffic, the clutter in the room, the patterns on the carpet, the decorations on the wall, the ornaments on the shelves, the noise from the corridor, the slamming of doors, the way the staff chatted to each other, the bright contrasting colours of staff clothing, their bright dangling jewellery, the smell of garlic on the staff, the radio, and the list went on.

As a result, she drew up new guidelines. Staff were to wear subdued pastel-coloured clothes, to avoid garlic before coming on duty and to avoid chatting over Sarah's head. The clutter was reduced and soundproof curtains put up. The manager tried to change all the things that she had observed. She reported an immediate and drastic reduction in Sarah's challenging behaviour. The interesting aspect of this was that the manager had previously known the 'facts' about sensory difference for people on the autism spectrum but she now knew them in a different way.

Prior to this, there was a good knowledge base and a multidisciplinary team to plan care. There was plenty of motivation to come up with an effective care plan because people were being hurt as a result of the challenging behaviour, and there was a huge cost to the service. Nevertheless, in a six-week course, hearing the 'Spiderman' story was the critical point at which a cognitive shift took place. This event was the focus of this manager's essay.

As well as including accounts from people with autism, this course has also been attended by a significant number of students with autism and their relatives. This has always seemed odd to me; surely *they* are the true experts? Yet, when asked why they attend a course that they should really be teaching, they usually say something along the lines of 'I need a paper qualification to get the professionals to take me seriously'. This is a real indictment of some professional behaviour.

I have learned some profound lessons through marking essays describing the lived experiences of people with autism who have attended the course. Some of these stories have caused me to rethink previously held beliefs about autism. Some are shocking and scarcely believable. Some retain their power to shock many years after being first read. Stories from these essays form some of the chapters in this book. Others chapters are from people whose paths have crossed mine and whose stories have had an impact. All except two of the accounts in this book are from people on the autism spectrum, or their siblings or parents. In some cases the authors fall into more than one category – for example, being both a parent of a person with autism and having autism themselves.

My aim in presenting these stories is to give the reader a chance to reflect on the realities of life for the writers. I hope the stories will prove easy to read, being free of lengthy footnotes, references and other conventional academic trappings. These are true stories and it is hoped that practitioners will read them slowly, allowing themselves time to reflect on what life with autism might really be like.

KatyLou, one of the mothers who writes in this book, describes the sort of professional support that it is helpful, and the sort that is not:

...[the best professionals are those] who try to understand what it's like in a parent's shoes and even more importantly talk to parents on equal terms, not as experts doling out expertise, but simply people helping people, no matter how wonderfully knowledgeable they are. But the ones who will to me be forever memorable, for how they failed us, are no doubt continuing to look down on the rest of us from the ivory towers of their very questionable expertise.

This book provides a series of personal stories, rather than a battery of professional tools. Slow reading of these accounts should offer insights similar to the one gained by the service manager who heard the 'Spiderman' story. Testimonies like this one can highlight ways of being more useful as 'people helping people'. All these stories have touched me in one way or another. I hope they will touch you too.

The authors

The following chapters are in the words of the people who own the stories. The writing is an eclectic mix, with a range of styles, lengths and core themes. Some were written by the person themselves; others were told to me, or to Kate Mee, and then transcribed. One is a series of email communications. Some are shocking, some focus on everyday matters, and others may appear strange. The stories are from very individual perspectives, and if all the authors were in a room together it is unlikely that they would agree on many issues. In fact, friendships between some of the authors have become strained due to differences in opinion.

My aim in presenting these accounts is that they should remain authentic, so there have been few attempts to mediate their core messages or edit the content. This offers the reader the opportunity of a secondary level of learning that is beyond the story in the narrative. For example, some of the accounts express the deep anger felt by the writer and there is little attempt to rein in the emotion. Some of the stories are presented in great detail, whereas a neurotypical account might have taken the form of a shorter summary. This can be seen as another way of attempting to stand in someone else's shoes, to understand the world as they see it. I made this selection from a wide range of stories; the decision was based on which struck me as resonant. Each chapter has a very individual voice and I considered it important that the stories should be told in the voice chosen by the narrator.

I believe that becoming aware of very differing life experiences and perspectives on autism can help us become more effective professionals. They can enable us to move beyond simple stereotypes, which might lead us to conclude that 'autism is like this'. The experience of autism is obviously individual and so each story is unique. Yet there *are* some universal themes, and each reader will be struck by particular themes that resonate with their own experiences and understanding. The concluding chapter includes some of my own reflections on the impact of these stories.

Each chapter starts with a brief introduction and ends with some reflections written by me. I had originally intended to let the chapters stand alone but it was suggested by neurotypical reviewers that some guidance for the neurotypical reader would be useful. The introduction to each chapter therefore gives some indication of the origin of the account, and the conclusion offers some personal reflections on practice based on the themes in the chapter. Of course that are many other themes in each chapter and I hope the reader will reflect on whatever aspects have resonance for them. If some readers decide to ignore my introductions and reflections, perhaps little will be lost.

Each author has chosen whether to use their own name or a pseudonym. A similar decision has also been made where family members are concerned. Each author has also decided whether or not to name particular places.

Section 1

Three women getting on with their lives

1
A person with autism

Julia Clifford

Julia is a woman with autism. She has generously shared this account of her life, which she had already written with a view to publication. She offers some vivid detail about her day-to-day life. For example, when describing her literal understanding of the world she tells us:

> "Whenever I pass an estate agent's, there are always notices saying: 'Your home is at risk if you don't keep up payments on your mortgage'. I always have visions of people's homes being destroyed by meteorites if the home owner goes into arrears. I often have this urge to say to estate agents 'in reality the home isn't at risk; all that is at risk is the people's ownership of it'."

Julia's account might well prompt us to question why neurotypical professionals describe people with autism as having 'impairment of imagination'.

Introduction

It may seem bizarre to many people that I genuinely hoped my sisters were correct when they told me they thought that I might be autistic, but it can be reassuring for an individual to know that their condition can be and has been properly identified. I was relieved when a doctor confirmed their suspicions, as autism fits my symptoms and my behaviour extremely well. I am writing this chapter as a way of exploring and trying to understand my autism.

Social skills

First and foremost, I looked up the meaning of the word 'society' in a dictionary. The definition it gave was: 'fellowship, company or a body of persons united for the same object'.

The problem with autistic people is that the way their brains have been wired means they have a poor concept regarding the laws governing how the other members of human society work. Those who are on the autistic spectrum have their own personal set of rules and regulations, which are often more than a little out of step with their contemporaries. To be autistic is to have a problem with other people, dealing with their reactions and interpreting the human environment in which we all have to live.

The word 'autism' comes from the Greek word autos, meaning 'self'. Autistic people have a fundamental problem with themselves. They cannot help sometimes coming across as totally egocentric. They are very good at pursuing their own personal agenda and often don't realise that they are doing this and don't fully appreciate the impact it might have on others. They may come across as lacking in empathy. They are the world's loners, many of whom lack the ability to make friends or establish 'normal' relationships. But 'no man is an island, entire of itself' (John Donne).

However, in many situations when they are by themselves they don't always feel lonely. They often enjoy the pleasure of their own company and find other ways to compensate for their lack of human companionship.

It is not that autists don't care about others; neither is it a case of them being unwilling or unable to make a positive contribution to society. The real problem they face is that when they try to make a positive contribution to society they often handle it in the wrong way. They need a great deal of direction and help with this issue.

Those on the autistic spectrum often don't hate their fellow human beings. It is actually the behaviour of those who respond negatively to their needs that autistic people have a problem coping with. When it comes to the crunch, some autistic people are very good Christians who understand the need to forgive others who wrong them! Unfortunately the non-autistic members of society don't often realise their need to ask forgiveness from the autistic people they may have hurt, albeit unintentionally. Autistic people are often exceptionally vulnerable and they are often put into situations with people who are quick to exploit them. But autistic people should bear in mind that they too may be guilty of not apologising to those whom they may have harmed as a result of their behaviour and inability to understand the needs of others.

Examples of problems with relationships

As a child, I had huge difficulty mixing with others and making friends with children my own age, at school, at Church and in the Brownies. This often resulted in me being left to my own devices. I was often happier and more at ease with the adults at Church than the other children. I was on friendlier terms with a lot of the Sunday School teachers, the clergy and the old ladies/men. As an adult, I would say that I prefer the company of people who have a clear 'role'.

At school, I was accused by a 'friend' of using people. I am sure that I probably do. It's not done with deliberate malice but it is more like an automatic reflex. For example, as a child I made friends with a family of girls, not because of their personalities, but because they all had bikes that I could use. My main interest in another friend had nothing to do with his personality but the fact that he owned a computer that I needed to use. I have this lifelong tendency to get other people to do jobs for me – if I am too nervous about handling them myself. Because these are people I regard as my friends, I can get angry and annoyed if they have valid reasons (and sometimes reasons which I don't think are so valid) for not wanting to get involved in the way I wanted them to. Although it has taken me a good few years to work out this phrase, I now tell people that 'I very nearly lost my life, very nearly lost my home and ended up living inside a Nazi state because too few people made appropriate phone calls on my behalf!'

I have a problem with eye contact. My school friends thought I was deaf because I tended to look at their mouths instead of their eyes – as if I was lip reading. Plus, on many occasions, I have problems working out whether I am being addressed or someone else is. A priest who helped me with my lay reader training said that I had a problem engaging with people. Even now I often look at people's hands, the floor or the ceiling when I am engaging in conversation. I am very good at telling which people are married or engaged because I can tell by the rings on their hands.

I find it difficult to take an active interest in other people's hobbies. The last time I got taken to the British Museum, I just sat reading a book. I was once taken to the Oval to watch a cricket match. I just read one of my books throughout the whole match. Much to the embarrassment of my brother and sister, I started cheering when the game got rained off. My family, all of whom like flowers, were buying flowers for my wedding. I showed no interest in this particular procedure and was extremely bored by the whole experience.

My manner can be aloof. I am very good at cutting out people completely, particularly if I feel they have upset or pushed me too far. I love being on my own a lot. I adore my privacy. Even as a small child, I was more than happy to play by myself. At the age of 11, I was overjoyed to be given my own bedroom and spent abnormally long periods of time by myself in my room. I don't like unexpected visitors or interruptions, and I love finding valid reasons for not having visitors. As long as I am well, I seldom feel lonely. I have what I would call 'a fortress mentality'. I am very happy to sit on my own in cafés, pubs and libraries.

Examples of when I come across as lacking empathy

In a letter to Social Services, my sister Anne mentioned the way I have a problem with empathy, saying that I was prepared to cause chaos and havoc regardless of the cost to others. I did not agree with the way she expressed this view. It is just that in my case it takes a long time to work out how my behaviour is going to impact on others, even though I work hard at this issue and have done for many years. I have no intention of showing deliberate malice or indifference. I find it very hard to demonstrate my feelings. I often feel that when people have hurt me, their suffering is self-inflicted.

When Mary, my younger sister, started learning to write – without fully understanding what she was writing, she wrote a message that I had dictated to her: 'Mary is a very silly little girl'. Feeling it was great achievement, she showed it to Mummy and Daddy. Once when I was at secondary school I made a comment about a friend who had been off sick a lot: 'Hasn't she died yet!' Understandably, my other friends were disgusted and shocked. On another occasion at home, I said: 'I don't know about the starving millions of Belsen but I wish Mummy would hurry up with our lunch!' Daddy said it was wrong of me to make fun of the people who died there. I must confess I was trying to copy someone's style but as per usual I got it wrong. In hindsight, I must have been a horrible child on many occasions.

Personal hygiene, grooming problems and mobility problems

I often don't bother washing myself first thing in the morning when I get up, and have to be reminded to take a bath. I also forget to clean my teeth, or can't be bothered. I have a problem washing my bottom properly after I have opened my bowels. If I run out of toilet paper on occasions, instead of rushing out to buy more, I will just use J-cloths or something similar. My carers say this isn't a good idea.

I don't worry too much about wearing plastic gloves when I clean out the rabbits. I am quite happy to handle rabbit droppings using my bare hands. My nails get dirty easily from cleaning out the rabbits. I don't always wash them unless I am reminded to do so. During my teens, a very good friend of mine pointed out that if I ever hoped to get a decent boyfriend I should stop picking up rabbit droppings and just shoving them in my pocket.

I hate cutting my nails and always have done! I even hate it when other people try and cut my nails. The person whom I will tolerate doing this is the chiropodist.

I seldom worry about cleaning my glasses unless there is a piece of dirt on them obscuring my view. I often have to be reminded to clean my glasses.

To quote my friend Lyn, I am 'simply not domesticated'! My washing-up skills leave a lot to be desired. I like drinking black coffee because it is just the same drink over and over again. I may only wash my favourite beaker once a week. My carers aren't happy about this.

I am naturally very clumsy. It is easy for me to break ornaments and picture frames and to spill things. I easily fall over my feet. I have done this since childhood and I am very good at falling over things when I don't want to! I can't hold a pen properly. I never have been able to. I have what I think is called the 'palmar grip'. My handwriting is very distinctive.

15

Communication skills

'To cause to be common with other, to impart news and to share with others' – this is how my dictionary defines communication skills. However, autists could be described as 'uncommon people of society' (pardon me for being pedantic but 'common' is defined in my dictionary as 'usual or general'). Those who are on the autistic spectrum can't always share with others and there are many occasions when they don't want to, in the way that others want them to, and in the way that is generally regarded as acceptable by other members of society.

On the other hand, there are situations in which autists do need to share with others. When things go seriously wrong for them they can indeed feel alone, frightened, stigmatised by society, and in those situations they are often desperate to communicate their individual needs with other people.

Autists have a problem expressing their abstract thoughts or understanding other people's abstract thoughts. I can now see why I didn't always get brilliant marks in formal written exams is because so often the question ended with the word 'discuss'. In the heat of the moment, I usually interpreted this as 'write down everything you know about this particular subject'. In reality the word 'discuss' means that the candidate has to put forward an argument relating to specific requirements contained within the question.

Problems with having a literal mind and working out what other people really mean

When I was a Brownie I was told that we had to do one good turn a day. I took this phrase literally, meaning I only had to do one good turn, and only one. When I was about seven years old my mother asked me to wash up. I told her I couldn't because I had already done my good turn.

When I was about eight years old, a lady, who didn't know me very well, asked if I wished to 'spend a penny'. I thought it meant that she was going to take me to the sweet shop. I didn't realise until she explained it properly that what she really meant was 'Do you want to go to the toilet?'

When I was a child my dad worked at the British Museum. We had to go through a door that said 'STAFF ONLY'. But because I was genuinely allowed through this door, I told everyone I was obviously a member of staff.

On one occasion I got onto a bus and asked for a return ticket. The bus driver asked me where I wanted to go to and I just automatically said 'Here of course'.

I once bumped into my first social worker's vicar and he informed me that she had gone on sick leave. The vicar said the chances were that 'she would bounce back'. As my first social

16

worker was very rotund, I replied by saying she was the right shape to bounce back!

When one of my carers took me shopping and we brought the food back home, she asked me where I was going to put the food. I just replied by saying 'in my mouth'.

My family and me always think it is rather strange when square envelopes come through the letterbox with the words 'this is not a circular', as it seems that they are stating the obvious.

When I was in the St John's Ambulance during my school days I was amused to see that the sign in hospital that said 'LABOUR WARD' was written in blue, the colour of the Conservative Party.

Whenever I pass an estate agent's, there are always notices saying: 'Your home is at risk if you don't keep up payments on your mortgage'. I always have visions of people's homes being destroyed by meteorites if the home owner goes into arrears. I often have this urge to say to say to estate agents 'in reality the home isn't at risk; all that is at risk is the people's ownership of it'.

When I was still with my ex-husband, a couple of kids came round wanting 'a penny for the guy' just before Bonfire Night. So I went and gave them a penny. When my ex-husband asked me who had come to the door he wanted to know if I told the kids to go away and get lost. When I told him that I had given them a whole penny – no more, no less – he burst out laughing, saying that doing that was probably worse. When I explained this to Mummy, she too just laughed and said 'Our Julia has always had a literal mind.'

Examples of problems with expressing myself verbally

It is very hard for me to express my thoughts verbally. I struggle to get the correct words out of my mouth. I compensate for this by putting pen to paper and writing my thoughts down. I often have to prepare a script, either written or inside my head, before I have official or even unofficial conversations with people. This can include doctor's appointments. The best ploy I use for expressing my points verbally is changing the sentence structure so that the subject matter of the sentence becomes the first word I use, and I use it like a statement. For example:

'Meditation. Is that within your remit please?'

'Autism. I'm pretty sure that I am autistic.'

When my mental or physical health deteriorates, I can get frustrated and angry. I get bad-tempered if I feel I am not being understood properly, especially if I think that the person I am speaking to is being patronising, nasty or ignorant. I have often tried to explain to people that, even if they don't understand what I am saying to them, deep down inside I know the feelings I am trying to express. It is very easy for me to end up talking at cross-purposes and frankly it does make me cross!

I often have to rely on other people's words and quotations to express my abstract thoughts such as the Bible and the Prayer of St Francis of Assissi.

Examples of speaking on narrowly focused subjects

Rabbits/animals

I am good at talking about this subject and usually have deep meaningful conversations with people about this several times a day. I can discuss:

- Different species of rabbit
- How they behave in the wild
- How to interpret their body language
- Where they stand in the Carl Linnaeus system of nomenclature
- How they compare with hares
- Which breeds make the best pets
- How to understand their behaviour
- And the fact that rabbits have eternal souls.

The Holocaust and the life of Ann Frank

When I was 13 I talked obsessively about the life of Ann Frank; even my mother once commented that I was becoming too fixated on her. I can also provide a detailed accurate description of the vast majority of Nazi concentration camps/extermination camps and ghettos, which victims died where, and what happened to the perpetrators of the Holocaust.

When I was younger, before I got married, I developed a huge infatuation with someone to the point where it became overwhelmingly obsessive. Fortunately I am well and truly over it now, but I would talk about him obsessively to anyone whom I felt I could trust.

I can also talk obsessively about legal issues, history and theology.

Conversational skills

I am very good at having one-sided conversations with my friends, many of whom have been very good to me. They have had to listen to my problems and I often assume that they will be seriously interested in the difficulties in my personal life. Under the circumstances, it can be easy to go on and on about the challenges within my own life and to forget that they have lives of their own. My conversations can often come across as being very self-focused unless I am very careful about this issue. When things go wrong, very often I am not.

I am good at saying the wrong thing, especially when I am angry or stressed. My social worker says that when I am stressed I can be very impulsive, especially about saying the wrong thing. I am also good at muddling up my words.

Thinking style differences

My dictionary defines the word imagination as 'the faculty [i.e. the ability] with which we form a mental image or new combination of ideas'.

As for the word 'image', the best way to describe it is a representation of a person, thing, statue, picture or idea. Even words that come into a person's mind can be described as an image.

Autistic people usually have problems with imagination skills. This doesn't mean that they don't have imaginations but they think differently, and are often reliant on other people's thoughts, ideas, fantasies and experiences in order to build their own personal imagery. However, it does need to be remembered that those with autism have their own set of experiences relating to their own private world. But the problem with those on the autistic spectrum is that they can be very myopic (metaphorically speaking) and don't understand the correct way of using their past experiences to build up a better future for themselves.

One common experience in my life is that 'history often repeats itself'. It is very difficult for an autistic person to make the right connections in their mind regarding past events. They don't always understand that what they have experienced in the past and present can influence what happens in the future. They have serious problems using the information that they have gained from their past experiences in such a way that it can have a positive impact on their future.

It is impossible to change the past and it can be very difficult for people on the autistic spectrum to move on when things go wrong. But, with the correct level of help and guidance from professionals, even autistic people can learn to ensure that the mistakes that have occurred in the past – their own and other people's – don't necessarily have to be repeated. Instead they can look forward to happier events. One real problem those on the autistic spectrum face is that they benefit from living in their own 'comfort zones' and do not know how to cope if external events, including the actions of other people, threaten their comfort zones.

Love of routine and sameness

I have daily and weekly routines. I go through the same activities when I get up and in the evenings. Around 90 per cent of the time my routine is to ensure that I spend my evenings alone inside my house with only my pets for company. I like going to bed at roughly the same time each night and it can be much earlier than a lot of people. The main exceptions to this rule include watching my favourite television programmes or attending social or official appointments that I have no excuse for not going to, such as weddings or meetings.

My social life is also governed by routines. I always go to the same pubs/cafés. I hate it if people break their promises, including being late for, or cancelling appointments. When I read the 'Professor Branestawm' books at junior school, I remember the Professor saying that he always turned up for appointments exactly on time – not a second later, nor a second sooner. When I explained his technique to Mummy, she said that it was wrong to do that because the polite thing to do was to turn up at least 5 minutes beforehand.

I hate it when evening or day visitors upset my viewing habits. Even if the phone rings when I am watching Casualty, Holby City or one of my detective stories, I will usually tell the person to phone me later. I also feel nervous about watching new TV programmes and need a lot of encouragement before I am tempted to change my viewing habits. If I am involved in one of my solitary activities, which is very important to me personally, I get distressed or frustrated if I am interrupted.

When I first started school I couldn't cope with being there all day – Mummy dealt with this problem by allowing me to go home for lunch. This continued until the final year of primary school. The transition to secondary school was particularly difficult. It was the first time I had attended school without my sister. The other girls seemed to adapt a lot more quickly than I did. Secondary school involved dealing with a different set of teachers and a different set of girls. Because of my behavioural differences, I had problems making a new set of friends and often went about this totally the wrong way. The school building was a different style to my primary school and was often very cold. I can remember on the last day of term, when I had completed my first year at grammar school, I went home and vomited. The thought of going into a new classroom, having a new set of teachers (including a new form teacher), was more than my system could cope with.

I found it very difficult to adapt to life after full-time education. Moving into employment was a real challenge, and has been a life-long problem for me. When I first left school I found it very difficult to understand the aims and objectives of employers/employees, as they are often very different from the aims and objectives of school teachers and other pupils. Consequently I am far happier with the concept of self-employment.

Sometimes I have found it difficult coping with bodily changes – such as periods and the symptoms of illness. When I was about eight years old, I had a sudden growth spurt, which took some getting used to. I found it embarrassing developing breasts and it took a long time before I was convinced that it would be a good idea to wear a bra. I remember saying to my mother when I was about 11 years old that I would probably have had enough of life by the time I reached the age of 21 and really didn't know how to look beyond that. One useful thing about being infertile is that, although I did often think of having a baby I don't think I could have coped with all the changes and demands that are involved in child development. Children and their needs do change very quickly.

Impulsiveness

Autists don't always appreciate the need for forward planning. I have this problem and have been known to act impulsively. For example, I once turned up on the doorstep of a private nursing home, assuming they would be able to offer me instant respite care. The establishment had been mentioned as somewhere that could provide respite but this needed to be planned.

Concrete thinking

Dingbats is a board game that involves solving rebuses, puzzles in which a common word or saying is hidden in a cryptic or otherwise unique arrangement of symbols. Because of my concrete thinking, I've always hated playing this game. It relies on the type of abstract thinking skills I just don't have.

I am very interested in theology. In my twenties I developed a serious problem that proved to be a huge block to my faith. It was to do with my understanding of infinity and that God has no beginning and no end, and has just always been there. My friends were very patient with me and explained that God's infinity can be compared to a long toilet roll that has no end and no beginning.

Autistic people often see things in black and white. For instance, I automatically regard good people as those who are always kind and gentle with me; I feel it is wicked and cruel for people to lose their temper with me. I feel it is exceptionally wicked for people to accuse me of telling lies when I know I have been telling the truth. In the past I have always believed that I was the one who was in the right and that it was others who were wrong. I still often think that. But looking back, I know I haven't always been the easiest of people to get on with.

Working out what other people are thinking

I have already written about literal understanding, I take things literally because I don't always understand what the person meant or was thinking. It is also very difficult for me to work out if people are telling the truth or telling 'porkies' – I find sarcasm and some types of humour particularly difficult to understand.

A male friend who used to drive me to work took me to work one morning in a different car. He told me that he had just bought himself a new one. I automatically believed him. A few days later he was back in the old car and he told me that he was joking about treating himself to a new car; his old car had been in the garage for its MOT. I don't notice the changes to people's facial expression or body language when they are not telling the truth. I never do!

Details

I am very good at noticing things on the ground such as dead birds, other people's lost correspondence and broken manhole covers. I also tend to notice things out of the corner of my eye such as boxes of tissues, pictures and notices in pubs. Plus I am also good at noticing things in the sky!

Obsessions

I can become obsessively attached to things. For example, when I was in my teens I became very attached to a purple skirt. I carried on wearing it long after it had worn out, and it took a lot of persuasion from others before I would throw it away. I also had a very strong attachment to a wrist watch which my aunt had given me (it never worked while I owned it). On one occasion I had to take it off during a lesson. I was upset when I left it behind at school, but fortunately a very kind schoolteacher came and brought it round to our house.

As an adult I tend to hang on to my correspondence and paper work for years and years. I have an obsessive attachment to my books. Even if I have read them, I don't like to be parted from them and hate the thought of getting rid of them.

I have a particular interest in/obsession with journalism that began with writing stories, and I even began producing my own children's magazines by the age of seven or eight. These were called 'Daisy'. When I was a little older, I started writing poems, fictional stories and even writing about factual events in my own family and school life. At the age of 15, I had my first story published in the parish magazine. I now produce my own educational literature and have quite a few paying customers. Keeping Eleanor Claire Educational Services up and running has indeed proved a very positive obsession. I don't think it is ever going to make me rich but it does tide me over, especially during a financial emergency.

As can be seen from this example, some of my symptoms can genuinely be very useful, as they can enable me to develop positive hobbies that have led to the type of employment opportunities that I can cope with.

Information overload

Although in one sense I can be myopic (metaphorically speaking), in another sense I can be said to see more detail and remember more information than so-called normal people. This can lead to information overload. When I am experiencing information overload I can get anxious and frustrated, and at these times it is extremely difficult for me to express myself. My sleep patterns suffer. I find it harder to judge what is safe and what is dangerous.

Other difficulties

Motor skills and repetitive movements

I have hopeless body mapping. I can fall over and crash into things very easily. I have been known to fall out of the bath or to fall down stairs. However, the fact that I was taught balancing techniques has helped me. I learned these through ballroom dancing and ice-skating! If you stick out your arms like wings, it improves balance.

I went to both ballroom and Latin American dancing lessons when I was younger, though I was pretty hopeless. I was very stiff and one of my teachers complained that I walked on tiptoe a lot. When I was at school my younger sister used to laugh at the way I ran. She said my posture was very strange, in that I would run with my arms right by my side. I would clench my fists and all people could see were the soles of my feet.

For many years I have enjoyed sitting in the lotus position and just rocking from side to side. It can help calm me down. I especially enjoy rocking from side to side when I am listening to music. When I am listening to my favourite CDs I have developed my own 'dances' and movements. Please note I am not a very good dancer! I practise my own dances, wearing my roller skates – in front of a mirror.

Eating habits

When I was quite a young child, I found eating meals boring and a lot of the time I just didn't feel hungry. I find being thirsty much more difficult to cope with than being hungry.

As a child I was an extremely faddy eater. This problem has remained with me all my life. Foods I refused to eat as a child included ice-cream, blancmange and custard. Plus I hated eating stew. When I went to Girl Guide Camp, my mother gave the Guide Captain a list of

23

food I couldn't eat. She just said that I was allergic to them but in reality I probably wasn't!

In adulthood I was diagnosed with an atypical eating disorder. I started having it during my school days. I went through periods when I had an obsessive desire to lose weight. I would often throw my packed lunches away. I have carried on throwing food away during adulthood. There have been many occasions when I have been dangerously underweight and it has triggered dangerous levels of reactive hypoglycaemia. It is also worth mentioning that on Breakfast TV there was an item in which certain members of the medical profession said there was possibly a strong link between autism and anorexia.

I am prone to irritable bowel syndrome and on one occasion my GP recommended that I went on a gluten-free diet. This was when I was in my mid-twenties. Funnily enough, in a lot of the books I have read recently they have said that many autistic people benefit from gluten-free diets!

Sensory issues

I notice things out of the corner of my eyes, such as things that are at ground level, in the corner of the room or at sky level. During adolescence, I had a problem with eye contact and still do on occasions. I am also very good at concentrating on one section of a person's body. When I was at junior school, and earlier on at secondary school, I was very good at staring at other girls' feet as I was obsessively interested in the types of shoes they were wearing. I am still good at noticing people's shoes.

There are certain sounds I genuinely can't stand, such as the screeching of car brakes or the persistent crying of toddlers.

I have always had extremely funny skin. I have never tolerated the cold and I am extremely fussy about the type of clothes I wear. I am not keen on wearing jeans as it feels like being in a straitjacket. After returning home from school as a child, the first thing I wanted to do was always to remove my shoes and socks and walk about the house bare-footed.

Reflections

Julia thinks that neurotypicals should seek forgiveness from people with autism for the hurt they have caused, 'albeit unintentionally'. Do you think this is fair? Should you seek forgiveness?

Julia is happy to be by herself. She devises ways of excluding visitors from her life. Does the person with autism you support seek time alone? Do they have opportunities to be alone when they choose?

Neurotypical services often use terms like 'person on the autism spectrum'. Julia describes herself as 'an autist'. Should professional neurotypicals adopt the term used by the person with autism (or whatever is the appropriate term) or should we stick to our 'official' definitions? Does this mean that we are putting ourselves in the position of knowing best?

2
An Asperger marriage
Gay Eastoe

Gay takes an active role in many aspects of life. She has achieved many things, including a long-term marriage and raising four children. When her life is seen against a backdrop of significant autism effects, these achievements are very thought-provoking. Meeting Gay at an Autism Partnership Board caused me to reflect on what I thought I knew, and led to me asking her to contribute a chapter to this book.

Gay offers an account of marriage to a neurotypical man. They have raised four children who have now grown up and left home. She describes successfully negotiating a long marriage and a large family whilst struggling with her autism. She concludes:

> "We have shown that an 'Asperger Marriage' does work, as long as the neurotypical spouse is prepared to accept – in their entirety – the routines, rituals, social ineptness, special fields of interest, and fear of change that are critical for the Asperger spouse if 'meltdown' is to be avoided."

This account stresses the importance of accommodation. For example, Gay describes the issues presented by windows:

> "In our home I have a problem with doors and windows. I do not like any of them open. I do not like sitting where air is moving past me. If they have to be open for aeration the doors can only be open at less than a 45-degree angle and windows only slightly. Richard has solved this problem by opening doors and windows when I am out."

Before beginning the main narrative it is necessary to relate a little about myself. I am a twin (born in 1953) and my twin sister does not have Asperger Syndrome. I have had to deal with my autism throughout my life on my own. I have always found socialising and communication very difficult but I managed because I had to. Then by chance in 2001 I required a hernia operation and my life changed markedly. It was the loss of control during anaesthesia that

26

brought about a marked change in my persona. Over a period of about one year, I gradually reverted back to the person I was as a child, teenager, undergraduate and postgraduate. This was accompanied by panic attacks, extreme anxiety and depression. My speech is affected, and at times my hearing. Faces terrify me.

In February 2002 I saw a psychiatrist and the report described me as a person who falls within the autism spectrum of disorders (i.e. Asperger Syndrome). She wrote:

The lack of empathy, emotional reactivity and absolute lack of warmth which came through at the interview, and seems to have been there ever since she was a child, strongly suggest this as does her speech impediment which she says has been there since childhood. Her obsessional features, her anarchistic traits, adherence to routine and fear of change as well as her solitary interests and rather unusual hobbies and collections also point to this diagnosis.

Prior to receiving this report, I had diagnosed myself as having Asperger Syndrome, which was later confirmed by my doctor. I also have dyslexia, obsessive compulsive disorder, and catatonic-like deterioration. In my opinion it is important to appreciate that an 'Asperger Marriage' can only work if the neurotypical spouse understands autism and is prepared to accept all that it entails. My life story as an Asperger is recounted in my book *Asperger Syndrome: My Puzzle* (AuthorHouse UK, 2005).

It was at Leicester University in the autumn of 1972 that I first met Richard as a fellow undergraduate in the Geology Department. By Christmas 1974 we had become good friends. In many respects he was quite like me because he was rather shy and quiet and we enjoyed similar activities. It was pleasant to have a boyfriend, but I was really amazed that a young man should actually take an interest in me!

When the inevitable came with the end of our undergraduate years, I went off to Sheffield University to study for a PhD and Richard headed to Bedford College (University of London) to likewise study for a PhD. Still together but miles apart! Richard was my special friend, someone to talk to, someone I could rely on, and above all someone who cared for me. During this period apart we used to see each other about once a month (except during the summer months when Richard went to Norway to do his fieldwork). Sometimes I would travel down to London by train and stay in his parental home, and at other times he travelled up to Sheffield and stayed with me in my accommodation.

In 1978 shortly after Christmas we became engaged, and married in July 1980 in a small church in Alnwick (in Northumberland). By then I had been awarded my PhD. Richard by this time had changed his career direction. He had studied law at the London College of Law and was engaged in doing his Articles in a Sheffield city centre law firm. On finishing his Articles in 1982, we moved up to West Cumbria for Richard to take up his first post as a solicitor in a law firm in Whitehaven. Little were we to know at the time but Richard would remain there for 27 years! Whilst Richard went to work I did some voluntary work and, being a keen runner, I ran. We spent our weekends fell-walking, a pastime we both loved. So it was that our day-to-day life had a strict routine, which is so very important to someone with Asperger Syndrome. We did not socialise with other people, as I did not know how to find people to socialise with! It is now 2013 and we are still living in West Cumbria!

Our rented flat in St Bees was soon relinquished when we bought our first home in the village – a move hastened by the realisation that parenthood would be upon us in the autumn of 1983. At the time it was inconceivable to live anywhere but St Bees because I had got used to living there. On the birth of our first baby (Emma), our lives changed dramatically and we were both astounded at how much work such a little bundle seemed to generate! As a mother with autism, the loss of control, new routines and unpredictable demands posed problems for me, which I had to learn to live with.

When Emma was almost two years old, we began to visit a lady each week who had a little girl of a similar age. This was good for Emma because she was learning to mix. I was ever-mindful of the fact that children need to learn how to relate to others, even though this task posed enormous problems for me. We did attend a mother and toddler group once in the village but Emma did not play with the other children and the other mothers did not speak to me. Events such as this, which are taken for granted by neurotypical mothers, posed immense problems for me and I was so pleased when we could at last go home. We never returned.

Emma and myself just spent our time together with very little socialising in the neurotypical world. Only 20 months after Emma's arrival, our son was born (Peter), and this meant a new routine to accommodate him! Establishing the new routine took several weeks but as time passed I gradually became accustomed to my new role as a mother of two young children. Having two very young children was undoubtedly hard work.

Some two years later, our second son (Phillip) was born and that meant yet another routine! Three young children under five years dramatically increased our workload. When Richard was at work I could have done with some grandparents at times to give a helping hand, but that was not to be as they lived in the Northeast and they had their own lives and agendas. We saw them occasionally. Richard was great with the children and spent much of his free time with them. He was regularly up at 5am, washing the nappies out before I was even up! When Richard was at the office, I could have done with an extra pair of hands.

Something that people perhaps do not appreciate is that, as an Asperger mother, I could not ring people up for a chat or to talk about matters relating to babies and children because I just did not have other people to ring up.

Play school and primary school for the two older children was soon followed by moving home to a house in a small hamlet about 4 miles east of St Bees. The larger house and very spacious garden gave us much more space and we loved the quietness of the area. When Phillip was five years old, our numbers increased to six with the birth of our fourth child, a little boy (Duncan); and yes, a new routine had to be devised! This time I had a trio of 'little helpers'! One aspect of their childhood I could not help my children with was 'teaching them how to socialise and have friends'. This was an area they had to explore themselves.

In 2007 our lives were to change again in a rather dramatic way when Richard experienced 'burnout'. As a result of this, he had to leave his job and has not worked since. It was, after all these years, very strange for me to have Richard at home 'full time', so to speak, because I had been used to having the house to myself during office hours. Again, another change to our routine! Following this, Richard has gradually taken over much of the housework and does the shopping. This change has given us both more time to pursue our individual and mixed interests. We are a good partnership!

So the years passed by and in 2010 Richard and I found ourselves living alone for long periods of time, as our three eldest children had 'flown the nest' to begin their own lives and for the academic year Duncan was away at university. At first it seemed strange with just the two of us at home but we soon became used to it and were pleased that the children were making headway in the 'big wide world'.

It is now 2013 and our family circumstances have again changed. Gone are our four young children, to be replaced by four young adults. Emma is now married and has provided us with three young grandsons; Peter lives in York; Phillip is married and lives in Aviemore; and Duncan will begin his final year at university after the summer vacation.

Richard and I spend a lot of our time on our own together. It is important to understand that my problems with socialising and communication also affect Richard. My parents are dead and Richard's parents are very elderly. We do occasionally see something of Richard's sister and my siblings but they all live at a distance.

Perhaps the hardest thing Richard has to deal with is my fear of faces (especially the eyes) because at all times he has to be vigilant to not make eye contact with me. Anyone's eyes can affect me, whether a stranger or an acquaintance. Looking at eyes instills great fear in me and affects my speech, such that it can become totally incoherent. I am limited as to where I can go on my own, and more often or not Richard has to come with me.

I can manage to go to our local swimming pool on my own, and I usually cycle or I am dropped off by car and then walk or run home. (I am at present engaged in the final stages of a 6,824-mile swim, raising funds for our local 'Hospice at Home' charity.) I can go to see my GP on my own (either cycling or walking) and also visit the hairdresser and very occasionally a shop (usually walking). For seven and a half years (finishing in July 2012), I visited a local special school as a volunteer helper, which I enjoyed immensely. I usually went straight after swimming and then cycled home. I am given to understand that I was a great help to the staff with my knowledge of autism.

I am currently Vice-Chair of the Cumbrian Autism Board and attend six meetings annually. As these meetings are at a distance, Richard drives me there, installs me and then returns to collect me two and a half hours later. I have been unable to drive since 2005 because I experienced massive panic attacks, usually when I neared a junction. I knew I needed to brake but for some reason my foot must have hit the accelerator, which resulted in my not being able to stop the car until it was nearly too late. I believe that I must have seen a face as I was reaching the junction that caused me to act in this manner. As I experienced this phenomenon several times, I feared I might hurt someone so I had no alternative but to voluntarily relinquish my car. Something else I experience in a car is that as soon as we have driven beyond my 'comfort zone' I invariably fall asleep and this is another reason I can no longer drive.

Together we enjoy running, cycling and walking. We regularly take part in running races (5-kilometre to half-marathon distances). We gave up ultra running, and I gave up marathon running a few years ago. We run the races together, with Richard usually just behind me. I have to be very careful not to look at anyone's face because if I do my body seriously slows down, and in the worst-case scenario my body hurts so much I have to literally stop, walk a bit and then start running again. It is really kind of Richard to do this because he is actually faster than me at the shorter distances.

Together we have walked to all the named tarns in the Lake District National Park (217); all the Wainwright summits (214) and all the outlying Wainwright summits (110); and we have completed the ascents of all the fells (646) in the Lake District that exceed 1000 feet. I list all my achievements. Lists are very important to me. Collecting data has the advantage that a collection cannot criticise, reject, demand gratitude or expect success, whereas human contacts expect an emotional reaction and at times a demonstration of affection.

We do not go away much and if we do it is usually only for a few days at a time. Like many Aspergers, I fear change. To me 'sameness — safety'. I need to have a routine such that I know what is going to happen all the time. I must know exactly what is going to happen the next day. If there has to be a change from my routine, then I need to know well in advance so I can prepare myself mentally. To neurotypicals, my behaviour probably seems very strange and is difficult to understand because most people thrive on change and doing new things. Richard probably finds this aspect of my Asperger difficult to comprehend and at times even rather annoying, but he is very good about it because he knows it is the way it has to be for me.

Meals in our household are perhaps rather different to those in other households. We always have exactly the same evening meal so Monday's meal is always the same every Monday, as is Tuesday's meal every Tuesday, etc. I always eat exactly the same food at breakfast each day and at lunch each day. I have to lick out every yoghurt pot and pudding bowl at the table. I do not know why I do it – I just feel compelled to act in this way. I am very particular concerning cutlery and bowls. I always use a small spoon and never a dessertspoon. I always use the same bowl, and would be very upset if someone else used it. Richard does the weekly shopping and is very good at it. For me, there are too many people in a supermarket and too much danger of things falling out of my hands and smashing if I see a face.

In our home I have a problem with doors and windows. I do not like any of them open. I do not like sitting where air is moving past me. If they have to be open for aeration, the doors can only be open at less than a 45-degree angle and windows only slightly. Richard has solved this problem by opening doors and windows when I am out. If they are still open on my return, I have to check the window angles immediately. Everything in our home has to be in its right place and if it is not I have to move it directly. I dislike intensely 'bits' on the floor and have to pick them up immediately. I cannot bear bits of grass in the house. The latter really upsets me.

My obsessive compulsive disorder (OCD) is something else that Richard has to deal with. This is a condition that I would rather not have because it places me under a lot of stress and anxiety. On leaving our home or going to bed, I have to repeatedly check that plugs are out of electrical sockets, water taps are off, fridge and freezer doors are closed and that nothing has been left on top of our Aga. Richard performing these checks is not a solution – because I feel that I have to do it all myself.

I am given to understand that, as an Asperger ages, their autistic symptoms and characteristics become stronger, and also the person is apparently more susceptible to developing some form of dementia. This is something I think about, and we as a couple have discussed these possibilities and also various strategies for these eventualities if required in the future years.

In conclusion, we have shown that an 'Asperger Marriage' does work, as long as the neurotypical spouse is prepared to accept in their entirety the routines, rituals, social ineptness, special fields of interest, and fear of change that are critical for the Asperger spouse if 'meltdown' is to be avoided. We have been married now for 33 years and hopefully for many more years!

Reflections

Gay has managed to organise her life in a way that suits her autistic needs. Some of the key factors she describes are:

- A supportive neurotypical partner
- Ownership of and control over her own living space
- The power to exclude certain people from her life
- A family income that allows for independence
- The opportunity to spend significant amounts of time with her special interests, and a life partner who can share these interests.

How many of these factors are in place for the person with autism who you support? What is the impact on them when these things are not in place?

What might be done to put them in place? Can you offer to accommodate their needs in a similar way to Richard's accommodation of Gay's needs?

Gay describes her extreme response to eye contact. She thinks that it was the issue with eye contact that caused her to lose control of a car she was driving. Do you work with anyone who has similar problems? How do they manage to negotiate any situations, such as shopping, work or pubs, where eye contact might be the norm? How good are you at maintaining communication without eye contact yourself?

3
A mother and person on the spectrum
Julia Pilkington

Julia wrote this essay for assessment on the autism course at the University of Cumbria. It describes her late diagnosis of autism and considers sexist bias in diagnosis. This chapter is the complete essay. She tells us:

> "Over my lifetime, I have developed ways of coping in different situations by hiding my true self behind a situation-relevant facsimile born of observation of others and application of academic learning. I had no idea that other people were not doing this as a matter of course. I got so good at this over time that it has taken me over a year so far to start rediscovering my natural self and I constantly have to check with myself whether a belief, action or reaction is true or false."

This is the only chapter in the book that includes references, as the literature played an important part in her gaining an understanding of her condition and the gender bias women face in getting diagnosis.

My name is Julia, I am 48 and I received a diagnosis of Asperger Syndrome (AS) aged 47. I was born with cerebral palsy and went through mainstream school till the age of 18, took a job in a library, got married and had three children. I then worked in primary school as a non-teaching assistant, gaining my specialist teacher assistant certificate. I qualified as a nursery nurse in 2000, and special needs assistant in 2001. I also took responsibility for setting up and running out-of-school provision. I worked in mainstream primary school for a further five years, then left suddenly, having experienced burnout. My husband left a year previous and I was left to bring up three teenagers as a single parent – and all this without really knowing who – or what I was!

It was trying to understand why I had suffered burnout that led me to a diagnosis of AS. Initially the GP diagnosed reactive depression but this never felt right. Whilst seeking a diagnosis of AS for my son and taking part in the assessment process as a parent, I identified with many of the diagnostic criteria. A good friend had received a diagnosis several years previously and suggested this could be the real reason behind my burnout.

Incidence in women

In 'The Pattern of Abilities and Development of Girls with Asperger Syndrome', Attwood's experience of the ratio of males to females presenting for diagnosis is 10:1 in favour of males but he notes that research suggests that it should be 4:1 (Attwood 2009). I have read literature that agrees with the 4:1 ratio – Hawkes (2009) and the National Autistic Society website being examples. However, Marshall (2004, p. 7) saying, 'Asperger Syndrome is ten times more common in boys', confirms Attwood's experience.

Wing (2002, pp. 63–64) agrees with the ratio of 4 boys to 1 girl with AS and suggests that there are far fewer able women with autistic disorders than men. However, she also cites a Swedish study in mainstream school (1991) that suggested the 4:1 ratio but which then subsequently included a group of children who exhibited some of the criteria needed for an AS diagnosis and found a ratio of 2.3 girls to 1 boy to be more likely. This indicated that autistic conditions may be more difficult to spot in girls and suggested girls' superior social skills as a possible reason. Nichols *et al.* (2009) reports that in epidemiological studies of autism spectrum conditions (ASCs), male to female ratios vary from 2:1 to 16:1 and that there has never been a study conducted on AS specifically.

My own experience during diagnosis was that, on the day I attended, the ratio of men to women was 1:1. Subsequently, I have met many AS women who more often than not have no 'official' diagnosis. More accurate assessment of the male to female ratio is needed, for if clinicians believe the 10:1 or 4:1 ratio to be correct and they fail to take on board the possibility of AS girls presenting differently from boys, then girls will continue not to be recognised. Many will be damaged as a result of having to navigate society without context or self-understanding.

Why girls are misdiagnosed

The points discussed below are taken from '*The Pattern of Abilities and Development of Girls with Asperger's Syndrome*' (2009), an archived paper from Tony Attwood's website. Attwood suggests that the characteristics of Asperger Syndrome may be expressed in a different way in girls and that 'clinicians may be hesitant to commit themselves to a diagnosis unless the signs are conspicuously different to the normal range of behaviour and abilities.'

Hagland (2009) agrees that the presentation of AS females can be different and notes that some of the special interests shown may be less unusual than their male counterparts, citing collecting dolls and interest in personal hygiene as examples.

My own special interests, consistent for as long as I can remember, have been reading and watching films. These alone would have never got me a diagnosis. If I had explained that books were my friends, that they always helped me relax, or that films gave me a great deal of information on social situations and how to deal with them, offering a means of escaping into fantasy away from a very confusing world, the picture may have been different.

In his next point, Attwood notes that parents or schools refer many more boys than girls to psychologists after they exhibit anger and aggression. This, he says, reflects a stereotypical view of behaviour differences between the sexes that can give a false impression of the incidence of aggression in the AS population. Bridget Orr, interviewed in the *Guardian* on Wednesday 4 June 2008, says 'I used to go to special schools and classes that were dominated by rowdy and moody boys, and even the misconceived stereotype of people with autistic spectrum disorders is that of a humourless and awkward-looking nerdy man with an attitude problem.' She goes on to talk about how difficult she found it to fit into either the autistic or the mainstream world as a result.

My own son was referred to an educational psychologist after exhibiting challenging behaviours at school and was immediately diagnosed with attention deficit hyperactivity disorder (ADHD) and given Ritalin. At 16, we began searching for a diagnosis of AS after recognising that he fitted the diagnostic criteria, which he now has, and as a result he is much less prone to aggression, having a better understanding of his dual diagnosis and what it means to him.

My own school and home life went relatively smoothly and I never exhibited challenging behaviour in school so as a result my differences went unnoticed.

Attwood then goes on to describe how individual personality can influence coping strategies and thus may inhibit detection: 'some are reluctant to socialise with others and their personality can be described as passive. They can become quite adept at camouflaging their difficulties and clinical experience suggests that the passive personality is more common in girls.' Wing (2002) groups expression of social impairment into four types, including 'passive' and 'active but odd', both of whom exhibit more willingness to interact with others, although she does not suggest any of these groups are more likely to contain girls.

I never stood out as being different. I recognise that I was always more of a loner as a child, but as I grew up I had a few trusted friends, most of whom I am still in touch with. (Most of these now have a diagnosis, or have children being assessed.) I could get by in social situations but tended to be on the periphery, something that eventually made me realise I lacked the skills of those around me, and this was one of the factors that made me seek a diagnosis. However, I do not think this was ever picked up on by others except, perhaps, that they thought me shy. If I was in a situation where I was confident, such as talking about a specialist subject, I was, and still remain, able to take part.

In his next observation, Attwood suggests that girls may miss out on diagnosis because their natural peer group is female and they are therefore more likely to be included and their differences tolerated and they tend to receive help in social situations. Nichols *et al.* (2009) suggests mentoring as a tool for girls already diagnosed. My own peer group as a child was a group of four girls, three of whom I now believe were AS. We all relied upon the other one to act as a social interface in times of uncertainty. I still count this woman as one of the people I trust to 'tell me how it is' in the real world.

Attwood continues by suggesting that AS girls' social skills are liable to be better than those of boys, as he has observed a willingness to learn and a motivation to acquire them in social groups. Marshall (2004) cites Christopher Gillberg as being of the opinion that girls are misdiagnosed because they have better social and communication skills. Hagland (2009, p. 21) states: 'some clinicians believe that women with AS tend to be more sociable than men with the condition'.

Attwood notes the tendency of women on the spectrum to have an innate ability to empathise with their children, which he finds to be lacking in AS males. Nichols *et al.* (2009) cite a study by Bacon and colleagues in 1998, noting that autistic girls in the group displayed pro-social behaviour and empathy when another child was in distress. Personally I am able to relate to my children on an emotional level, whilst I have been told, by one male friend with a diagnosis of AS that he didn't know what his children wanted from him. Conversely, I have male Aspergian friends who relate well to their offspring.

Another reason Attwood cites for girls to be under-diagnosed is their ability to mimic social behaviour. This was the case for a woman who, after unsuccessfully seeking a diagnosis, was quoted on the Asperger Adult Support Network website:

They did find many things that fit the AS picture, but not enough to make a diagnosis. What did they expect after having to survive alone in a neurotypical society, that I would not have adapted, adjusted, subdued and conformed to the rules of the neurotypical game? Obviously they could not realise that a woman with Asperger's is the chameleon of the Autism Spectrum, that our innate empathically wired brain allows us to 'copy' neurotypical behavior and 'wear' it like a cloak, a cover, a cape, a costume over our persona so that we can fit in and survive. My high intelligence and eye for detail helped me create such a costume, and the people (one person actually) who interviewed me failed to notice that.

Another way in which girls can be missed, according to Attwood, is if they have had drama lessons and learned about body language through role-play and by acting out scenes whilst memorising dialogue which they can apply in real-life circumstances. He points out that where an AS women adopts another persona as a coping strategy, it can lead to misdiagnosis of a multiple personality disorder. The first books I read on autism were the autobiographies of Donna Williams and, although I found them interesting, I did not particularly identify with her characteristics.

However, what I did identify with was her presentation as several different individuals with different qualities to be used as coping strategies in whichever situation presented itself – she talks about this in her book *Autism: An Inside Out Approach* (1996). Over my lifetime, I have developed ways of coping in different situations by hiding my true self behind a situation-relevant facsimile born of observation of others and application of academic learning. I had no idea that other people were not doing this as a matter of course. I got so good at this over time that it has taken me over a year so far to start rediscovering my natural self and I constantly have to check with myself whether a belief, action or reaction is true or false.

Using play as a means for observing lack of social imagination is a commonly used tool for diagnosis of an ASC and Attwood notes that girls on the spectrum may *seem* as if they are using social imagination when playing with dolls, when in reality they are not. He suggests that they may be recreating scenes they have seen in real life or films. He also states that talking to dolls into later years may lead to an inaccurate diagnosis of schizophrenia. Nichols *et al.* (2009) say that girls have been noted to be better at pretend-play and score higher on diagnostic assessments as a result. I did have dolls as a child but I never played with them in an imaginative fashion, merely as objects

Talking about specialist interests, Attwood comments on the fact that many women choose to write and express their creativity through poetry or prose because of a love of words and rhythm. It is certainly true that many Aspergian women choose to write – Donna Williams, Wendy Lawson, Gunilla Gerland and Temple Grandin among them. Because there is so little factual information out there for AS women, their books are a valuable resource for us females, who resonate with what is being said and recognise we are not alone.

Men on the spectrum, he says, are more inclined to 'traditional' scientific or fact-based interests. In Julie Brown's book *Writers on the Spectrum* (2010), some males discussed – such as Lewis Carroll and Hans Andersen – write fiction but all the females cited are poets, diarists and those writing autobiographies. Brown also suggests that those who are AS write in order to make sense of their world and themselves. I write mainly for those reasons, sometimes keeping journals, writing poetry (an indication of my less than perfect memory, I remember and recall snatches of my life) and factual stuff about my life experiences and never write outside of them.

Other women I have spoken to do the same and much more than the males I know. Only one male is listed in the section on autistic biographies. Maybe this is an essential difference – women seeming to write for different purposes from men and, as a male AS friend commented, getting across a more accurate portrayal of what life is like for Aspergians.

The last point Attwood makes in his piece refers to his observation that some AS women have an unusual child-like quality to their voice and seem to prefer to 'maintain the characteristics of childhood'. In her article 'An Aspie in the City', Carlin Flora says of the interviewee:

> Looking around Kiriana's apartment—at her collection of colored Easter eggs and logic games, her Edward Gorey books and whimsical drawings—it occurs to me: She's a successful young woman who still inhabits the magical domain of a child.

Attwood also notes that, like AS boys, many AS women do not buy into the concept of wearing fashionable clothes and furthermore do not use cosmetics or deodorants. Williams (1996) reports that an AS female she knew was unable to perceive her own voice with meaning. Conversely, she observes that a boy with AS saw using his own voice as too much of an exposure of self, so perhaps using a child-like voice is a means of self-protection for some.

If you project vulnerability, with intent or unconsciously, it can promote protectiveness from others. I have observed AS and Predominant Neuro Type (PNT) males who respond in a protective manner to women who present in this way. Unfortunately such a strategy can also lead to bullying and accentuate differences, leading eventually to a lack of self-esteem. This can be made worse by them not buying into the societal expectations of 'normal' female expression of self through fashion and cosmetics. Nichols et al. (2009) state that difficulty arises when girls are 'becoming aware of being different from their peers … entering puberty and facing adulthood' (p.153) and suggest that this challenges self-esteem.

By way of contrast, there is evidence online in websites, blogs and forums that many AS females feel feminine, and object to the assumption that all AS females have a science-oriented, systemised male brain and are tomboys.

Blogs such as 'An Aspie Life' by Lynne Soraya, on the Psychology Today website, help to promote self-esteem by giving other women a chance to relate to each other and to read that they are not alone. The comments posted on this site reflect the diversity of Aspergian women and also the similarities, helping to create a feeling of Asperger 'normality' that does not rely on being accepted by the majority.

In conclusion, Attwood identifies the need for objective research studies on AS in girls and calls for 'epidemiological studies to establish the true incidence in girls and for research on the clinical signs, cognitive abilities and adaptive behaviour to include an examination of any quantitative and qualitative differences between male and female subjects'.

Nichols *et al.* (2009) agree that perhaps girls are being under-diagnosed because they are being assessed by professionals using criteria based upon a male stereotype and that although many, including Attwood, have speculated that girls express AS differently, there is a lack of literature recommending specific diagnostic criteria. The exception they cite is from Koenig and Tsatsanis (2005), whose suggestions for assessment stress the need to move away from the stereotypical male bias with its concentration on rigid, repetitive routines and restricted interests with accompanying disruptive behaviour.

By using careful observation over time and allowing for society-based sex differences in socialisation, communication and behaviour, using PNT girls of the same age and cognitive level as a basis for comparison, a clearer picture of presentation could be gained. They also suggest that whilst girls remain under-diagnosed there will be no true representation of AS females in research projects, and things will continue as they are. In my experience, most of the females I know are undiagnosed or self-diagnosed in adulthood, and those diagnosed in childhood do not receive adequate help in school, colleges or at work.

Diagnosis and beyond

I will now discuss my diagnosis, comparing the process and the report to documents suggesting best practice in the area, and examining the content of my report for similarities to, and subtle differences from, the traditional male biases discussed above.

The Aspect Consultancy Report Executive Summary (2007, p. 5) recommends that 'Individuals themselves should never be put into a position where they have to pay to get a private diagnosis'.

As stated in my diagnostic report, I decided on a private diagnosis after supporting my son with one done through the NHS, where the funding took two years to secure. The waiting was so stressful for us both that I decided to go private, through the people who had assessed my son.

'Better Services for Adults with an Autistic Spectrum Disorder' (2006, p. 10) states: 'People with an ASD and their families say diagnostic services are important. Knowing where to get diagnostic help, getting help in a timely way and receiving post-diagnostic support and information are all important.' The account below shows that my diagnostic process covered all these points.

I had already known the person doing the assessment report for two years, had met the diagnostician at my son's diagnosis and had visited Sheffield for interviews during the process. This meant that I was familiar with the setting and procedure, thus allowing me to concentrate on the process. I first had an interview with the person doing my assessment report, with two of my closest friends, to give answers to some of the questions about my presentation. I then received the report he had prepared and was invited to attend for formal diagnosis with the diagnostician.

My daughter came to support me and to confirm her observation of my differences. At all times we received explanations of what was to happen and the criteria being used for the assessment. It was also checked that I actually wanted a diagnosis. There is also a note in my diagnostic report pointing out that current diagnostic criteria are based on deficits, and apologising if the points made come across as negative. The report is divided into sections on social communication and interaction, theory of mind and executive functioning. In addition, there is a section on sensory differences, not needed for diagnosis but indicative of particular needs.

Social communication and interaction

This section mentions my interest in books, music and walking and my lack of interest in toys and dolls whilst creating my own world to live in. It also mentions my trampoline that became my friend. It also mentions my need to create a separate persona to deal with new social situations and my intellectual understanding of social 'rules' that I have difficulty putting into practice. This reflects some of the points made by Attwood (2009) above – namely the less 'odd' particular interests, the ability of females to hide behind created personas, and our more accurate intellectual understanding of social rules than AS males.

Theory of mind

In this part it is noted that I assume the best in people and am never able to read their intent. I do not follow crazes and am indifferent to peer pressure. I also frequently assume people know what my experiences have been without me having to tell them. This agrees with the currently accepted diagnostic criteria and shows the similarities between men and women on the spectrum, as mentioned in the quote from Caroline Faherty, *Autism Aspergers Digest* (July/August 2002): 'Women are affected by autism in the same ways as are their male counterparts; however, they are doubly challenged by the added assumptions that society places on the female gender.'

Executive functioning

My adherence to set routines to manage my stress level and the stress increase when things do not go according to plan are again typical examples of Aspergian behaviour agreeing with current diagnostic criteria. However, I often have to adapt these routines or abandon them without notice, even though it takes me to the edge of my coping capacity and can have a knock-on effect lasting several days. This is indicative of society's expectation of women having to adapt or multi-task and adds another layer to the problems Aspergian women face on a daily basis.

Catherine Faherty says, 'There is subtle interaction between two sets of issues. 'Problems related to the [autism] spectrum are combined with problems of society's expectations of women.'

Sensory issues

Apart from disliking certain textures and a mild intolerance of light and loud noises that can lead to sensory overload, I have little sensory difficulty compared to others I know. The major problem I have is difficulty comparing my size with that of others around me. I have an inaccurate perception of my physical self, which means I have to rely on the judgements of others. This has led to my having major body image problems for most of my life, promoting feelings of inadequacy, low self-esteem and guilt. This, more than any other aspect of my AS, has affected my daily life in an adverse way but since my diagnosis I have been able to readjust my thinking and feel better about myself as a result. Nichols *et al.* (2009) recognise that girls on the spectrum have problems defining their physical selves.

After attending for my diagnostic interview I received my diagnosis, which – together with the assessment report – contained suggestions for further reading, websites and explaining about benefits that may be available with advice on genetic counselling for the wider family. Since diagnosis, I have been able to email and visit the person who carried out my assessment whenever I needed help and he has continued to offer support to my son and myself on a regular basis. I have taken part in a research project specifically aimed at women with a late diagnosis of AS and have secured Disability Living Allowance, enabling me to live comfortably on benefits.

Once I had left work, I began helping a friend to offer support to other Aspergian adults. During this time I became more 'immersed' in the world of autism on a practical level and this helped me gain a better understanding and acceptance of my own and others' differences. In particular, I came into contact with more and more disenchanted AS women who were often unable to learn about their own AS or get a diagnosis because they were seeing to the needs of partners and/or children on the spectrum. Women are society's natural carers and often put themselves last on the list in family situations. As a result, we are in the process of setting up a women's self-help group with the following aims:

- To provide a regular forum for discussion on subjects that matter to members of the group
- To provide support for women dealing with their own, or with others' AS, via swapping ideas and giving access to training in specific areas
- To put women in touch with others in similar circumstances to create mutual support networks
- To explore how AS affects women, as opposed to men, and how it affects their ability to cope with their family, work or personal lives
- To encourage women to take part in research, either by professionals or within the group, to gain greater understanding of how AS affects women in particular
- To create links with other AS-friendly organisations offering specialist services like diagnosis or family support
- To share free therapy sessions within the group to help counteract stress and to give a bit of 'me time' to busy women; therapies could include counselling, relationship help, Reiki, EFT and others as suggested.

Conclusion

My personal journey has been easier than a lot of Aspergians – male and female – who I have met, and I am using my diagnosis and knowledge to help give support to others and project a positive image of what Aspergians have to offer society. I am proud of who I am, and want others to be proud of themselves instead of having to 'hide' who they really are. I wrote the following poem recently and it illustrates the difference between society's perception and the reality of being an Aspergian woman.

What they see is NOT what they get

They see a 48-year-old adult…
What they get is a child of 4
They see a woman experienced in the world of work…
What they get is a naïve trusting soul confused by rules of interaction

They see a 'good' parent…
What they get is someone winging it, reacting and hiding behind old routines

They see a confident, happy, outgoing individual…
What they get is a worried mass of coping strategies wanting to be liked

They see a competent citizen…
They get a backlog of experiences regurgitated to order

They see an educated eloquent woman…
What they get is a self taught, parroting, observant facsimile

They see an ordered, organiser with a plan…
What they get is a maker of order out of chaos clinging on for dear life

They see a reliable, loyal friend –
(That part is TRUE)

They see an innovator, an ideas person…
What they get is logic and common sense

He sees a rock, an interface…
What he gets is a lonely, scarred being doing what has to be done
Despite herself – or is that to spite herself?

But above all what they get is…
Someone who wants to please, to be able to make everything 'right',
To give love unconditionally, in whatever form, to those that will accept it

Someone who wants to 'be', to have fun, to share happy days and nights
To cherish the moment and beyond, dreamy and calm in a sea of unknowing
To be loved and accepted for what she is

Brave enough to expose her weakness, accept her strength and live
As the vulnerable lost girl she is becoming on the outside,
Feminine, pre-Raphaelite beauty radiating from within.

Update

Since writing this, a lot has happened in my life so I thought an update might come in handy. I worked in an Asperger Consultancy that I helped found for around a year and, through this, gained a lot more experience of working with AS adults, their families, carers and professionals working with them. It was a very valuable experience and during this time I became involved in moves to implement the autism strategy resulting from the passing of the Autism Act in

2009. I am currently co-chair of the Lancashire Autism Partnership Board and work alongside its members to promote better services for autistic adults. The board has members from services, autistic individuals, parents and care providers, and by working together we are beginning to achieve results, although it is a long, slow process. Service personnel are gaining a better understanding of how services can better meet the needs of autistic adults and those individuals; their families and carers are learning more about the constraints services have worked under historically that have prevented change taking place previously.

I was also able to set up the women's group I had thought of, and it ran pretty successfully for a time. It took the form of an informal meeting at a local café where AS women, with and without a diagnosis, were able to chat about whatever took their fancy. The numbers attending varied and eventually I made the decision to put it on hold. I have recently been talking to a local autism project with a view to resurrecting it in a different format.

Since attending the University of Cumbria course, I have completed my Post-Graduate Certificate in Asperger Syndrome through Sheffield Hallam University and done a couple of talks for the University of Cumbria on AS, from both a parent and individual perspective, as well as writing short pieces for inclusion in books.

At the time of writing, I am still getting to grips with my AS and how it affects my life. Although I am able to manage without the help of services, I have to be very careful to manage my workload and my lifestyle to avoid becoming overloaded.

All in all, I am glad to have received my diagnosis and, through that, to have been able to help others gain a better understanding of AS. Working on the ground with autistic folk and those involved in caring for their needs was rewarding but very stressful. Working with members of the board, I try and change thinking on both sides to achieve better results through common understanding. I hope that this will result in better experiences for AS folk with services, something that at present can be extremely traumatic and have far-reaching effects.

Reflections

Julia develops a convincing argument that definitions and diagnoses of autism are inherently sexist. Women, such as herself, have been missed because autism manifests differently in women.

The simple but important question for health and social care professionals is: Are you skilled enough to spot and respond to the needs of women with autism?

References

Books

Brown, J. (2010). *Writers on the Spectrum: How Autism and Asperger Syndrome Have Influenced Literary Writing.* London: Jessica Kingsley.

Gerland, G. (2003). *A Real Person: Life on the Outside.* London: Souvenir Press.

Hagland, C. (2009). *Getting to Grips with Asperger Syndrome: Understanding Adults on the Autism Spectrum.* London: Jessica Kingsley.

Hawkes, H. (2009). *Asperger's Syndrome: The Essential Guide.* Peterborough: Need2Know.

Marshall, F. (2004). *Living with Autism.* London: Sheldon Press.

Nichols, S. et al. (2009). *Girls Growing Up on the Autism Spectrum.* London: Jessica Kingsley.

Williams, D. (1996). *Autism: An Inside-Out Approach.* London: Jessica Kingsley.

Wing, L. (2002). *The Autistic Spectrum.* New updated edition. London: Robinson.

Reports

ASPECT Consultancy Report Executive Summary (2007). A National Report on the Needs of Adults with Asperger Syndrome, compiled by Luke Beardon and Genevieve Edmonds.

Autism Aspergers Digest (July/August 2002).

Department of Health (2006). 'Better Services for People with an Autistic Spectrum Disorder: A Note Clarifying Current Government Policy and Describing Good Practice'. London: DH.

Online articles

Attwood, T. (2009). The Pattern of Abilities and Development of Girls with Asperger Syndrome. http://www.aspergerfoundation.org.uk/infosheets/ta_girls.pdf

Flora, C. (1 November 2006). 'An Aspie in the City'. *Psychology Today*, p. 2. http://www.psychologytoday.com/articles/200611/aspie-in-the-city

Moorehead, J. (4 June 2008). 'It's not just boys who are autistic'. *Guardian newspaper.*

http://www.theguardian.com/lifeandstyle/2008/jun/04/women.familyandrelationships

Periodicals

Faherty, C. (July/August 2002). 'Asperger Syndrome in Women: A Different Set of Challenges'. *Autism Aspergers Digest.*

Section 2
Going through the education system

4
Four stories from the edge
Thomas Madar

Thomas taught on the autism course in Carlisle. I have always found his stories very memorable and captivating. This chapter is a collection of events from his life as he used to present them on the course. Two themes that run through his account are rejection and isolation, which he believes have had long-term adverse effects on his life. At one point, he says:

> "The rejection of an application to join an expedition to Morocco led by a church pastor resulted in feelings of disappointment and rejection which took several days to overcome. Over the long term, this event contributed to feelings of social inferiority and rejection to be addressed by counselling sessions more than ten years later."

My introduction to the Christian faith

The University Christian Union meeting was a hive of activity. Tea was being served. A well-known local speaker had just given an account of his life with the Christian faith and was inviting people with problems, health issues or who sought conversion to the Christian faith to come forward to be prayed for. At this stage, a friend I had known for some time impressed upon me that the only way in which I could get to Heaven after my death was not by expressing kindness or good works, but by conversion to the Christian faith, by accepting Jesus Christ as personal Saviour and Lord by means of prayer. So I went forward, uttered the required prayer, and became converted to the Christian faith.

From my primary school days, I became conscious of the need to consider where I would finish up after my death. Regular Sunday school attendance at the age of ten impressed upon me that if I was kind and helpful to others, gave frequently, and worshipped God and Jesus regularly, I would go to Heaven and be with God. If I was a nasty person who stole from and murdered other people, and forgot about God, then He would forget about me. I would finish up in Hell. From these times onwards, I strove to be on the right side of God.

Most of my secondary school years were spent at a series of private boarding schools on account of my special educational requirements. At a well-known preparatory school in Wiltshire, my introduction to the Christian faith was taken further with timetabled lessons and regular attendance at Church of England services. Compulsory attendance at religious classes and regular church services continued until the end of my school-based education in the mid-1970s. My awareness of where I would spend eternity was greatly augmented. To ensure that I finished up at the right place when I died, I became confirmed in the Church of England and started to attend church services during the school holidays.

At university, my interest in eternity and the Christian faith was an effective key to making friends and participating in social activities. I regularly attended Anglican Society and Christian Union meetings and joined Bible studies and prayer meetings. By this means, I became known to the friend who led me to Christian conversion.

From the time of my conversion until the present day, my Christian faith has been a primary source of making friends, enjoying social contact and finding appropriate support. I illustrate this by giving three examples.

In the mid-1980s, I was living and working in Chelmsford as a software engineer. I was suffering badly from post-traumatic stress as a result of being bullied at school and a very unfortunate career experience shortly after having left university. I was plagued by feelings of social inferiority and was subject to visible mood swings. The pastor of my church became aware of my emotional ill health and felt it 'in his bones' to refer me to a Christian counselling centre. There, I received a course of counselling which was effective in fighting my depression and restoring me to a sound state of emotional health.

A few years after this, I was studying for a post-graduate degree at my former university. As a result of my membership of the Christian Union and a local Elim Pentecostal church, I made several close friends with whom I went on walks and shared other social activities. Indeed, such was my ability to make friends at this time that it was as though I had been cured of having an autistic spectrum condition.

In the early 2000s, I was working as a software developer at Boots the Chemist in Nottingham. I was again troubled by feelings of social inferiority arising from a history of being patronised, talked down to, or even bullied by other people to whom I looked for friendship. My circumstances were not helped by the fact that I was being dominated by another person on the autistic spectrum, well known to me, who had a somewhat aggressive personality. At this time, I was a member of the Derby chapter of the Full Gospel Businessmen's Fellowship and made a regular appearance at their prayer and dinner evenings. An influential member became aware of my troubles and referred me to a counselling service in Loughborough.

Once on their register, I was assigned a counsellor who enabled me to overcome my feelings of low self-esteem by means of appropriate cognitive behavioural therapy. He also offered assertiveness training, so I was able to escape from the domination mentioned above.

An attempt to join a Christian-led expedition to Morocco

I was in the final year of my first-degree studies at university. The advertising literature on my desk looked very enticing. A local church pastor was looking for students to join him on an expedition to Morocco at a very reasonable price. Now, for some years, I had been intrigued by this country and was yearning to visit it. When I was at school, a camping expedition to this destination was organised one of the staff, but my parents were unable to afford the cost. Now, with sufficient funds in my pocket, I could go!

Attached to the advertisement was a form asking for my name, address, and a deposit of twenty pounds. I sent this off as instructed. Back came a reply asking me to write about myself. I wrote back a long letter with the following content:

- Detailed physical characteristics including the fact that I was short in height, had dark brown hair and had thick lips
- Details of what I was studying
- Details of my leisure activities, including cycling
- Details of where I lived and where I was studying
- A few details about being a recent convert to the Christian faith.

Certain of an invitation to join the group, I took out travel insurance.

But what I received back was most upsetting. It was a lengthy scrawled letter stating that this expedition was a mission to spread the Christian faith in that country and that only those who were 'called by God to spread the word' could go. As I was expecting an adventure holiday, I was not welcome. Attached to this letter was a cheque returning my deposit.

It took me several days to overcome feelings of intense rejection and bitter disappointment. Over the long term, this event contributed to feelings of social inferiority and rejection to be addressed by counselling sessions more than ten years later.

On reflection, what should I have written in that critical letter? I should have been aware that when the pastor issued his request for me to write about myself, it was an *unwritten direction* for me to *sell* to him my level of enthusiasm for the Christian faith, and my eagerness to tell others about it. This letter should therefore have concentrated primarily on an account of my Christian faith and my enthusiasm for it, and only subsequently on everything else. Had I done this, I would have been on my way to Morocco in that pastor's minibus.

An attempt to join a well-known social club for university graduates

The level of noise in the overcrowded bar was overwhelming. I had just cycled to a popular venue frequented by a club for recent university graduates so as to sample one of their social evenings. At first, I could not distinguish anyone from the crowd, but then, I noticed a group of young people sitting at the furthest end of the bar area. They beckoned me over...

I had recently started work as a software engineer for a well-known engineering company and was keen to get to know the local area and the people who worked in it. I became aware of a social club for recent university graduates, people of my age, which met on a weekly basis for a variety of activities. Membership of such an organisation would be ideal!

I applied for membership and was told that I would have to attend at least six meetings, over six weeks, as a prospective member. During these meetings, I had to get to know at least four members of the committee and become well-liked by the other members, whether on or off the committee. At the end of that time, the committee would meet and vote as to whether to accept or reject my application for membership.

The weeks passed as I attended the requisite number of meetings. These encompassed a variety of activities ranging from safari suppers, through country walks, to 'bring a bottle' parties and pub evenings. My social performance was variable. Sometimes I was able to attract friendship and conversation from others as intended. At most other times my approach to people was awkward, and this was a positive disincentive to engage me in conversation. At one cocktail party, I vividly remember approaching one couple to talk about my newly acquired television, only for them to show no interest and to promptly depart in another direction. On another occasion, I became very aggravated after a bottle of wine, which I had intended as a contribution to a 'bring a bottle' party, slipped out of its bag and smashed on the pavement outside the venue where the party was held. It took a long time for my mood to calm down to the extent that I could hold an easy conversation with others.

The time came for the committee meeting where my fate would be decided. With trepidation I waited, and a few days later, an envelope from the club dropped through my letterbox. I opened it, and to my profound dismay, the letter inside told me that my application had been unsuccessful. On that same evening, I rang the chairman of the committee to enquire why my application had been rejected, and he declined to give me the reason – in case I would sue the club. All I was told was that the decision to reject me was nearly unanimous.

On reflection, with my autistic spectrum condition as it was, I should not have ventured into an area where the level of a person's acceptance depends solely on their personality and social skills. At the very least, I should have made the club committee aware of my autistic spectrum condition and its implications, from the very first time that I met them. Should this have happened, they would have either made a special allowance, or would have rejected me at a very early stage. This experience emphasises the relative lack of Christian compassion shown by a number of secular organisations. Note the timing of these events, more than a decade and a half before the advent of the Disability Discrimination Act; now, this club would have legal proceedings taken against it!

A long-distance cycling trip

It was the summer after I graduated from university with my first degree. Being a recent convert to Christianity, I was on an expedition organised by the Christian Union. This involved travelling by minibus to Grosseto in Northern Italy to take part in the refurbishment of a Christian missionary centre nearby. As the vehicle drove slowly along the picturesque road, I wondered what it would be like to make a similar trip by bicycle.

A few years later, in the early 1980s, I had my chance. It was the summer after another graduation, I was living at home with my parents, and, with a bit of money to spare, I felt that a few weeks exploring the Continent by bicycle would do me good. I found for myself a volunteering position at a camp, which involved the restoration of an old school as a community centre. This was situated near Ripoll, a small town at the Eastern end of the Spanish Pyrenees. Around this, I organised for myself a cycling expedition extending as far as Alicante on the Spanish Mediterranean coast. Great attention was paid to the details. Each day, I knew exactly how far I would ride and where I would stop and left the details with my parents. I did not neglect adequate travel insurance and a sufficiency of foreign currency and traveller's cheques.

The ride began in early July. Being a fit cyclist, I allowed myself nine days to ride the 800 miles to Ripoll. Having little concept of the therapeutic value of a traffic-free environment, I stuck to the major roads. An abundance of youth hostels and campsites meant that I could travel cheaply.

My outward route lay through Paris. I found the centre easily enough, but emerging on the right route out was another matter! After more than an hour's searching, I found myself in a high-rise housing estate. There, with the help of a bus station street-map, I managed to work out where I was and the right route to take.

On the fifth day, I was racing along the N10, well on schedule for an overnight stop at the youth hostel at Ruffec. I saw what I thought to be the route in, but, because on the Continent people drive on the opposite side of the road, it was actually the route out. Before I realised my error, a white car suddenly appeared on a head-on collision course. Immediately I swerved, but was knocked off onto a grassy verge, as the left-hand front fender hit my rear wheel. With some relief, I found myself uninjured and was able to get up from the grass. My bicycle appeared to be undamaged. The occupants of the car emerged from their vehicle and showed concern, but I told them that I was all right and they went on their way.

When I tried to wheel my bicycle into town, I found that the rear wheel was badly buckled, though the rest of it was undamaged. With some difficulty, I made my way into the centre of town and found the youth hostel. I was traumatised and in need of some rest. The restoration of my cycle to roadworthy condition would have to wait until morning. That night, I prayed to God that He would help me on my way.

The following morning, I managed to purchase a new rear wheel and rear tyre, of a similar quality and appearance to the items that were damaged, from one of the local bicycle shops. The cost of these parts was 240 French Francs (about £25 in 1982). Using the tools I had brought along myself, I substituted new for old and was on my way by 11 in the morning. The old wheel and tyre were so damaged that they were beyond repair.

The Pyrenees were truly spectacular and involved long stretches of climbing, which I had never experienced before. I had lunch at a hotel on the Col de Puymorens, at 1900 metres, before descending and entering Spain at Puigcerda. It became extremely hot and the sudden deterioration of the condition of the road was very noticeable. Another climb over the La Molina pass awaited before I was well and truly over the Pyrenees and enjoying a downhill run to Ripoll.

I arrived for camp a day early and had to spend the night at a hotel. The following day, I was able to join camp for an extremely successful fortnight, helping to decorate the old school for use as a local community centre. The freedom from social rejection that I had enjoyed at university continued at this camp: despite my idiosyncrasies, I became an accepted and valued member of the community. My only regret was that, as the fortnight ended, our work became rushed, with a consequential deterioration in quality. Great pressure was put upon us to get the work finished on time, but it would have been better to have left a good job unfinished than for us to have finished it badly.

Following on from this camp there was a four-day dash to Alicante at the height of the Spanish summer. It was incredibly hot, making the use of water bottles essential. I stuck to the coastal route to enjoy a near absence of hills, a tempering breeze from the Mediterranean, and a wide choice of cafés, restaurants and campsites.

At Alicante, I stayed at the youth hostel for four nights, visited the local tourist attractions and sampled bathing in the Mediterranean. With the latter activity, I took a calculated risk: I hid my passport and cash under a towel before entering the water and was lucky to find them still there on my return.

At that time, the youth hostel, its dormitories, and the cupboards in these dormitories were accessible to anyone from the street. Whilst I was away exploring the town, a thief used my nail scissors (carefully laid out near my bunk) to break open another hosteller's suitcase in order to steal valuable items. Another hosteller's towel and the bungee cords used to fasten bags to my rack were also taken. I did not notice anything amiss until after I returned – to find these scissors in the hands of another hosteller, who demanded a camera and some cash in return for them.

Since it was my scissors that had been used to break open that suitcase, I was the first to be suspected of stealing these items. An audience with the youth hostel director followed. I was ushered into his office and he called the municipal police. I was severely questioned and all my bags were thoroughly searched before my innocence was established. I was extremely relieved not to finish my expedition in the embrace of the Spanish justice system.

Over the next fortnight, my journey back to England was rapid and relatively uneventful. I took a different route back through Spain and France, which involved smaller roads and a rather more picturesque route. My route took in Lerida and Andorra: I did some of this travelling by coach, on a school skiing holiday in the early 1970s. There followed a spectacular climb, over the 2,400-metre Port d'Envalira pass, an overnight stay at Pas de las Casa, at over 2,000 metres above sea level, and a rapid descent into France. From there, my scenic ride took in the Central Massif, with an approach to Clermont Ferrand via the Puy-de-Dome.

At Clermont Ferrand, my request for directions to the youth hostel resulted in me being conducted to a similar hostel in the town centre. When I found that none of the showers were working, I carried out a little simple plumbing work to convert two non-working showers into one working shower.

From Clermont, I continued my scenic ride to England, bypassing Paris and avoiding becoming lost in that city.

The above adventures testify that a person on the autistic spectrum is not incapable. If anything, a raised level of anxiety forced me to think and plan ahead better than a lot of others, so as to ensure that the expedition was a success. Despite obvious idiosyncrasies, I was extremely effective when it came to carrying out tasks that did not require too much verbal communication, and this made me an effective team member at the camp.

Not being subject to advertising and social pressures

As a person on the autistic spectrum, I have built up a track record over the past 45 years of not being subject to social and advertising pressures. I resist change and have not conformed to trends that I found unnecessary and uncomfortable. I find all but the quietest forms of advertising profoundly irritating. Listed below are a number of examples of me resisting advertising and social pressures:

- At secondary school, I continued to enjoy Baroque and romantic classical music long after my peers switched their allegiance to the latest popular sounds. Indeed, such was my enjoyment of this that I took up O-level music in my sixth form years and secured a pass in this subject with my A levels.

- At the same time, my clothing preferences remained extremely conservative. I continued to dress quietly and smartly long after my peers were starting to look increasingly casual.

- In stark contrast to my peers, I preferred a visually quiet environment and did not decorate my personal space with posters.

- Owning and driving a car (or even a motorcycle) did not appeal to me. While my peers were keen to take the fastest route to owning and driving their own set of four wheels, I was content to continue using a bicycle and the train as my primary modes of transport. In the early 1980s, my parents succeeded in persuading me to learn how to drive: I passed my driving test on my second attempt in 1985, and consequently spent several hours behind the wheel of my mother's Saab. With the advent of the Network Southeast Railcard at about the same time, it became much cheaper and easier for me to travel by train and bicycle than to drive a car, and this finished my driving career. However, I still have an up-to-date driving licence, which I use as an identity document.

- Owning the latest electronic gadgetry does not appeal to me. Owning electronic gadgetry that is reliable, repairable and works as it should appeals to me greatly. If my mobile phone is capable of voice and text communication, then this is all I require. Besides, I find electronic gadgets that break down shortly after purchase extremely aggravating.

Reflections

Thomas has always craved friendship. The Church has offered him opportunities to make friends but he has experienced rejection and isolation in most other spheres of life, including school education, and early instances of work. His difficulty in reading social cues and understanding convention, and the insensitivity of others, have combined to damage his mental health and self-esteem.

Consider the person with autism with whom you work. Do they wish to have friends? Thomas wishes to have friends and socialise in social settings but prefers to get on with work when he is at work. Where does the person with whom you work have the opportunity to socialise? Is that their choice?

Thomas did not 'get' the implicit message that he had to 'sell himself' when applying for the mission to Morocco. In what spheres of life does the person you support experience implicit social convention? It might be in work, personal relationships, education, support service provision and your personal communication with them. What support can you offer to help make the implicit explicit?

Thomas finds certainty and, therefore, security in his Christian faith. Where does the person with autism you support experience certainty?

5
A life violated... A life missing
Cornish

Cornish was the first known autistic person (his preferred term) to attend the autism course at Carlisle. I was surprised by how much support he required to do so, and his fear was palpable on a pre-course meeting he asked for. It was only when he submitted the following essay that I understood exactly why he had such a fear of education. He has since gone on to achieve a masters level qualification and has published and taught in the field of autism. My own experiences with Cornish are described in Chapter 6. This chapter gives his account. Cornish is very angry about his stolen life. He expresses his feelings with force and uses language that may offend some readers. There is no intention to cause offence but, in accordance with my intention that the authentic and unmediated autistic voice should be heard, Cornish's narrative is presented as he has chosen to express it.

Cornish describes the school system as 'legalised hostage-taking' and is not sure that the neurotypical world has anything to offer him. He concludes:

"The life that I have ended up with is not my own. My life consists solely of something that has been done to me. Had the neurotypical world not interfered with mine, then obviously things would have been very different ... most pointedly ... a lot less trauma than I could have ever visited upon myself. Therefore ... my own life is missing, the one I thought I was going to live never materialised, it was and still is systematically denied to me. Therefore ... I have a life missing. Anyone seen it?"

Cornish wrote about his first morning at school in the 1960s as an assignment. He had left school with no qualifications and asked for support in writing at degree level. This was a transformative time, as I slowly became aware of the great harm that had been done to him by the education system, how his ability had been missed at school and how much it was costing him to come back into education in his fifties.

I had no idea ... no suspicions whatsoever of the horror that awaited me when I reached four and a half in August 1963...

I had no idea that the institution of compulsory schooling even existed. At four and a half, I had no idea of what constituted the greater world at large... I didn't even know that anything outside my immediate understanding existed... I didn't need to... I had my autistic bubble, and at that time that was all I was aware of.

At four years old it had only just occurred to me that these upright things that walked about actually had people inside them. And take my word, the thought had never crossed my mind that people and bodies were the same thing; or rather, I hadn't been able to properly conceptualise the existence of others around me... The only real thing that I was aware of at that time ... was me. So I had pretty much ignored them as they didn't represent anything real in my world. Much of what I understood of the world as a toddler came from my direct sensory experiences and internal processes, rather than any direct or indirect external input, i.e. from my parents, or the broader social context. I found it hard to take in much of what anyone said ... including my parents ... because nothing that was said held any interest or relevance for or to me, and again, it didn't occur to me that anyone was communicating anything meaningful or that anything reciprocal was required.

Perhaps, having read the above paragraph, you might think that being cut off from the outside world would be isolating and maybe disturbing, but to me it was like having a whole personal universe all to myself, where I was free to explore at will. It was a world of absolute sensory wonder, magic and discovery, where everything was fascinating, where all things needed discovering and all theories needed testing ... a world of absolute bliss. This was how I thought the world functioned back then, running on a natural order, which ordered and perpetuated itself in a beautiful, peaceful existence. Once I became aware of others, I thought everyone had their own unique and prized world of their own. It never once occurred to me that the majority of people shared a different world to me: a very different universe, where they shared very different thoughts and thinking from me. I also thought that everyone was free to do with their life as they wished without interference or internment ... *how fucking wrong was I...?* (Obviously I certainly was not thinking in those expletive terms at the age of four ... but that does sum up definitively my feelings at the time, and how when I think of those times ... it still brings back those heartfelt emotions.)

There seemed to be thousands of kids and mums when I was led through those gates. Everyone was milling around in a blur of arms and legs, in a never-ending assortment of shapes and colours.

I looked at the soot-blackened buff sandstone building which loomed oppressively above me. Overbearing and darkly overwhelming ... I was drowning in fear and anxiety ... my mind suddenly drowning in what was happening to me...

'This can't be happening to me!!!' my mind was screaming...

And a feeling which I had never encountered before took over the whole of my being ... absolute and abject terror!

I was drowning in dread, drowning in sudden anxiety ... drowning in the slow realisation of what was being done to me.

'Oh no, no, no, no, this cannot be happening.' My world suddenly felt very unsafe... My world was suddenly coming apart at the seams.

Some large green doors opened, and everyone started to move towards them.

All at once everything that was good in the world disappeared, the light in my soul immediately went out and my life from then on would be filled with darkness and terror... a living nightmare that was a daily Hell of absolute despair. My poor unsuspecting autistic universe was shattered beyond all repair, as I was forced against my will into the neurotypical universe... a universe that I never knew even existed until that morning. I passively surrendered as I realised that my life had never been my own. I had thought it was mine... but I was wrong... and in that moment I knew my life was over as the *'shock of capture'* (look it up) overwhelmed me. Everything that was magical and wondrous was over... All that was good in the world disappeared in an instant ... never to return. The light went out, and my life of misery started.

I was ushered towards these kids. I didn't know any of these kids. I didn't want to know any of these kids. I didn't want to stand with them. In fact, I didn't want them anywhere near me.

Their noises, namely their voices, began to grate in my ears, becoming painful, and – they smelled – and they smelled really bad. Not having spent much time around kids it was a total shock... Why did they smell so bad?

Also, I didn't know that there were so many kids in the world ... hadn't ever thought about it... Where the fuck had they all come from, what were they for and why were they here?

We were led into an enormous hall. I'd never seen, never mind been inside, such a big room with such a high ceiling, windows that were high up and huge, and enormous doors that seemed to be more about remaining shut ... keeping people in, and then...

All in one go, as my bubble shattered I saw the NT world that had eluded me for so long. In one overwhelming moment as all of my hypersensitivities swung round to see it in all of its horror, the NT universe dragged me down into a never-ending abyss of blackness that I didn't even know was there.

All of the echoes of voices, children and adults, all the scuffing and shuffling of feet bouncing off the walls, floor and ceiling, was making me disoriented, dizzy and nauseous. The light was bouncing off every painted surface, scattering and refracting everywhere. It was like being inside a giant kaleidoscope ... and everything was descending into sensory overload and utter chaos.

Deep inside, a silent scream had been screaming silently as the feeling of being trapped began to grip my stomach, and panic threatened to close in and run away with itself.

I wanted to tell my mum that something was very, very wrong here – that I wasn't supposed to be here. This place was very frightening and I didn't like being with so many people. Especially people I didn't know or particularly like. I already knew all the people I wanted to know. I didn't feel I needed to know any more people. I was petrified... I didn't belong here... *Every fibre of my being was screaming...*

'DANGER – GET OUT NOW!!!'

But I was utterly powerless. I tried to say something to my mum, but nothing seemed to come out... I was a rabbit caught in headlights.

I was trapped... Someone or something was now in control of my life... My days of freedom ... my liberty to explore and learn about my world ... had only ever been an illusion ... and the shock crippled me. My cerebral functions began to shut down, and in that maelstrom of terror, I began to lose my sense of self, and a very, very frightened little boy began to die a long and painful death. Not a death of the body ... but a death of the soul.

Panic began to grip me. Again, I wanted to tell my mum that something was very wrong and that I wasn't supposed to be here. I really didn't like this place. I didn't like being with so many people... I DIDN'T BELONG HERE!!! What seemed like an eternity passed...

I became aware of some grown-ups saying stuff at the front of the hall, and then we were led off to a smaller room. Why? Why was I here, what was going on? I just had no idea what was happening, why was this happening to me ... I had done nothing wrong!

In this room the walls were painted bright again, with those horrendous fluorescents flickering away ... *and* ... I noticed my mum talking to this strange woman. They seemed to know each other somehow, and I managed to work out that this woman seemed to be in charge, and then, in that moment, I realised that my mother had set this up for me!!!

I felt utterly betrayed. That moment, that I remember so well, was the moment that my trust in my parents was completely blown... This was beyond my comprehension, why would they do this? What had I done that was so wrong as to warrant this sort of punishment ... and ... I learned my first important lesson at school...

Grown-ups are not safe to be around, they are never to be trusted. And I never did again.

You may be puzzled by the last paragraph. But ... I had never been in a situation that had ever taken away and denied me my freedom and liberty on a daily basis. I got chastised very rarely at home. I had far too much interesting stuff to discover and learn about, so I never really got into trouble. Then I suddenly found myself in a place that was run on a foundation of punitive measures, where any misdemeanour was punished with shouting and scary words, and physical violence from grown-ups. This was the dark oppressive cloud that hung over me for the whole of my time at school. I simply could not comprehend that anyone, let alone a grown-up, would want to wilfully inflict pain and violence on me. How could this happen? And this terrifying concept kept me awake night after night, and petrified through the day ... because I could never predict when it would be my turn. How could any sane person be OK with putting small, frightened children under these conditions?

Today things are not so different from when I was at school. The anticipation of something horrendous happening to you is still a real killer for any Aspergian, and always keeps you on the edge. Young or old, if you are autistic, you don't ever get away from this ... because this is exactly what is taught.

The light scatter in this new room was difficult to cope with. I struggled with bright vibrant blues and reds that seemed to dance before my eyes, only to then find that they belonged to objects across the room. My perspective was all messed up; I walked into chairs because all the wood was the same colour. I walked into walls because they were so shiny that I couldn't determine where the painted surfaces began. I was under an absolute sensory battering; I had never experienced anything like this in my short life.

My mum finished talking to this woman, sat me in a corner and promptly left. And I thought that she had left me for good. The only logical explanation I could come up with was ... *this was a place for the really bad children. Therefore ... I must be a really bad child, and that's why she's left me.*

Only problem was ... I couldn't remember having done anything bad enough to warrant this. So maybe I was just a child no one liked, and that was why I was here. I then proceeded to amalgamate both of these concepts into my psyche ... and that's who I became as a child ... someone who had done something so terribly wrong (but I couldn't remember what), and because of that, no one liked me. That was the best I could reason, given the situation at the time.

For some reason the kids had gathered round this woman and she started speaking to them. The meaning of what she was saying was completely lost on me, and so I kept on sorting the coloured wooden blocks that I had found on the table where I was sat into their appropriate sequence of colours.

Absorbed in what I was doing ... trying my best to shut out the horror nightmare that had suddenly become my world ... I never noticed the seemingly never-ending shadow that was looming over me... I hadn't noticed the woman approaching. She said something to me that didn't make any sense, and I just looked up at her fearfully.

'Come and sit with the rest of us,' she repeated.

The words seemed to slow in my mind. I'd heard perfectly well, but couldn't react. It was like being in one of those dreams where you are trying to get away but your legs are stuck in something sticky and gooey.

Why couldn't she understand that I didn't want to sit with the children? I just wanted to go home. I didn't like children very much anyway. Why would I want to go anywhere near them? What was wrong with her? What was wrong with this nasty grown-up whom I had done nothing to? Who was she to keep me here against my will? More to the point, how could she get away with doing this?

Getting no response from me, this woman grabbed my arm and hauled me over to where the other kids were sat.

The touch on my arm was sudden and unexpected, and not only did it feel like fire on my skin, but what the fuck!!! ... an ABSOLUTE VIOLATION of my person!!! No one ... *but no one, ever touched me except my mum, and that was void from now on.*

62

'Sit here,' she said, and plonked me on a chair.

My resentment was building apace. Who the fuck was this woman, whom I'd never met before, to tell me what to do? She meant nothing to me, and as far as I was concerned, I was nothing and fuck all to do with her. She was scary, and I didn't like her one bit. She wouldn't let me go... I had no idea who she was, or what she wanted from me. I found her and the rest of the kids very threatening, and very menacing.

As I looked at my contemporaries, I couldn't work out what they were about. They didn't seem to like each other at all. They were constantly bickering with each other, loud and very aggressive. Punching and pulling and pushing and biting each other, the level of cruelty and how vindictive they were had me scared out of my wits. I hated the lot of them. They were just like the other children I had tried playing with in the past ... cruel and nasty. I found their behaviour scary and intolerable. I had never experienced this level of aggression before.

(Incidentally Professor Robert Winston states that 'we are at our most violent between the ages of three and seven'. Well, speak for yourself Prof. Winston, because *I* never was!!!)

I understood the wind and the stars, the rain and the sunshine, the call of birds and the breeze in the trees. I had taught myself to read by the time I was three. I was already educating myself ... and here I was, as good as locked in a room full of complete psychopathic, homicidal imbeciles... My life was well and truly over.

'This can't be happening,' I kept repeating to myself over and over again. 'This just can't be happening.'

I had no one to turn to. For the first time in my short little life I knew what it was to be completely abandoned. Helplessness descended, and my sense of who I was ... was becoming lost and fragmented in the horror and confusion. I was lost in a world that hadn't existed until a couple of hours ago... I was lost and frightened, and it seemed no one cared.

Nothing was making sense. I was falling deeper and deeper into a sea of despair and anxiety. Too many things were happening for me to process ... too much ... too much. My whole world had imploded in on itself... The whole of creation, it seemed, had turned against me and my very soul.

I desperately tried to make sense of things. I could only come up with:

'Well ... it must be me... I must be the problem.' After all, none of the other kids seem to be reacting like me... so it must be me. 'It's me ... I'm the bad boy.'

I was already losing touch with reality... I was already losing my grip. How had I ended up in a place where all they do is trick you into making mistakes so they can immediately punish you at every given opportunity? To humiliate and frighten you into whatever it is they want you to do. And all the grown-ups at this place were the same, as I found out... None of them would let me go. I was their prisoner, whether I liked it or not.

I had been forced, against my will, into a world more nightmarish than anything I could possibly have imagined... I was being forced into the maw of Hell itself!!!

On that day, my sense of self was obliterated. If every day from now on was going to be the same ... made up of dread and terror ... then what was the point of living? What was the point of life? I had been quietly seeing to my own education and wanted to get on with it. Why was this being done to me?!!!

What was left of me in that moment vowed to reject anything and everything associated with school. I could feel the scars and injuries being left on my soul, second by second.

I sat in that chair, unable to get my head round anything that was happening. I began to settle into an inner orbit of black despair and depression. And yes ... my history of forty years of chronic depression started right there and then, that morning. Everything around me was in a state of complete chaos, and logically, I began to accept this as part of the punitive measures being meted out in this place... It was all part of the punishment.

Deep inside, on a soul level, I began subconsciously broadcasting a galaxy-wide distress call to the home world... Fifty years on, I still am.

Feeling increasingly detached from the situation, I noticed the woman's voice becoming more and more threatening, and louder and louder.

Why did she want me to listen? Why did she want me to take notice of her? What the fuck did she want?

I hadn't approached her. I didn't want anything from her ... so what did she want with me? Moments later, I found out the price of not understanding. As the confusion within me had built over the few hours I had been there, I had withdrawn more and more into myself, as any self-respecting Aspie does under such circumstances. Lost inside my own torment, *a hand suddenly appeared and very rudely slapped me hard across the face!!!*

We hadn't even made it through the morning, Miss Wood of 1963. That was the first time I'd ever been hit like that … and that is a slap that I remember every day of my life, because that was a slap that was unwarranted and undeserved and something I am unable to forget.

It was totally unexpected, and I was completely shocked and beaten. I had nothing to go up against something like this. These were grown adults… I was just a little kid. What could I do? And, from that moment on, I began wishing that I'd never been born. I could do nothing against these big bullies.

The second thing I learned at school was:

Everything you do here has consequences. Whether you are aware of what you are doing or not, the punishment is guaranteed. The punishment is terror.

The third:

The terror is always there and never-ending, and you can't get away from it (even when you have left school).

I look back at the intensity of my emotions at that time. To my mind, if I'd had a heart condition or something similar, there is no doubt that I would have dropped down dead by the end of the day. Dying of fright used to be a constant obsessive fear of mine that persisted well into my thirties. I was convinced that if I did this I would be in more trouble than I'd ever experienced so far. This was a bit nuts, considering that I would be dead of course. But this is how fucked up that day had made me. Since then, my life has been dedicated to not 'getting done' for anything… I still dread committing even the smallest misdemeanour… That's how fucked up I still am.

People over the years have refused to believe that being sent to a school (mainstream or otherwise, it wouldn't have mattered) could have such a devastating effect on me. And I sincerely mean it when I say that it wasn't until September 11 2001 that an example that shook the world came anywhere close to how much fear I went through on a second-by-second basis. And I'm talking about the passengers on board the second airliner, having just watched the first one hit the Twin Towers. That's the sort of sheer panic and fear I'm talking about. It was that intense… In the face of that sort of threat, I never felt safe with these adults. I was always under the impression that my life was in jeopardy, that it could be snuffed out whenever they wanted, at a whim. THAT was my days at school!!! Back in the classroom…

> *I just couldn't get what these kids were about; they flocked around this woman like they knew her. Well I didn't know her … and I didn't want to get to know her. I'd never seen her before in my life, so who was she to take command of it? And the kids … they just flocked around her. Couldn't they see what was happening here?*
>
> *'You're all locked up here as well,' I kept thinking. 'Why can't you see?'*

They all seemed be accepting the situation and, even more scary, they all seemed to think as one, which was a new and strange concept to me, and another thing to be frightened of. They were like a separate species from me, and that's exactly how I viewed them, and everyone else who displayed similar behaviours. I could find nothing of myself in these people. Forty years on, and having a post-grad in Asperger's, I now know why!

Before starting school I existed in a completely different world to the one I'd just been thrust into. School was re-describing the world from the one I'd been born into, and was now presenting an evil sadistic one. I think it was Prof. Winston again who said:

> *'Starting school is when children first meet the darker side of human nature.'*

They know this … and yet it is still supported by the majority? It makes no sense at all!

Break time came without warning. A bell went off. I was sat, 'shock upon shock', holding my ears when I noticed that all the kids had disappeared. That woman was approaching again … I wasn't sure if she was going to hit me again. She never said a word; she grabbed my arm again and hauled me outside. With my arm smarting, I stopped, amazed to see a mass of kids milling about in the schoolyard.

> *'What the fuck is going on now? Why are we out here all of a sudden?'*

This was freaky shit building on freaky shit, and was scaring the shit out of me. Nothing was making any sense whatsoever!

I found myself backing away from this madness that I wanted nothing to do with, and into the woman's legs behind me, whereupon she just shoved me out into this maelstrom of insanity.

Not knowing how these kids' minds worked, I didn't know what to expect. I am a naturally gentle passive person... I had no idea what was coming!

After seeing that woman slap me in class, word soon got around, and from that day on the kids just zeroed in on me, and I was subjected to constant and systemised humiliation and bullying for the rest of my years trapped in this insane system of abuse.

As I ran from these kids, who thought it wonderful fun to pick on me for sport, I managed to find a place to hide in the outside toilets, and, there without warning, I was suddenly and wholeheartedly projectile-vomiting.

My fear and anxiety had finally got the better of my physiological system, and this was a pattern I was to endure every morning before going to school for the next 11 years. My breakfast was never in my stomach for more than forty minutes for the whole time I was at school.

Because I had no idea of what was expected, and what was acceptable for them, and what doing wrong was to them, I never knew what was happening from one moment to the next. I simply had no idea, by their standards, what I was doing wrong. I was teetering on the edge of an abyss every moment. I couldn't tell anyone how incredibly miserable I was because I simply didn't have the academic terminology available to me, as I have now. I could not explain the unexplainable to anyone.

I was also under the impression that being miserable to the point of suicide might be a horrendous misdemeanour, and the correctional process that was being implemented didn't seem to be working. I just couldn't take the chance of something worse being done to me, to make me into something they wanted me to be, and that I very obviously wasn't ... so I ended up saying absolutely nothing!

The rest of that first day was a never-ending nightmare. I had no frames of reference that would make any sense of my being there. And I plunged deeper and deeper into a self-hating pit of despair. I was totally surprised when my mother came to get me at the end of the day. For one false moment of hope, when I thought that the day was just a one-off, my despair lifted, until I was informed that this was going to be done to me practically every day from now on.

Every night I would eventually cry myself to sleep when the dread of the coming dawn finally overwhelmed me with exhaustion. Every morning I would wake up and wish with all my heart that I'd never been born... I just wanted the pain to stop... It never did.

I wish I could say that I was an isolated case, and that these days things have moved on. But things haven't changed much, and I wasn't an isolated case. I have talked to Aspergians of my generation and every one of them has a similar story to tell. The problem is ... their kids are experiencing exactly the same issues and abuse as they and I did in mainstream school ... and some in the autistic specialist schools fare just as badly.

If it had just been me, someone who has to deal with the trauma that is the legacy of *Forced Cognitive Manipulation*, if it had just been me who has to put up with the frequent post-traumatic night-time terrors, if it was just me who fears the world of the neurotypical, then I would accept the logic of the evidence that I was something of an anomaly...

BUT I'M NOT!!!

I would urge anyone reading this to explore such luminaries as John Taylor Gatto and his seminal book *Dumbing Us Down*. Many Aspie survivors of neurotypical compulsory schooling have pointed this very accessible book out to me and I'm always recommending it on to others. Other authors who question the ethics and the validity of compulsory schooling, such as Clive Harber in *Schooling as Violence: How Schools Harm Pupils and Societies* and Ivan Illich in *Deschooling Society*, make my case for me. So it's not just me who knows something is very wrong with the treatment of our young children – especially autistic children. At the end of each school day, I was always left with the feeling that I had been somehow tampered with. It felt like I'd had someone rummaging around in my underpants... Every day I felt like I had been somehow horrendously raped and violated. The violation is still happening... It is still being allowed to carry on!!!

In my experience, all that compulsory schooling amounts to is:

'LEGALISED HOSTAGE TAKING'.

Children are being taken on a daily basis... Friedrich Nietzsche said:

'What is the point of being healthily adjusted to a very sick society?'

The aim of compulsory schooling is to perpetuate this sickness, so it is wrong to use our children to perpetuate the illusion that school is the best place for our kids to be and learn.

Yes I may have a massive chip on my shoulder, if that's the way you want to view it. If that's what it is, then remember… I never gave my consent to be part of it … and it will always be the price that I and many others pay on a daily basis… My deep trauma, that is now part of who I am, was NOT MY CHOICE!!!

The life that I have ended up with is not my own. My life consists solely of something that has been done to me. Had the neurotypical world not interfered with mine, then obviously things would have been very different … most pointedly … a lot less trauma than I could have ever visited upon myself. Therefore … my own life is missing, the one I thought I was going to live never materialised, it was and still is systematically denied to me. Therefore … I have a life missing… Anyone seen it?

Postscript

Cornish was in email contact with me as this chapter was finished. We thought the following, taken from three emails verbatim, might be of interest to readers. They are challenging!

I just thought I'd bring you up to date a tad. I'm currently receiving post-traumatic stress disorder counselling from our local Mental Health Team. Before you start thinking that it's been the chapter that brought it all back up … it wasn't. What it has done is my feelings of anger and violation haven't decreased any over the years, and I don't want the rest of my life to be dominated by these feelings. Regardless of the promising steps of folding time back on itself according to one of my current favourite Aspies, Dr Brian Cox, we can't turn the clock back. But the nightmares have been getting out of hand again for quite some time, so hoping things have moved on since my last involvement with them, I'm seeing a counsellor on a weekly basis, and try and put some of the stuff to bed, or just make it behave a bit better. Happily things have moved on a bit, which is encouraging. The counsellor recognises her limitations when it comes to Asperger's, but she is more than happy to listen. It looks like we might be able to affect some of the Demons I've been given. The counsellor has said from the beginning of our sessions that after examining my records and having read this chapter that owing to the chronicity and longevity of my trauma, we don't know if anything will really help. So many opportunities lost.

I was watching the Britain's Got Talent show the night that Susan Boyle put in an appearance. The audience immediately reacted before she'd even said a word … and so did the judges. Straight away it was very obvious to me as usual that we were looking at an

Aspie sleeper. The looks on everyone's face said it all ... and she was judged and immediately dismissed ... until she started singing ... and the rest is history. However, the day after, the press were vilifying her and especially what the *Daily Express* had to say, which disgusted me to the point of writing in to their website. Amongst the rest of the comments left, I explained my position as a consultant and that SuBo was obviously Asperger's, which no one had picked up on. I want to stop the discrimination because of the label. A couple of hours later when I had another look ... they had taken my comments down off the site. Well, as you can imagine, I was furious! And now in today's news feed there's an article on SuBo saying that after being diagnosed as a child with a brain tumour, last year she was finally given a diagnosis of Aspergers. AARGGHHHHHH! I keep saying to myself over and over ... this shit has got to stop. How can I convince the professionals that AS ID and diagnosis can be done much more effectively by visual assessment alone? That one's a bit rhetorical, I don't expect an answer will ever be forthcoming to tackle it.

Susan's story tugs at me so hard because I know what it's like to live with the confusion and pain of not knowing just what's been going on all of your life as an Aspie. If someone like me could be given the opportunity to identify and diagnose, then we could stop these stories of 'collateral damage' happening. I, for one, am sick and tired of receiving and bearing the brunt of professionals' 'blind ignorance'. Susan had to endure a childhood of pain and torment because the NT professional that originally saw her could not see that he/she was looking at an autistic face. And I could give you the number of clients I've seen that I have had re-diagnosed as Asperger's, after having been given a bi-polar diagnosis or some other nonsense that the professional has thought up because he can't think of anything else.

And this is the thing that terrifies me. Most clinicians will always mis-diagnose because most clinicians are NTs and are neurologically incapable and unable to visually see and identify who and what is sat in front of them when it comes to autism. This is what has let me down since getting involved with the local mental health teams from 1980 onwards. The diagnosis that I received throughout my time with the mental health teams was constantly Depression. Damned right I was depressed ... bloody well suicidal for most of the time.

If I'd been seen by one of the clinicians that I use for diagnosis, I would not have had to put up with the life I've had. Why these particular clinicians? Simple ... only another autistic person can immediately spot another autistic person. Not all Aspies can do this, but most can. All of the people I have helped get a diagnosis have been based purely on my visual assessment ... then diagnosis from a clinician. People ask me ... 'but how do you know I'm Aspie?'... and I always reply 'no getting away with it... 'You've an Aspie face!' And there is no getting away from it!

There is also another important point that has come up recently and that is, especially amongst the older Aspies that I know, they find it uncomfortable to be seen by an NT. They feel that it should be their autistic right to be able to choose an autistic professional should they want to. Don't for a minute think that there aren't many professional Aspies within the NHS, because there are lots. It's just that many feel that it would be professional suicide to 'come out Aspie', as one GP was telling me a while ago. So how do we solve this? Answers on a postcard or just email them to me.

It only takes one NT to turn our gift into a nightmare!

Reflections

Cornish's life has been dominated by fear, which he likens to being a passenger on the second plane to crash into the Twin Towers on 9/11. He thought he would die of fright. Does the person you support experience fear? How can you support them through this?

Cornish has explicitly stated that he has little wish to be included in a neurotypical world. In fact he finds it presumptuous that we might think it would be beneficial for him to be included in an NT world. To what extent does the service you work for insist upon inclusion? Is inclusion part of the mission statement? Does the person you support have the opportunity to choose when they experience inclusion? Does that person have a choice about how they experience exclusion or inclusion?

6
The lecturer and Cornish
Steve Mee

I got to know Cornish when he attended the autism course. I was course leader at the time. He asked for help to turn the story in the previous chapter into an essay. Supporting him during the course brought me face to face with severe limits to my understanding. The resulting reflections have proved to be transformative.

In the previous chapter Cornish described his first morning at school in shocking detail. His whole school life experience was one of relentless trauma. His mental health suffered and he seems to have been trying to get over this ever since. He describes his life as having been stolen.

I first became aware of Cornish when he sent an email asking me to phone him, as he wanted to prepare to come on the University of Cumbria autism course. This caused me some confusion, as he was registered with the university by his given name, Stephen Cornwall, but his email was signed with his preferred name, Cornish.

He was not the first person with autism to attend the course but he was the first to request a pre-course discussion. At this point I became aware of two conflicting thoughts, which do not reflect well on me at all. On the one hand, I was proud that people with autism appeared to value the course and that we appeared to have successfully met their requirements so far. On the other hand I thought (here goes!): 'What a faff! I'm busy enough without an individual student demanding individual attention, and why has he named himself as an adjective?'

This thought seemed to have a life of its own, emerging from somewhere dark. It put me in mind of a cartoon in which an individual attempting to make a hard decision has an angel whispering in one ear 'give the money back!' while a devil whispers in the other ear 'go on take the money, no one will know'. This duality of thought is something we, as professionals, can usefully become more aware of. Rather than deceive our neurotypical selves that we always act in objective, non-discriminatory ways, we might be aware of the devil whispering in the other ear. Or am I the only one who has two voices? I subsequently wrote about this issue in my book *Valuing People with a Learning Disability* (M&K Update, 2012).

Cornish's manner was very assertive over the phone; he was quite clear about what he needed. He asked to see the route to the classroom, the classroom itself, the seat he would have, the curriculum and the details of the assignment. His friend Lois, the author of Chapter 12, supported him on this visit. As I approached reception, I wondered if I would be able to meet his needs and whether I would even recognise him. I need not have worried about that. The leather cowboy hat, long grey hair, goatee beard, shades on a dull day, leather waistcoat, jeans and boots all gave him a very distinctive appearance. I introduced myself – and was shocked at how nervous he seemed. He was visibly shaking and his trembling voice suggested a state of deep anxiety.

We visited the classroom and he chose a seat in one corner, as he likes to have his back against the wall. The fluorescent lights were a big problem so we hoped for sunny days during the course. The shades and wide-brimmed hat were not a style statement (another neurotypical judgment of mine) but a way of reducing the effects of artificial light. As I waved Cornish and Lois off, I did not really believe he would be attending the course.

He *did* attend, and Lois attended too (to support him) and also complete the course herself. He was vocal in class and frequently corrected lecturers and fellow students. He often made reference to his own experience of autism. After one class, he told me there had been an issue for him that day. The lecturer had been describing the problem with personal space for people with autism. She made the point that neurotypicals can tolerate very close proximity if they are not facing the other person – for example, when sitting next to someone or standing in a queue – whereas a person with autism might find this as stressful as being face to face with someone else.

She said, 'You know how it is when you are queuing for your flight to Spain for hours...' Cornish told me that he had not liked this because he himself had never been to Spain. She had said, 'You know how it is when YOU are queuing for your flight...' However, he then said that he knew that she had not really been talking to him but his autistic self was telling him she was. This was a moment of real reflective learning for me. My neurotypical devil was asking how this could possibly be an issue if he knew she was not really using 'you' in a personal sense. It was as if he had a choice in the matter; he was choosing to let the autism direct his thinking and cause problems when he knew it was not the reality.

And then I thought about my own response to a certain situation. I know someone who really winds me up. I seem to respond to certain triggers every time we talk and I believe that he deliberately uses these triggers because he knows they work. Before we meet I give myself a talking-to, promising myself that I won't respond and will let his comments go over my head. But five minutes into our get-together, I rise yet again to the same bait. It put me in mind of Michael Holding, a West Indian fast bowler, who frequently bowled out the England batsman Mike Gatting. He often trapped Gatting into hooking to deep fine leg by setting the field and bowling a bouncer. Gatting knew Holding would set this trap for him and yet he fell for it time and again. He remembers saying to himself 'don't hook, don't hook' as Holding came in to bowl the bouncer. He was saying 'don't hook' the moment he hooked and was caught yet again.

Cornish responding to what he knows is an illogical autistic response, my defensive response to the wind-up merchant and Gatting falling for a trap he knew was being set are all examples of the same human tendency. We all know what we *should* do but we then do something else – in response to a deeper motivation than conscious choice. When I really thought about Cornish's story, I realised I had previously 'othered' people with autism, not allowing them a full range of nuanced human behaviour available to us all. My neurotypical preconception was wrong yet again.

As Cornish described in the previous chapter, he left school with post-traumatic stress and no qualifications at all. The University of Cumbria follows the typical higher education procedure in allowing people to study at one level higher than they have previously achieved. With no previous academic achievement, Cornish was registered at the introductory level (4). People with no prior achievement usually have to work hard to develop an academic way of writing, frequently requiring a lot of tutorial support to achieve level 4. However, Cornish told me on week two of the course that he needed to complete the course at level 6 (degree level). Apparently he had been told that he could start the Sheffield Hallam University masters course if he successfully completed the University of Cumbria module at degree level.

This was most unusual and I tried to warn him about the severe challenge he faced, quite apart from the issue of how to get round the university protocol. He had no problem with taking the risk and stated, 'I'm autistic, you tell me the rules of passing at level 6 and I will follow them to the letter.' Fortunately the head of school had the necessary understanding to enable us to sidestep the protocol. Now it was down to Cornish, with my help.

He asked me to meet him at reception the day he came for a tutorial. As I approached him, he looked straight through me. I said 'hello' and he then recognised me. He told me that he did not really see faces and tended to rely on hair outline. I had had what little hair I have left cut the previous day, so he had not recognised my outline. He was supported on this trip by his friend Julia Pilkington, the author of Chapter 3 and a future student and lecturer on the autism course.

When we entered my office, I could see yet again that he was shaking with fear. He handed me some work that he had previously written and wanted to know if this would be useful for the essay. I was stunned by how well written it was, and shocked by its content. He showed me a shorter version of Chapter 5 in this book. He then started to tell me his story, which was so arresting that I fetched a colleague in to hear what he had to say. It seemed to me that he had managed to crystallise the essence of the problems faced by people with autism. As we talked, he said he was not feeling very well. I asked what the problem was and he said my office was too untidy. He felt dizzy and said that if he was not sitting he might actually fall over. A colleague who shared my office had hung a crystal in the window. This was slowly rotating and sending beams of light round the room. This was causing him to lose his train of thought altogether. I had to take this down before he could continue.

Cornish had come to ask about essay writing but he had presented me with a story. I needed to explain how to turn this into an essay. We all know that an academic piece of work needs to contain references. This is an interesting issue for me. I was an undergraduate in the early 1970s, a time when there was no great emphasis on including references. For example, when writing an essay contrasting explanations of social change by Marx and Weber, a student could write safe in the knowledge that the lecturer knew what both authors had written and they knew that you, the student, knew what they had written. It was pointless to regurgitate the sources, and the student was marked on their ability to argue the finer points in their own way. In this case, it was possible to earn a good mark with no references apart from the two prime texts.

Nowadays, the norm is to reference everything and you lose marks if you don't – for example, 'people with autism breathe (Jones 2013)'! I found myself saying to Cornish that he needed to take the story, identify aspects of his autism and link it to the literature. I gave an example involving his sensory difference concerning busy environments and lights that made him fall over. He needed to go back to the literature and find out who said that this was a problem for people with autism. He replied, 'I say it is a problem, I'm autistic.' I had no answer other than, 'Those are the rules, mate.' He shrugged and went off to change his story into an essay.

Interestingly, I have since had to say to him that, for his narrative to be of use in this book, and of probable wide interest to people, he would need to 'de-essayify' it and turn it back into a story. This has made me reflect on the way in which we neurotypicals label people with autism as blind followers of rules and regulations. Yet here we are in academia, following a set of rules about setting and marking assignments that I, for

75

one, find very difficult to defend or believe in. The truth is that we all – autistic or neurotypicals – follow rules.

Cornish produced his essay. It was astounding. He was awarded a mark of 94%. He has subsequently gone on to achieve his post-graduate certificate in autism. What did Miss Wood not see when Cornish entered her class in 1963? It has been noticeable that the people with autism who have attended the course at the University of Cumbria have usually not achieved their potential at school.

Cornish's story had one last effect on me. In many ways, his experience actually resembled my own. We are a similar age and so school was similar. I did not get school at all. Why were we there and why were we expected to do these apparently pointless things? Why did they want us to learn to read? Bizarre as it seems now, I thought boys had no need to learn to read, as it was a girl thing! Looking back, I think I could read but just refused to do so. This was compounded when a teacher told us we would be 'doing English this morning'. I thought 'English' was a nationality and, for some reason, thought we would be learning about the war with Germany! When the class started and I realised that we were yet again just doing reading and writing, I ignored the lesson. I think I assumed the teacher had no idea what she was talking about. Any subsequent 'English' lessons were similarly ignored.

When I moved up to junior school, the recommendation was that I should be put in the 'remove' class, which was the terminology of the time. I was to be put into the class with people with a learning disability. In fact this did not happen – and it is odd to think that my academic title is now 'Reader'! After my meeting with Cornish I was haunted by the thought of our similar experiences in early education. Perhaps I was neurotypical enough to manage to get back on course and so our paths diverged, but we started from a very similar place.

I have learned a lot from Cornish and have come to realise that, despite us being on either side of a label divide, we have more common ground than difference. He always signs off his emails with 'Stay Groovy'. I try my best.

Reflections

I became conscious of how my neurotypical 'lens' affected the way I perceived Cornish's behaviour and needs:

- His attire and choice of name appeared 'attention-seeking'

- His desire to check his environment was a 'faff'

- His need to always have to make a point in class became a bit irksome

- His response to the idea of waiting in a flight queue seemed optional, and therefore unnecessary.

When I reflected on my responses, I realised that I had 'othered' Cornish. I had not allowed him human frailty and complexity. It was only when Cornish told his story that I started to see the full picture.

Do you really know the full story of the person with autism whom you support?

We all like to think of ourselves as non-judgemental and supportive. But if you think about your response to the people with autism you have supported, can you truly claim to have made no negative judgements? Have you ever thought of them as 'making a fuss', 'choosing to behave like that' or 'tiresome'?

I felt entitled to 'take some credit' that I appeared to work well with people with autism. Do you experience any self-esteem benefits from your work with people with autism? Might this sometimes prove to be a problem?

7
Surviving at school
Christopher in conversation with Kate Mee

This chapter is based on a conversation between Christopher and Kate Mee. However, Kate's contributions have been removed, as the focus is on Christopher. Christopher was taking his A-levels at the time when this account was recorded. He has had constant battles throughout his time at school. He does not really understand the problems that neurotypicals have with him. He is just 'him' and does not understand the autism label at all.

A quotation from his account was used at the start of the Introduction to this book.

The thing about autism, if you suffer from it, is that you can't tell the difference between yourself and someone who doesn't. You can't think any other way. You only have one perspective, and from your perspective you can't tell that anything's wrong. Other people say you've got it. You're different. There's something wrong with you. They give you this label. There's nothing you can do about it. It doesn't matter what your perceptions about yourself are; it's other people who define you. I wouldn't know I was autistic if people didn't tell me I was. So it's not what *I* think that's important; it's what other people think. No matter how much you hate it, no matter how much you try to change yourself, it doesn't go away. It's like the scars left by a hot iron brand; you can't run and you can't hide. You're autistic and there is absolutely nothing you can do. You have no idea how soul crushing that is.

I worry about upsetting people. Treat people as you wish to be treated yourself – that's the categorical imperative. People don't treat me like that. Some people are careful, some people aren't. Some people try to use empathy, whereas others don't. You can usually tell who is doing what because the people who don't try to use empathy just try to piss you off because it is funny. People have done it all through school. I'm year 13 but I can remember them doing it in year 7 and 8. They used to try and wind me up deliberately.

Why do I believe certain things? I don't know. From experience I like to think I've learned about the world but when I think back all I've got is a belief and justification of what's behind it. For example, you know Mrs X's son? In my opinion he's a right bell-end and I'm glad I haven't seen him in two years. When he was in year 11 he was trying to piss me off and he was doing it consistently. I can't remember how, and that's part of the problem, I can't remember what he was doing. So I avoid him even though I can't remember what he did, I just know he pissed me off. It's like a set belief. It's like Brian Jones in year 11 – he joined in with Mrs X's son.

I don't know why they pick on me. Maybe it's because I'm sensitive and think in a different way. Maybe its because I get pissed off easily. I honestly don't know. But for as long as I can remember, I have been beaten up, annoyed and pissed off by all sorts of people.

I can remember two things about the first primary school I went to. The first thing is being in a little side room with a support teacher, playing with some Lego bricks or something. The other thing is lying on the floor in the playground being kicked repeatedly. I don't know why and I don't really care any more. The two people who generally beat me up didn't really get on very well with each other, or at least their families didn't. I think, due to some sort of problems between their families, they got bullied themselves by the other family members. Someone told me about it while I was still at that school about nine or ten years ago. I ended up getting a kicking off these two. I don't think it was because of their family conflict. It was because of me and the way I acted. I think I was a little shit. With hindsight, I think that because I was bullied I got a bullying mentality into my own head. I didn't know that at the time but people have told me. That's when I had to go to another school.

I spent the best part of a year at the pupil referral unit in town. It's a temporary school for children who have problems, while they are waiting to be moved onto a different school. They don't teach you much. I remember one lesson where they taught you how to use a compass. I learned about northeast and north-northeast! I'm not sure what happened. I know I used to read a lot of books because people have told me I did. I don't think the lessons taught me much.

Then I went to another primary school and I was still violent. I don't know how many people I hit, and it was sometimes for trivial reasons. One time I feel particularly bad about was with a lad who kicked a pigeon that had an injured wing. I thought that was cruel, and I picked him up by the throat and threw him. In hindsight I don't know why I did it but it made me so angry at the time. It was spur of the moment. At that school I managed to break a sink. I broke a lock on the door; because the door was locked I pulled it and the lock in the middle stayed firm but the bolts at the top and the bottom ripped off. I caused quite a lot of damage at that school before I left! I was probably a bit better by the time I left, to be honest.

I left and went to senior school. I almost went to the grammar. If there had been a choice of going to the comprehensive as a second choice and I had the chance of taking the exams for the grammar I might have tried going. My sister had that option, which pissed me off. Pretty much all of my friends from the primary school went to the boys' grammar so I was pretty pissed off about that too. My best mate went, although I haven't really spoken to him since his mum died about four years ago. It was when I was in year 7 or 8, his mum died of cancer. I think I saw him once after that and I haven't seen him since.

I recently had another problem with someone I thought was my friend. I try to avoid him now because I piss him off. I'm not entirely certain how I pissed him off but he was shouting at me. What happened was I was explaining something to him about dates. When you are talking about the date 1776 that is the 18th century right? But I said to him that it was the 17th century. He said 'No it isn't. You've got that wrong.' I didn't really understand what he was saying and I was thinking about it but it must have been my expression or something. He snapped at me. I told him I was just thinking about it. I didn't know what had happened. Then he shouted at me so I left. I'm not completely sure why he shouted at me but I know really; it is because of me. I pissed him off. If I could change it I would.

There might be other reasons he was fed up with me. He is sensitive at the moment but it was me who pissed him off so it is justified. He is a bit unreasonable but in the end it was justified. I don't want to piss him off any more so I avoid him.

I have tried talking to him about it in the past but it has made it worse. I can't remember what I said. Have you ever had a conversation but you can't remember a single word that's been said but you can remember the general message? But if someone was to turn round and say to you afterwards, 'Could you repeat what I just said?' you would just not remember.

All through school, my friends stayed away from me when I was violent. It was an absolute nightmare trying to make friends. It was one of the reasons I was shit scared about coming to this comprehensive. I haven't really made many friends. The only two people who I really spent time with, well, I just used to follow them around. I was accepted by these two in the end. This was in year 7 and 8, although, well, it might have even taken longer than that, perhaps up to the end of year 9. I'm not sure if I would call them friends, but I don't know what else to call them. And then I changed populations in year 10 which was the best thing that happened to me because I met new people. It was a fresh start, meeting people like you [Kate] and your friend.

Up until changing populations, I had still been violent. In year 7 I had four isolations. In year 8 I can't remember whether I had any isolations but I was still in trouble for being violent. I was really aggressive right up until that point, and I changed. I'm not sure what happened, or why I changed, whether something snapped or whether it was a more gradual thing, I

80

don't really know. I started thinking about life and really started to regret it. I suppose I am a violent person but I try to suppress it as much as possible and stay away from violence. I just try and avoid conflict.

There is another odd thing about me. I hate to say it but I'm doing what I want but I don't really want to! I love being the centre of attention but I hate the fact that I love being the centre of attention. It's drawing attention to myself and I kind of figure that is why people try to piss me off so much. Because I draw attention to myself I mark myself out a little bit, and people grab that, do something and realise that I get pissed off easily and carry on doing it. I know I should keep a low profile and that attention-seeking will get people trying to piss me off but I still do it and I hate the fact that I do it.

It's a bit like the debating society. I'm not very good at debating; I think about a point and then shout it out from the other side of the room. I've been in two debates in the sixth form. I lost the first one and won the second one about the United Nations. I still feel really guilty about that. Literally the day before, I had almost nothing prepared. My first speech was crap and the teacher told me I ought to try doing this. He suggested I should propose that people should be asked to pay an extra dollar on an aircraft flight and that would go towards helping people. It's only a small increase in the price but think how many people would make a fuss about having to pay an extra amount on their fare.

I looked at an article and I based my speech on that, pretty much; small things make a big difference. So it was the teacher's idea really. And then I was up until 12 o'clock the night before and I'd got my first speech done and I was happy with that, but the second speech I hadn't started and so the teacher effectively wrote it. I changed a few little bits around but the second speech was effectively written by the teacher and it was just me acting. The teacher said I was doing a good job, going over the top with all the emphasis, the movement, keep doing it. It made me put a bit more into it. I think that's why I won, I connected more with the audience than everyone else. Even though everyone else fit the brief better. It was my presentation, not the actual content.

I don't like saying I won it; it was the school that won it. It was a little bit me but a lot the teacher. I know if I was the teacher I'd be thinking 'I helped him win that'. I haven't spoken to him about it. I feel like I should but I can't bring myself to. The reason I like debating is that half of it is acting. It's putting the emphasis on the right bit. For example, just moving a comma in a sentence you can completely change its meaning. You can play tricks with numbers, but with words you can really make them bounce.

Reflections

Christopher finds the label 'autistic' hurtful, like the searing of a hot iron. Have you ever labelled someone as a result of carrying out an assessment? How did that person respond to the label? Might you have done things differently?

Whilst at senior school, Christopher changed significantly from someone who was regularly aggressive towards his peers to someone who managed to keep himself out of trouble. He cannot remember what caused this to happen. Those of us who work with people with autism should always remember that change is possible; people are no more fixed by their autism than the rest of us by our neurotypicality. Do you manage to work with the possibility of change in mind?

8
Into university
Samuel

Samuel has left school and has just started a degree course at university. He communicated with Kate Mee and myself via email. This chapter is taken virtually verbatim from his emails. I was particularly struck by his resilience during a period of transition that is difficult for any school leaver. When I asked if he would like me to chase up the support systems on his behalf, he chose to tackle it himself. However, he has struggled to fit in, as shown by the following description:

> "On the first day of university they started with an activity that involved 'getting to know people'. It made me really uncomfortable and was irritating. It was an activity that 99% of the rest of the forensics group excelled at but I didn't (sadly) due to my autism. I didn't want to offend or give the wrong impression to people and so this resulted in me removing myself from the activity. I felt inferior compared to the rest of the group."

My course is forensic science, which is stereotyped as being about crime scene investigation (CSI), though it can be used in other professions. I chose the course because I found it interesting. It was pure science at its best, with testing different types of evidence, testing ballistics and seeing scientific theory being practised for good. Also my dad is a police sergeant so it seemed logical to go for that course.

My first term has been a difficult process, and not at all an enjoyable one. I suspected it would be like this from before the start of university life. On the first day of university they started with an activity that involved 'getting to know people'. It made me really uncomfortable and was irritating. It was an activity that 99% of the rest of the forensics group excelled at but I didn't (sadly) due to my autism. I didn't want to offend or give the wrong impression to people and so this resulted in me removing myself from the activity. I felt inferior compared to the rest of the group.

It also became clear later in the term that my support that had been agreed was not being placed in operation. I was supposed to have regular meetings with the learning support each week but only received two of those meetings, and that was after having to call the learning support to state that. Initially I didn't want to fuss but it was proving to be a 'handicap' to my learning. The only support that I received was a note-taker who was only there to catch information that I might not get, and that was it.

I felt awful for most of this half term and wanted to just give up and leave. People were not helpful. My classmates see me as an outcast, and pretty much everything I said to my best friend Kate in a text a few months ago has come true. She asked me which would I find worse, going to university or not going? I responded by saying:

> What's worse is going around doing stuff to secure a future where people like me are looked down upon as inferior to them and so the 'normals' place you in areas which ultimately highlight inability and so you earn no respect from the people surrounding you. That's worse than missing out – the feeling of inferiority in a place where those who don't have disability can do stuff that you can't because you were constructed incorrectly.

It has been difficult and I'm not enjoying university life but my family has been supportive (if not a little pushy) in the matter and they say to me that if I give up now I will only be proving to these people, and all those who thought I was not good enough, that they were correct. So I will continue. I've been though one hell (sixth form, where I was treated awfully). I've now entered another but that is just typical for people like me. I'll carry on and come out a better man than all those who treat me wrong. To answer your question, I am not enjoying my first term and doubt I will enjoy the second. (Sorry for rambling, I'm sick of all this stupidity when it comes to people like me.)

I know my classmates see me as an outcast because they give me funny looks, like I don't belong, and talk to me slowly as if I'm not as intelligent as them. When I talk they look like they regret talking to me, as if I'm going to go on forever. This rarely happens as they seem to avoid me at all times – except one person who I really dislike. When I told him I was autistic, he went around stating the fact that I was autistic, with a 'look at my autistic friend, does he look marvellous with my curtains?' type of attitude, so I tend to avoid him.

I get the impression that I'm discriminated against because I don't fall in line with what is characterised as normal. They can't see people like me fitting into normal society without having someone holding my hand. And then at the end of the day it's never the autistic who has achieved but the normal person behind that has in their view. I've had help throughout my school life until university but it was my hard work that managed to get me where I am today.

It's not my autism that is the obstacle affecting my academic life. It is the lack of help and the bureaucracy from my university that has proven to be the real obstacle for me and people like me. My request is simple. I just want help and a little bit of extra effort in helping me. But no, they say, that might be unfair to those who aren't autistic, or we need to negotiate with student finance on how much help you get because it's inconvenient for us. I'm sorry, does the fact I want to be educated, to have a possible academic career in the subject, which is the right of every person alive, inconvenient to you? They say it's not fair to people who aren't autistic if I receive help. I say it's not fair to deny someone help, whether they are autistic or not.

I find it upsetting to see a world where people don't understand the needs of autistic people, and why do people turn around and say we don't want you here, or we want you here but we won't help you? They either discriminate because they don't understand, or it's inconvenient they ended up with us. Sometimes they positively discriminate in order to show how diversity aware they are and show themselves as model people. This puts a negative light on autistic people, as others say to themselves, 'Why are they getting extra help and we are not?'

That is what I feel is happening.

What would be most useful would be someone who was available to help me with social issues, as I mentioned earlier. I need someone to point me in the right direction when it comes to work so I don't lose marks. I'd like to have regular meetings with my lecturers to see how I'm coping, rather than them just assuming I'm doing OK. The help I need is someone who understands where I'm coming from and keeps me on track with work, but is not patronising and doesn't treat me like a child who has just learned to spell. I'm a human being who was built differently who needs help, not an entirely different creature who has to be slowly integrated into society – otherwise people will think he/she's a freak.

I haven't been patronised by lecturers, though I was patronised by people at my sixth form and I am being patronised by my classmates at university. They say 'It's good you've managed to get here despite being autistic' and they talk to me slowly, one word at a time. Recently I was in a lecture room, the lecturer was late arriving and one of my classmates (not sure of his name and to be honest I don't really care) told everyone a joke. Other classmates were in the room, minding their own business. I can't remember the joke but I asked how that was funny and said that I didn't get it. Instead of trying to explain it to me, he then went, 'Just think Sam, it's a joke, laugh at it', which upset me. Everyone else laughed and I felt isolated and somewhat deliberately picked on. To some extent, I felt he knew I was autistic and told a joke I didn't understand to highlight my autism. I rarely mention my autism, as I don't want people to judge me.

The lecturers don't patronise me but they ignore what is happening around me, as if they don't want to be involved or don't want to know it is happening. If they had meetings with me, this problem might have been sorted out already, but they seem to simply ignore it. They have a 'close your eyes and ears and pretend it's not happening' mentality. They are nice people but they just never want to get involved.

My new classmates are not like my old school mates. They are not friendly, they are mocking. I'd rather not talk about these people who are just stupid, quite frankly. There are one or two who just get on with stuff and don't join in but they aren't the type of people you regularly chat to but just politely say hello or pardon me when you see them and that's it. The rest aren't really nice people from what I've seen so far in my time at university.

The people I am still friends with, from before university, that I'm still in contact with, are pleasant people. They don't shout at you when you don't get the joke and they actually explain it. They are people who are just nice, who don't make stupid comments. They ask me how I'm doing and try to get me involved and accept who I am as a person. They are fun, kind, considerate and just nice people to be around, who are smart enough to know what is appropriate, to be honest. The friends I have are very smart people and have made me feel happy and content with who I am. The people at university, on the other hand, are all about themselves and don't seem to care who they hurt when it comes to making themselves happy.

I guess a better world for me would be a world where one isn't treated as an alien based on whether or not one is able to understand certain elements of language, such as jokes or figures of speech. A better world would be one where people understand that if someone was built differently they might need help and shouldn't be seen as lazy or selfish. In a better world you could express yourself and not be ridiculed or patronised because you perceive the world differently from the norm.

But generally a world that is just nice, caring and where people can understand the difficulties of others. A better world is one where people understand and not a world where good women and men do nothing, because for evil to prosper, it takes good men and women to do nothing.

That would be a better world, a much better world.

Reflections

The rituals and practices in many everyday settings can exclude people with autism. Samuel chose to exclude himself from the first day on a course because of the 'getting to know you' icebreakers. The very activity intended to help students integrate as a class ended up excluding the person with autism. To what extent should day-to-day practices be changed to accommodate a minority? Is there any way such an icebreaker could be altered to include people with autism? Are there any aspects of your own day-to-day practices that might exclude people with autism?

Similarly, day-to-day social conventions, such as having a laugh, can exclude people with autism. Is it discriminatory to share a joke in the presence of people who interpret language literally?

Samuel hates not being accepted for who he is. He hopes to have a little acceptance and positive support:

> "But generally a world that is just nice, caring and where people can understand the difficulties of others. A better world is one where people understand and not a world where good women and men do nothing, because for evil to prosper, it takes good men and women to do nothing."

A question we might all ask ourselves is whether Samuel would look at our behaviour and think that we meet these simple expectations.

Section 3

From education to work

9
Looking for work – a job in itself
Richard Lewis

Richard is a school leaver with autism who is very concerned that his life should have purpose. He has contributed two chapters to this book. The first is his account of attempting to negotiate the world of job-seeking. He wants to work and for his life to have purpose. Richard's mum offers her perspective on events, shown in italics.

Having tried to use his local job centre, Richard's conclusion was:

"The whole system makes no sense to me. All I wanted to do was work, and I was turned away. Since this experience, I have been told by others that I should launch a complaint against jobcentre plus, but I don't want to do that. I never want to go there, or speak to anyone there again. I have learned of a few local schemes that are designed to get disabled people into work. Sadly, upon inquiry, they require a referral from jobcentre plus, which makes those options unviable. The experience has left a nasty taste in my mouth."

Hello, everyone reading this. My name is Richard Lewis, and I have Asperger's Syndrome, which is high-functioning autism, but I tend to refer to myself as an 'Aspie'.

Like many with Asperger's Syndrome, I have struggled in the world of work, from finding a job to managing in the workplace. To give you some background, I have done work experience, an apprenticeship, temporary work, full-time work and volunteering. However this story is mainly focused on my experience with jobcentre plus when trying to get help finding work. As the title suggests, this experience was not straightforward, and had plenty of challenges. I have asked my mother, who accompanied me during this experience, to write down her account of events, which I will be including with my account. So you can get two perspectives – one Aspie, one non-Aspie.

My son Richard has always had a strong work ethic. However, when his last job didn't work out, due to the company not being as successful as hoped, Richard found himself unemployed and, although having a voluntary job, needed to have a permanent paid job to report to on a daily basis.

My experience with the job centre started when my previous job came to an end. I was made redundant, as the company could no longer afford to pay my wages, having not made enough money during the recession. I didn't take this well, as I enjoyed the work. I was working full time and it gave me needed purpose and routine, which is very important to some Aspies. To keep myself occupied whilst looking for work, I volunteered with a local charity. Personally, work for me is more about the job than it is the money, as it gives me something to do, gives me purpose, and routine. Sadly I know I need to earn a living if I ever want to live independently. I kept searching for work whilst doing my volunteering work, and had secured some weekend work, which is enjoyable. However it only keeps me occupied for one day of the week, for eight hours, leaving the remaining six days to find something to do, as I hate being bored and without routine.

Richard had heard of a man at the job centre who could help disabled people into work via new training etc so he rang to make an appointment.

I rang a man who was meant to help registered disabled people into work, as by this point I had been unemployed for a few weeks, and had applied for a dozen or so vacancies with no success. I had been in the job centre before, only to check for vacancies, but now I had my appointment booked, and I wished to discuss whether I should declare my Asperger's Syndrome on job application forms. In the past I felt it worked against me, due to employers' misconceptions.

The appointment duly made, he set off on his push bike to do the 12-mile round trip.

I went to the job centre on my push bike as it was a nice day, and I am very keen on cycling. The trip there took me about 25 minutes, and would take a similar time on the ride home due to the hills and traffic.

When he arrived at the job centre, he was asked if he had registered online prior to the appointment. When he said no, he was turned away and was told to register online at home.

When I got there, I went in with my CV, qualifications and other paperwork, which I had transported on my bike with difficulty. I went through to see this person in charge of aiding disabled people, and he started by asking me 'Have you signed on online?' I remember saying, 'No, I don't want to sign on.' I was told nothing could be done for me until I signed on online. I asked if I could sign on, right then and there at the job centre. I was told 'No'. He gave me the web URL to go to so I could sign on at home. I felt cross, as I had to pedal back home, not having achieved anything, and I thought 'Why couldn't they tell me I had to sign on first, when I made the appointment?'

Feeling confused and frustrated, he came home and started to register.

I got home and went online and entered the URL I was given so I could sign on online. The URL provided didn't work. I entered it again and again, and nothing. I even typed the whole thing out manually several times, including the 'http://' at the start of the address. Eventually a quick Google search showed me they had provided the incorrect URL. I noticed they were transitioning from their 'Directgov' web service to a 'gov.uk' service. As I went through the gov.uk pages, I was bounced back to the Directgov website to fill out my details. I did do some web design at college, I am no expert at all, but I suspected whoever was in charge of this transition was ... to be polite, lazy. They were using the old website Directgov, which was supposedly 'shut down', as a redirect, instead of creating the form again under the new gov.uk website.

While he was filling in the details, I went searching for the information required about the tax area code regarding his last job.

I spent about two hours carefully going through all the options, making sure I filled in all the details correctly, with my mum checking it. As I finalised the details, the web page did something strange. Some code came up on the page – I had no idea what was going on. All the info I had input over two hours vanished, and it bounced me back to the start again! It was the last straw for me.

Richard had carefully been inputting the information when the website crashed, and all the details we had spent hours putting in disappeared. He went ballistic, total meltdown. He started throwing things round his bedroom whilst shrieking; he pulled a drawer out of his desk, which he ended up breaking. I was really scared, as this hadn't happened for a few years.

I don't really recall what happened. I just felt so angry and frustrated, losing all the information I had carefully been inputting on the web form. I remember being very angry, then looking round at my room, which was trashed, and running from the house to get some air.

After he left the house, I called the job centre and explained what had happened. I was asked to bring Richard to the office where they would do the details clerically (why couldn't this have been done when Richard first went?).

When I returned home, my mum told me she had been on the phone with the job centre and that we were going to complete the paperwork there. This just confused me, as they said that doing the paperwork there was not possible, and I felt upset as I had not had a meltdown for a few years.

We arrived and went through the various processes with three different clerks.

One of the clerks told Richard he would have to give up his voluntary work, because he had to be available for job interviews 24/7. Richard tried to explain that he had an arrangement that he could call in on the day and say he wouldn't be in if he had an interview. This, however, fell on deaf ears.

They told me I would have to stop my unpaid voluntary work. I didn't like this, I enjoyed my work, liked the people I worked with, and I had an arrangement with the manager I could have whatever time I wanted off. All I had to do was call in on that day. I was told that it was irrelevant and I would have to stop volunteering. With the prospect of my routine being shattered, I just felt I wanted to shut down, I felt dismantled.

He was then given a check sheet on which he had to tick off what he had done in searching for work. It meant cold-calling companies, checking various websites, checking local papers, etc. (which he was already doing).

With my routine gone, they said I had to look for work on various mediums several hours a day. I looked for work weekly with the paper, three times a week online, and called about vacancies weekly, a routine I felt happy with. I was told it wasn't enough, and now that I had no volunteering work I could do it for four hours a day. Now I just wanted to switch off.

After two hours of the 'quick and easy procedures' I could see Richard's eyes going to the floor and his body slumping in the chair.

I don't know how you describe a shut down – you don't want to be there, and you want to block everything out. One of the clerks told me I was not eligible for job seeker's allowance. I didn't care. All I wanted was help to get into work, and routine – I didn't care about money – and at this moment I had neither. I remember just before leaving, the clerk told us my mum and I would have to come in once every two weeks to sign on, as my mum had to vouch for me, or be a witness or something. I am not sure why but she had to be there for some reason, even though they said I couldn't have job seeker's allowance.

The clerk then told us we couldn't see the person who aids with disability for another month – even though I had cold-called and booked an appointment with him out of the blue. It made no sense at all. I remember after that we left.

We beat a hasty retreat and returned home. He was in a state of shut down. He was like this for a few days. We kept trying to encourage him to look, but he was just staring into oblivion.

I was very upset, as I no longer had a routine I felt I could execute. I don't really remember much of the next few days, other than being unsure what day it was, or what I was doing. During this time I found it very hard to communicate and felt demoralised.

Nothing was worth this, so I contacted the job centre and told them Richard would not be signing on any more, but would continue to look for work himself.

I remember my mum telling me I was no longer signing on. I was so happy. I was back at my volunteering work and loving my routine, which was back to normal. A week after signing on, I received a letter from the job centre, stating 'you are now eligible for your full payments of job seeker's allowance' after being told I was not eligible.

The whole system makes no sense to me. All I wanted to do was work, and I was turned away. Since this experience I have been told by others that I should launch a complaint against jobcentre plus, but I don't want to do that. I never want to go there, or speak to anyone there again. I have learned of a few local schemes that are designed to get disabled people into work. Sadly, upon inquiry, they require a referral from jobcentre plus, which makes those options unviable. The experience has left a nasty taste in my mouth.

I went to a different jobcentre plus a few months later, in a city about twenty miles away, while visiting friends. I walked in and saw various posters, encouraging job seekers to take up volunteering work. Upon inquiry, it turns out that job seekers are allowed to volunteer as much as they want, as long as they can become available for job interviews, which is what I had.

I am to this day still unemployed, but I am happy. I do my volunteering work; I have my weekend job, along with DLA, which keeps me going financially. That said, I am determined to find full-time work. I don't mind what work, as long as I enjoy it, and I earn enough to live on.

Altogether it was a dreadful experience, and I think dealt with insensitively.

Reflections

Richard needs the security of routine. He needs something useful and consistent to do, on a daily basis. To what extent does the person with autism you support have such consistency? To what extent do they have a life purpose?

The job seeker's systems proved impenetrable to Richard. Furthermore, they were inconsistent, ambiguous and inefficient. In fact it proved to be the case that the people who worked in this system did not understand it either! It is hard to understand how the system could carry out its stated purpose, to help people find work. Richard was made to claim benefit even though he did not want it, and this in an era when there is so much political energy devoted to getting people off benefits! This would be frustrating for any us, but for people with autism the consequences can be very serious.

If you work for a system that is accessed by people with autism, you might consider whether that system is logical, consistent, unambiguous and accessible. You might carry out an audit of the system and ask yourself: Is it autism-friendly?

10
An Aspie's apprenticeship in a county council
Richard Lewis

Despite the trauma of trying to negotiate his local job centre, described in the previous chapter, Richard did eventually manage to secure employment. This is an account of his experience. It is probably the case that many of the readers of this book will be professionals employed by the public sector. In summarising his experience of work, Richard says:

> "Looking back on my experience, I summarise that the public sector isn't completely Aspie friendly. For someone who requires logical decisions, straightforward instructions and understanding, from my experience at least, it was a poor fit."

'Logical decisions' and 'straightforward instructions' in public services; I'm afraid I laughed out loud when I read this!

Hello people reading this, my name is Richard. I have done work experience, part-time work, full time and as an apprentice. This story I will share with you is about my experience of being an apprentice for the local authority. Before going any further, I want to state that no real names are mentioned in this account to protect individuals' privacy.

This all started just over a year ago, in early summer of 2012. At this particular time I was unemployed, and had been for a few months. Over Christmas 2011, I had been working in a warehouse for a local company and I had really enjoyed it. Sadly after the Christmas rush, myself and several other workers found ourselves unemployed, having been made redundant. It left me feeling really down, as I enjoyed the work a lot more than I thought I would, and I seemed to get on well with my colleagues.

Anyway, at this time (May 2012), whilst looking in the local paper I saw a job advertisement from the council for a business admin apprentice, to work in children's services, to study at the local college. This seemed very appealing. I thought to myself it would be very beneficial.

I would be studying at the college, where I used to study. I know the site and staff very well. I would be working in the public sector; so there would be a pensions scheme, and this particular role in children's services meant I would be helping others like myself. I was thinking to myself this was a win-win situation.

I should state upfront that, before tackling this apprenticeship, I had obtained an A-level qualification in Business Studies, and that business as a whole has been one of my Aspie fascinations/interests for a few years, it being my best subject at school. I am a regular viewer of the TV shows *Dragon's Den* and *The Apprentice*, and I often wonder how big companies make money, profit margins, etc. This apprenticeship offered a level 3 qualification, which is an A-level equivalent, so on the qualification side I wasn't going to gain a lot. However, I was far more interested in the actual job. For me, work is more about the job than it is about the money. This philosophy on work comes from an Aspie's need for routine. When I was in my last job, I loved it so much because I had routine, I had a place to report to daily, and tasks to execute. The pay was just a bonus. That stated, let's carry on.

I requested an application form on the phone, and promptly received one in the post. I have always struggled with application forms, as I sometimes get confused. I always had a reader in exams at school for the same reason. I would misunderstand the question and give the incorrect answer. To combat this, I fill in all application forms in pencil, get them checked over by a family member, scribe over the pencil in pen, let the ink dry, then rub out the pencil underneath. It seems long-winded, but it's the only system I have to ensure I get everything right. That said, hopefully you can understand why I find the job-seeking process stressful, as it takes me far longer to execute than others, adding to my agitation. Once it was done, I sent everything off in the post, and waited.

A few weeks later, I received a letter notifying me that I had been shortlisted for an interview, which was to take place at the local college where I had studied. I was extremely happy, excited and nervous all at the same time. I couldn't wait to get my chance to show off my enthusiasm for work, especially in this apprenticeship. In the days leading up to the interview I bought a suit, from a supermarket, as being unemployed meant I had little money. I also did some research into the public sector, the local authority, and the department I was going to work for.

The day came, and I drove to college with all my qualification documents. I booked in at reception and made my way to the office where I was going to be interviewed. Being a past student, I didn't get lost. I waited outside the office until I was called in by three women who were sitting behind a desk. I jokingly thought to myself, Lord Sugar, Karen and Nick are ready (reference to *The Apprentice* TV show). I shook the hands of the people and, when gestured to, sat down opposite them.

I was introduced to the people, one being Suzanne, a tutor from the local college who I didn't know, but I explained I was a former student which I believe worked in my favour. The other two were both staff members of the council. One, called Beryl, was responsible for all apprentices throughout the council. The other was called Amy. I do not remember her role, but I didn't see her again after the interview.

The interview went well. They asked me questions regarding my interest in working in the public sector, and I inundated them with my research into the public sector and my fascination with business. There was also my own invested interest in the disabled. Being registered disabled myself, I was keen to be given the opportunity to help others like me, and I explained that I had given talks to schools, helping to raise awareness of Asperger's Syndrome.

As the interview concluded, I felt very confident, and happy that I had done my best to get the position. I shook hands with everyone again as I left. They added that they had a few more candidates to interview that day, and said that they would phone me in a week's time to tell me if I had been successful or not.

I went round the town and did a few jobs, spending the whole day out, which was unusual. It was about 4.30pm and I was looking round a shop, when my mobile phone rang. I checked and the caller ID was 'private', meaning the number was withheld. I answered cautiously, not knowing who it was. It was Beryl from the interview. We spoke for a bit about the interview and how it went; she then said words I will never forget: 'You've got the job.' I literally dropped everything in my hands, screamed out loud and jumped up and down on the spot, overwhelmed, feeling happy and excited. This, however, did prompt some odd looks from other shoppers nearby. I remember thinking to myself that they must have been pleased with me, to offer me the job the day of the interview, when they had stated it would be at least a week before they made contact, whilst they analysed the other candidates. A few days later, Beryl called again, with details about when I would begin.

A few weeks passed, and I was briefed that I was to go to the local college, where Suzanne (the tutor I met at the interview) would drive me up to the city, which was 60 miles away for some training for the first two days with the council. After that, I would start work in the local town. I didn't suspect anything, as the council was mainly based in this city, so I assumed they would send me to the resource, rather than send the resource to me. The drive was long, and not a lot was said. Another apprentice came too. She had secured a care apprenticeship with the council and was also going for this initial training, as she was from the same geographical area. It seemed all apprentices for the council county-wide would be attending, which made me feel rather anxious.

As we pulled up, we came to a small business estate; I thought it was a bit of an odd location, as none of the buildings were council buildings. However I tried not to let that phase me. We entered one of the buildings via a reception area. We waited about for a while; then a man in a suit came, and ushered us to a meeting room. We entered. The room was filled with other students, roughly twenty other apprentices from all over the county. We took seats at the front of the room, and the man in the suit left as we began to be addressed by a woman who works for the council, who would deliver a huge bombshell.

She explained that this was the location of the training provider. The company in question we will call Private Trainers (not the real company name). This was a huge slap in the face and very different from what, up until this point, I had been led to believe. Never at the interview was it stated that the training provider wouldn't be my local college, but in fact a private training company, based far away, who I had no knowledge of. I wanted to speak out and ask what was going on, but I was in a state of shock I guess, and I just couldn't bring myself to speak.

Things got worse as we started doing conventional team-building exercises. About 80% of these apprentices were city-based, so I thought it was pointless getting to know any of them. The only other apprentice who had been driven up with me was nowhere to be seen. Suzanne, the tutor from my local college, had also disappeared, which added to my distress.

By lunchtime I think the staff caught on I was not happy. I was rocking in my chair and stimming a lot (which for me is repetitive leg movements). I somehow managed to express my concerns to the council worker who was present, and the representative of the private training company. I was told that the change was made 'for my benefit', and that I could 'easily commute' there. I explained that the local college where I thought I was going to do my training was situated 6 miles from my house, about 15 minutes in a car, 20 minutes on a bus, or 25 minutes on a bicycle. I asked how I was going to easily commute 60 miles once a week, versus the 6-mile commute I already knew and had planned out in my head.

I was told buses or trains would be fine, or that I could drive. I inquired how I was going to afford to do so, and I was told that, in addition to my wage of £2.60p/h, I was entitled to up to £15p/w travel expenses. While there I checked bus and train timetables and displayed evidence that, in addition to my having to commute to my place of work, there wouldn't be sufficient funds to cover this additional travel. I was very upset as for weeks I had been looking forward to going back to the local college. I was told they would get back to me in the next few weeks with a decision about what to do with me.

I then asked where the other apprentice was, and the local college tutor. I was told that because she was doing a care course she would be attending the local college because the council deemed it more appropriate. This made me feel very confused, and de-motivated. I asked for more details but I was told that nothing more could be said.

The remainder of the training session was a blur. I was handed paperwork I didn't understand, shown information on a PowerPoint I struggled to process, and whenever I asked for explanations again it held everything up, which agitated the other apprentices. So I stopped asking and tried to figure things out, with questions about my training buzzing like bees in the back of my brain.

The following day I went to the local college, as planned, to await my lift to the city for my final day of training. I was told by the tutor Suzanne that the training day was to be cut in half, and that the other half of my day was to be spent at my place of work so I could get acquainted with my colleagues and see where I would work. I questioned why we should spend hours commuting and not just go to the place of work right away, and the tutor shrugged. This time the other apprentice was nowhere to be seen.

On the drive to the city I kept questioning Suzanne, asking why I wasn't allowed to attend the local college as agreed, who the new training provider was, and generally what was going to happen, and she couldn't give me an answer.

As we arrived, I entered the same room again with the other apprentices. They all stared at me. I took my seat, and we had a few presentations, and I was given more paperwork that I struggled to understand. I was then informed, after what seemed a very short time, that we had to leave – if we were to make it back in time for my half-day induction. As the commute would take over an hour, I judged it a bit of a waste of time.

An hour or so later I arrived at the office that would be my place of work, a building owned by the council, I would say built in the 1970s. I was dropped off by Suzanne, and I made my way into the reception area. There was no receptionist, but there was a telecom button. I pressed it and got through to someone. I notified them that I was the apprentice and, a few minutes later, my new manager (who we will call Joanne) came to greet me.

She took me round the various offices and departments, introducing me to all the staff. I wasn't in my best meet-and-greet mood, but I did my best with a small wave and nod of my head. We eventually made it to our office, where I was introduced to some of the other people I would work with.

The department I worked for in children's services dealt with statements for children with learning disabilities. I had a statement when I was at school, as I needed some support. As I mentioned earlier, I had a reader in exams. I state this because one of my colleagues, named Karen, opened with 'Hello Richard. Welcome to the madhouse' in a welcoming and joking manner, but then said 'I remember reading your file'. This sent shivers down my spine. I inquired 'What file?' and I was then informed what the department did. I was very interested and asked if I could have a look. I never remember seeing my statement before, and I have read up on Asperger's to give presentations on it, as it fascinated me. It hurt me when they said 'No you can't.' I felt extremely uneasy. Why couldn't I see my own file, about my diagnosis and statement? Let's say, after that episode I developed paranoia about information, which continued throughout the rest of the year.

That scare sort of tainted the rest of that day, but I remember being shown my desk, PC and so on, basically my own workspace. I was also shown the filing room where all statements were kept securely in paper files, and I was impressed with how well they were stored. It was a nice office. I was told that the statementing officers were mostly out of office, which they were that day, so I was only initially introduced to half the team. With that settled, they sent me on my way, and told me to come early the next day as the department had a meeting elsewhere, and we would car-share. I got home that night exhausted, and tried to push all that bothered me behind.

The following day I made it in early, and all of us (including one other member of staff who I hadn't yet met) got in the car. As we drove, my manager told me not to worry if I didn't understand anything, as it was my first day. After an hour or so driving, we arrived at the office where the meeting was to be held.

We all entered a massive boardroom where there were twenty to thirty people gathered around a large table. At one end there was a large TV set up to video-conference with another group of people at the other end of the county. I took a seat next to some random people, who I had never met before, who worked in children's services elsewhere in the county. Then we were doing introductions. People would state their name, job title, and what they did. Soon it was my turn, and I said rather nervously, 'Hello everyone, I'm Richard Lewis, a business admin apprentice, and it's my first day,' which was met with laughter and applause.

The meeting was soon in full flow. People were making points and using jargon I couldn't understand at all, but I didn't panic. As my manager said, it was my first day, and I wasn't expected to understand everything, but I did my best to pay attention, and to take in as much as possible. I remember that one person was angry that her department had been cut, and people had left, while a new multimillion-pound building was being commissioned, and that many were complaining about a new IT system that had been put in.

I should have mentioned I am interested in technology as well as business. I have used both Microsoft Windows and an Apple Mac, and have built my own PCs, and I tend to act as first port of call if friends or family have computer problems. That explained, what happened next will make a lot more sense.

In the next part of the meeting, a man in a suit, who I can only describe as your stereotypical milkshake salesman, came in – with a too perfect suit, haircut, bleached white teeth – hopefully you get the picture. He took his stance at the head of the table, and began to tell everyone that he was in charge of a new IT system (not related to the one I mentioned before), which was going to make all paper files in the statementing department redundant. I listened intently, as I felt he was using certain terms to try and trick the other members of staff, to make them fall into a false sense of security. If someone countered him, he would agree with them, win them over and carry on.

As he concluded, however, he said something along the lines of 'The system is completely secure,' which prompted me to raise my hand. He gestured to me and I said something along the lines of:

Nothing is completely secure. Remember Gary McKinnon? The person with Asperger's who hacked into the White House? If someone with a computer you or I could buy from a supermarket can hack into the world's most powerful country, then anyone can hack into your system. Yes you might ask who would hack into it? Maybe a parent with a grudge? A kid who gets bored? Or maybe some rough who wants to steal someone's identity? Who knows? The way things work with your paper files now is if someone wants to steal that data they have to physically break into the office. Via the internet and an IT system, someone from China could hack in, steal the data, and spoof an IP address to make it look as if someone from Germany hacked into your system. The data is compromised, and you're left wondering who the hell did it.

I just said what I thought honestly, I didn't think of anything else. It seemed the right thing to do, in a kind of black and white Aspie thought process way, looking back on it. He looked very nervous and trailed off after that. After the meeting my colleagues said I shouldn't talk to people like that, and then said I'd done well for speaking my mind, which confused me a lot.

For the rest of the week I was being settled into my office in my local town, given log-in details by the IT department, experimenting with specialist database software and trying to get the hang of things. I remember addressing my manager and I said, 'I have Asperger's Syndrome, which may mean I need an instruction repeating or rephrasing from time to time. I also want you and everyone else to know, if I do anything odd, or strange, or something unproductive, please just tell me. I can then try to fix the situation, it will be hard but it's better than screwing everything up.'

That was my way of saying, here I am, and let me be as helpful as I can. I have always been open that I am an Aspie, and I always try to be helpful. I do remember asking again why I couldn't see my file. I was told it was against policy. I asked what the policy was and I wasn't given any details, which annoyed me greatly, as I wanted to learn more about my diagnosis, as I was diagnosed very young and do not remember much about it.

About two weeks passed in my new role, which mainly comprised getting used to things – learning how to file things, getting my PC set up, getting my new email account working, learning the specialist database software, and getting used to some of the other office tasks like sorting out the mail. It was around this time that I inquired if any word had been given about my concerns with Private Trainers to Beryl, the person responsible for all apprentices. She assured me that all this would be dealt with at my first meeting/review with a training provider from that company. The good news was that my case had been heard, and they were going to travel to me. Also, the local college I was meant to be going to would be used as a training area, which I was happy about. That said, I was not as happy as I would have been if I had been trained by the local college in the first place, but this was beyond my control.

The date came, and it was postponed. When I inquired why, no reason was given, other than 'It will happen next month instead', so for the first month of my apprenticeship I had no training other than my initial induction. During this time I struggled to understand what I was doing for my actual apprenticeship work, which was for my qualification.

At this time I was introduced to more of the team, as statementing officers were using the office more often now. I had also befriended another apprentice in the same building. She, however, was about to end her apprenticeship, as she was going to university. I asked her why she was cutting the apprenticeship short to go to university, and she told me it was because she hated the Private Trainers tutor, found it a lot of work for little pay, and had no opportunity of a job come the end of the apprenticeship. Looking back, this should have been the first set of alarm bells to ring for me, but I just thought it was her department's problem, and her opinion on the training situation.

A few more weeks passed, and I was trying to get into my work. When filing I knew I kept making mistakes, and my manager Joanne kept having to go over the techniques again and again as I kept doing it wrong. I didn't want to; something just didn't click. It made me feel bad, as it was very basic, and I was taking up Joanne's time. Anyway I kept plodding on, not getting far with that particular task, but with all other tasks I felt I was doing well and when I asked for feedback my colleagues all seemed to be happy with me so I felt happy and secure.

A week later, two months into my role, the trainer from Private Trainers came down from the city to see me. The day before this meeting she asked if we could have the meeting at my place of work, as she couldn't book the local college, which again confused me. It led to me running round like a headless chicken to find a spare room we could use to meet in. The trainer also asked me to bring a copy of all my qualifications. I had the same trainer as the other apprentice in the building.

When she arrived and we were in the meeting room, she asked if she could see my qualifications. She explained my Business Admin apprenticeship would be composed of several modules, including ones in Maths, English and ICT. She stated that if I had a C or higher at GCSE in a particular subject, I wouldn't have to take that module.

Before we continue, I should explain that I have a B at GCSE in ICT, and a D in A-level ICT, meaning I was qualified not to have to do the ICT module section. In English, I had two C grades at GCSE so I again qualified. Maths, on the other hand, I had failed at GCSE grade. However, when I had attended the local college I had taken 'key skills' in which I obtained a maths qualification I was told was a C at GCSE equivalent. With all that under my belt, I felt confident I would get through this process, and have a good head start on this new qualification.

She looked over my qualifications, and said my English grades were good and I wouldn't have to do that, which made me feel relieved, but then she said, 'There's a problem with your maths and ICT,' which made me panic. She said, 'We cannot accept your ICT qualifications because of the exam board you sat them with, and we can't recognise your key skills in maths.' She said this in such a relaxed way, something in me just snapped.

My blood was boiling; I don't know what happened. I don't think you could classify it as a meltdown, but I just felt angry because of all the changes that had happened up to this point. This was the last straw for me. I said, 'I don't accept that.'

She said there was nothing she could do, and that I would have to sit an IT and maths module, but I was upset, on principle.

I retorted, 'I have never heard a university decline someone because of the exam board. That's a decision my school made, not me!'

My voice was raised and I think it shocked her, but she said there was nothing she could do about it. I was furious and said, 'Fine, I won't do it.'

'Do what?' she asked.

'The apprenticeship,' I stated.

She then told me to wait a moment, got out her phone and went into the corridor. A long time later she came in, and said my qualifications would be accepted.

At the end of that meeting she dropped another bombshell just as she left, saying that our meetings, instead of being weekly, would be monthly. This made me wonder what the hell was going on? My apprenticeship was meant to be weekly training, not monthly. When I asked Beryl, she stated this was correct, and that I could juggle qualification work with my existing work role.

As the weeks went on, I found it harder and harder to do my qualification work while doing my job role, as the demands became greater. If I did my qualification work, it put a strain on my colleagues, which made me feel guilty and meant that I didn't do as much as I would have liked to.

However, one good thing happened. One of the social workers from another department came in, and Karen explained that she was someone who had been involved in my diagnosis, the information I gathered she obtained from my invisible file. We chatted for a while and we were both pleased to see each other. All in all, meeting her was a good experience and I keep in touch.

Soon after, our team in the office were summoned to a meeting. Representatives from the entire building were present; the theme of the meeting was facility changes. I didn't know what was going on, but I soon caught on. Some superiors in the city were planning to move everyone in our building, and another building nearby, demolish them to make car parks, and then put us in an expensive, privately rented open office. A staff member from one of the other teams asked for numbers on office space. The number of people going in was about 110, and the number of desks and chairs for workers was 87. Now I struggle with maths, but even I know that's a shortfall. This was brought up, but these superiors waved it off and said, 'We will think of something', and they mentioned that a lot of people could work from home.

Either situation would be poor for me. I can't work from home as I cannot concentrate, with distractions like TV and books about. If I routinely go to an office to work, then I will work in that office as it's in my routine. The other idea of being in a massive open office made me feel ill. If you're reading this I assume you know that Asperger's includes sensory issues and social communication issues. The idea of hearing over 100 people talking all at once was too much.

At the end of the meeting I asked Joanne if I could see the manager of children's services, Dom, who was at the meeting. I explained my concerns to Dom, saying that I didn't know if I could handle working in that environment. He said he would relay my concerns. A few weeks later, Dom informed me that these superiors hadn't considered disabled colleagues when they planned this move, and that I had significantly delayed their plans, about which Dom seemed very pleased. However, it made me feel uneasy that these superiors hadn't considered disabled workers when they made the plan, and I thought: shouldn't they have been obliged to?

I carried on working. I couldn't get much work done for my qualification at work, so I did most of it at home at night, and I continued to struggle with some office tasks, regardless of being shown many times how to do them. I kept apologising and asking for feedback, but I was constantly told that it was all right and that I was doing well, so I continued to feel secure.

Three months in, my tutor from Private Trainers had to cancel again, and no reason was given. On the day in question when I came back from my lunch break Beryl was there, talking to my manager Joanne. I was surprised to see Beryl, as she was based in the city, about 60 miles away. She asked if she could talk to me, and led me to the same meeting room I used when the tutor came. We sat down and Beryl said, 'We're going to have a performance review.' My mind went back to training in the city and I repeated parrot-fashion, 'Performance reviews take place at six months in.' Beryl nodded and said, as she was nearby she thought she would see how things were going. I was feeling anxious and couldn't relay all my concerns, so I opted for a generic 'OK' response instead. She nodded and explained she was here because there were concerns about my performance, that my colleagues were concerned that I was not performing to the required standard, and that odd quirks like opening windows were not acceptable.

I was completely torn apart. I had kept asking my manager, who got feedback from all my colleagues, and up until now I had been told everything was satisfactory. I felt sick that I had been lied to. I knew I had struggled, but I remember stating that if they ever had any issue with me, they should bring it up so that I could try and adapt to become more useful. She then said my time at children's services would come to an end, and this would be effective at the end of the month. My routine of working was destroyed.

I knew a shutdown was coming; I was stimming like crazy, and trying very hard not to cry and scream. She then said that in a month's time I would transition to a new apprenticeship at the local library, but I wasn't taking much in. All this change was too much. I asked to be excused, barged into my office and told my colleagues that I was to go, and my heart sank when they told me that they already knew.

I ran out of the building, rain pelting down, with no coat or umbrella, and broke down outside, crying, screaming and curled up in a little ball. I felt so useless and powerless. Despite the heavy rain, I had no desire to go back inside. The fact that my colleagues knew about my leaving led me to an irrational conclusion that it was all a conspiracy to see me ousted, and that none of them trusted me. It took me a good hour or so to be in a fit state to return, by which time I was like a damp towel.

For a week I trudged along to work. I was nagged to work harder but I couldn't get my brain into gear. I couldn't understand what I was doing, or why. The end couldn't come quick enough. Joanne, my manager, could see this change in me, and asked Beryl if I could have the rest of the time off until the transition. She agreed. So for two weeks I relaxed at home, focused on my hobbies, and tried to recover.

Just before I was due to start at the library, I was summoned to a meeting. My parents, Beryl and the tutor from PrivateTrainers met in the library. It was explained that now my training would be a half-day every month, and not a full day every month, due to the fact that my training was on a one-to-one basis and not a group, as it was in the city. This was still a far cry from the original one-day-a-week's training that had been advertised but I just nodded and felt I couldn't argue with the decision.

I was then told that, due to limited resources, the library couldn't take me full-time. The cuts meant there was no job opportunity there, and that my apprenticeship would be split, two days at the library and three days at adult services, doing support for social workers, using a specialist database program. I wasn't happy with this either, but I nodded again and just accepted what was happening.

I was told by Beryl that I would be getting a helper to accompany me on my apprenticeship due to my difficulties. Remember I stated I had a reader in exams? I used to also have a helper who would aid me in classes, back in key stage 3, GCSE, and when I attended the local college. After that I had attended a school sixth form and asked for no help in class, and I did very well. So this felt like a punch in the gut. I had gone from needing an in-class helper in every class, to only needing a helper in exams, and now I was going back to having a helper all the time. It knocked my confidence, but, as with everything else, I just nodded.

As things turned out, I loved working at the library. The layout, the way the books were laid out – it was all logical, once I had memorised the layout. Shelving was easy, restocking was easy, and I was learning the IT system to check out books. I was good at dealing with the public and was able to direct them. I loved that job and the people I worked with were fantastic! Which is why it saddened me deep down that at the end of it all, regardless of the outcome, I would have to leave, as there would be no job in the future. Deep down, I felt I belonged there.

My other role was a stark contrast to the library. It was not public facing; rather it was a sort of technical support role, although we weren't IT, or IT support. As you can imagine, this caused confusion for people dealing with us. Our job was to assist social workers and maintain their specialist database software. For example, they would call if they entered data incorrectly, and we'd fix the problem. This side of the job was hard to pick up. The software was complex, and the department had its own terminology, which at times I could only describe as code, or a new language. That said, again my colleagues were brilliant!

I did mention I was assigned a helper. I cannot fault her as a person. Like my colleagues, she was brilliant. However, I was upset that it was felt that I needed a helper, after battling hard to prove myself capable during my time in school education. There were times when I felt we both misunderstood each other and got under each other's feet. There was also confusion about what help was going to be provided. The idea was that she would come in a lot while I was settling in, but then she would come less and less. For instance, she would say 'I am not coming in this morning, I will see you this afternoon', but if I had a task that morning I knew I would struggle with she said something like 'I won't be here all the time.' So I would struggle with the morning task and then she came in the afternoon, when I was getting on fine with my tasks, which annoyed and frustrated me.

My tutor from Private Trainers stated that, because my work placement had changed, the apprenticeship was starting again. I asked if my Maths and ICT qualifications were still in order, and I hesitantly got a positive response. Looking back, I came across as brash, but I didn't want to fight battles any more.

Another battle arose when she told me that the qualification I was studying for had always been a GCSE equivalent. I was shocked, as when I signed up I was under the impression I was studying for a level 3 (A-level) equivalent qualification, given my current qualifications. This came to my attention when I was told I had over-answered questions on a mock test, answering them to A-level standard and not GCSE standard.

Upon relaying this news to family and friends, there was a general consensus that the education side of the apprenticeship wasn't being taken seriously. The training had been reduced to monthly, and the qualification value had been dropped from A-level value to GCSE value. I began to believe them. I remember one family member saying, 'On your £2.60p/h wage, and that reduction, it's as if they don't care, it's as if you are slave labour to them.' That thought stuck with me for a long time. My friends at the time were also concerned. If I ever went to see friends I was usually quite sociable and would get stuck into things, but all this stress of not knowing what was going on at work was affecting me out of work as well. I was becoming a mute from loss of confidence, and I had little to no energy after a day's work.

This was all building up in my head. I tried to get this across to my managers, but I couldn't, and I was feeling very anxious and confused. One day in the library I was dealing with a customer, and I was struggling with the computer system to check out a book. I should also mention that my support worker wasn't around. Checking it out on the computer system took longer than expected, and I made some mistakes. I apologised to the gentleman and, as he left, I heard him mutter 'Useless' under his breath.

It hit me, like a brick wall, he was right. I couldn't get the apprenticeship right, I couldn't understand how it all worked, and I couldn't get my points across properly. I was useless. I hit another shutdown, I felt tears coming and I marched quickly, covering my face, to the staffroom, where the floodgates opened. I curled into a ball and screamed silently. I believed that the reason my apprenticeship wasn't going as I wanted was because I was performing poorly, and that I was useless, as the member of the public had said. My manager came in and offered to help, but nothing could be done. My colleagues sent me on my lunch break early. I insisted that all I needed was fresh air.

When I came back my support worker was there, and she looked horrified to see me, stating that I 'looked dreadful'. I tried to say I was fine and tried to push myself to work, despite feeling drained and sad. I managed another hour or so, but I was sent home early that day. When I got home, I isolated myself.

Two days later, in my other job, I was being inundated with tasks. We were in a small open-plan office, which I didn't mind too much, as there were normally no more than ten people there. However, today was different because people from other departments were asking me to do tasks. I couldn't plan, or process what I was doing. My helper came just as I was doing several things at once, working through my lunch break. The support worker said something to me. Looking back, I think the support worker was trying to use a calming tone, but at the time I picked it up as a patronising tone. I marched out and went to the staff room, where I suffered a meltdown.

I banged my head against the wall, punched the wall, kicked the floor, and swore. I was frustrated with myself for being so stupid, and for letting people walk all over me – like these superiors who decided I should study with PrivateTrainers and not my local college, who reduced my qualification, who reduced my training and who decided I was incapable of working without supervision. I felt I was hitting rock bottom with the shutdowns I had experienced, but this time I felt a flame of fight in me.

My helper came in, and tried to calm me down and talk me out of it. I remember shouting, 'I am sick of being used as fucking slave labour! Here I am, working my arse off, so that these bastards in the city can decide, let's make this change, fuck up his routine and it will be a right laugh! I'm working thirty-seven and a half hours a week for £2.60 per hour! My mates who work in bars at seventeen hours a week bring back more fucking money than me!' I said more probably, but it was lost in a hysterical rant that Malcolm Tucker would have been proud of. I was sent home early that day as well, and I could tell my helper was shaken.

That night I went home and I felt so guilty about what I had done, and felt depressed and powerless about it, as I am sure most Aspies do after meltdowns.

The following day I went in, and got a stern telling-off from my support worker, who told me how ashamed she was of me, how I shouldn't act like that and how she had never experienced behaviour like that before. I made a mental note that she must have never worked with Aspies before properly, as meltdowns and shutdowns are all part and parcel of the condition. They aren't good, and I am not saying they are acceptable, I am just saying they happen.

The week went on and I became a mute. I felt very depressed, and I didn't feel I was worthy of anything at all. At the start of the last week of November, I rang Beryl from a private meeting room and from a script I had written down I stated all my concerns – that I wanted my apprenticeship to return to what it was advertised as, a level 3 apprenticeship with one day a week's training with the local college.

She replied, 'We can't be specific with job adverts', basically telling me that it is how it is.

So I asked her 'Why didn't you say things might change at the interview?', to which there was a deathly silence. I actually thought she had put down the phone.

Eventually she said, 'The final decision is yours, but you know that this is how the real world of work is.' With that statement, I thought to myself, 'I can't work then, if this is how it is everywhere,' which made me panic even more.

That weekend I asked family and friends for their advice, and they all agreed. This was not doing me any good. My meltdowns and shutdowns were becoming more common, and with the effects on me (in and out of work) I knew my mental health was suffering. I wasn't going to get a job doing the work I loved, the pay was poor, and the education side wasn't worth it given my existing qualifications. With their support, my decision was made.

The following week, I handed in my notice of resignation to Beryl. I didn't tell my colleagues or social worker and everyone said I was suddenly happier, more energetic and more relaxed. I didn't want to tell them. However, eventually the truth had to come out. Most of my colleagues were heartbroken to see me go, but understood given the circumstances and were very supportive, which made me respect them all the more.

My helper bade me farewell and wished me all the best, as did Beryl. I also heard from my former colleagues at children's services who were upset to hear I was to go, but who also understood when I explained the situation.

Looking back on my experience, I conclude that the public sector isn't completely Aspie-friendly. For someone who requires logical decisions, straightforward instructions and understanding, from my experience at least, it was a poor fit. That said, it did open my eyes a lot.

I have since heard that the department that was going to offer me a job at the end of my apprenticeship was relocated to a large open-plan office shortly after I resigned. Most of the team now work from home, and I have been told that the department has now been disbanded. If I had stayed on, this would have meant another transition to another department, and the change in routine would have done nothing to improve things. So, looking back, perhaps I left at the right time.

Reflections

Although this attempt at working failed, it is hard not to be struck by Richard's resilience in the face of so many obstacles. He keeps trying, time after time, to gain employment. This should command respect. Have you recognised any resilience shown by the person with autism with whom you work?

All the systems Richard was exposed to lacked clarity and consistency, and caused confusion. He had too much to learn and not enough time to process what he was learning. The social side of office working, particularly in open-plan offices, was too much. On top of all this, there were constant changes, and this has been a feature of public sector employment in recent times. How can we support people with autism through such systems? How might we modify the environments? How might we clarify expectations and instructions? How can we build in the extra processing time often required by people with autism in new environments?

11
Andy and Tina's story
Andy and Andy's mother

Andy is a man with autism, cerebral palsy and a learning disability, and Tina is his mother. In this chapter, they each give their account of what happened to Andy in 2007, when he was 17. At that time, I was looking for examples of how people with a learning disability showed resilience. I interviewed Andy and discovered that his life was actually just 'bumping along'; it seemed that he was hiding away on his own, playing on his X-Box to escape the things that were going wrong in his life. His difficulties in relating to others, and their reactions to him, were causing him great distress. He said, 'Because I've been picked on, it feels like "Oh, I deserve to be in a better place." It feels like I've been there all my life. I want a decent place where I don't get picked on all the time.'

After I had recorded the interview, I gave Andy a transcript of what he'd said, and he took ownership of his story. In a sense, the transcript became his 'voice'. This turned out to have a big impact on his life. Tina describes her reaction to the transcript, and the way she and Andy worked together to achieve life-changing plans. At this time Andy said:

> "It feels like that last year I was in a bubble. I couldn't escape from all these problems but now I've found out that I've escaped it, it's burst like someone got a pin or something and popped the bubble and let me out. Not sure who popped it! It was probably my support workers, probably my social worker. Most likely I might have got a pin out of my pocket and must have popped it myself."

What a vivid simile for someone diagnosed with impairment of imagination!

This chapter starts with an introduction from Tina describing what had happened before Andy told his story. This is followed by an extract from Andy's story. The third section is Tina's account of the events that occurred after Andy told his story. The final section is from 2008, when Andy described what happened in his life in the year after the first interview.

Tina's story, 2007

Shortly before Andy told his story, contact had been made with social services. At this time he was isolated at home, talking to himself and immersed in a fantasy world, fearful of going out. Andy had been attending a vehicle mechanics course but had been asked to leave. At that time he was unable to pursue his interest in motor vehicles through his local college any further. His tutor had explained that Andy worked too slowly and was unable to stay 'on task' and follow instruction. With guidance from his tutor, Andy decided not to go on work placement in a commercial garage environment, as it would not have been possible for the college to provide appropriate support to ensure his personal safety.

We had a meeting with Andy's tutor to consider his future options, and this was when it was confirmed to Andy that there was no realistic future educational route available to him in respect of motor vehicles. I understand that this is something that colleges have not previously been involved in. If Andy had been 18, he would perhaps have been eligible for access to work support and this would not then have been a wasted opportunity for Andy to enter the workplace.

At this time I had stumbled upon a satellite unit from the local day services called Positive and Valuable Experiences (PAVE). This operated as a block contract with referral from learning disabilities social workers. PAVE encouraged individuals to access their local community, to run the office-based unit by manning reception, handling phone calls, and leading their own involvement in community activities. After I had made initial contact with social services, Andy was referred to the district team – because the diagnostic labels that had been attached to Andy read 'autism' and 'mild cerebral palsy'.

This was the point when I supported Andy to make contact with the Connexions service, and he linked up with the college's designated Connexions adviser. With the aid of his Connexions adviser, Andy started to consider other options. A statement of special educational need had supported him throughout mainstream school, and he then considered joining his peers from school on the second year of the pre-vocational training course operated through the college.

There was concern that Andy would not be funded by the Learning and Skills Council (LSC) as he had already completed an NVQ level 1 qualification, but fortunately his Connexions adviser picked up on the knocks to Andy's self-confidence (such as name-calling, other students refusing to work with Andy because he was different, tutor unable to break tasks down so that Andy could remain focused) that had resulted from attending the motor vehicle course. The Connexions adviser also started to work with Andy to establish contact with the local disability employment adviser, and to make contact with a local branch of Halfords about the possibility of supported employment for Andy.

Andy's story, 2007

I'm autistic. I had mild cerebral palsy but I had that at birth. If anyone asks me what my difficulties are I just tell them. I'm not scared to tell anybody.

I like touring cars. I wanted to be a mechanic. I can't be one now because of the support I got in the workshop and basically it's because the person in the garage has got to keep an eye on everyone and not just one person at a time.

I'm not able to go to college any more. When I found out I felt a bit gutted. Hopefully I'm going to find a job working in the store but not in the garage. I was disappointed because it was my lifelong dream to be a mechanic. I've had this dream and now there's barriers up saying I just can't do it. I thought, 'Oh my God, why has this happened to me? And why is everyone else, some people in the group, getting jobs out of it and I'm not?' Well I can understand that there are a few problems like my concentration and all that but what I can't understand is why can't I go into the garage to actually work? That's what I want to be.

I didn't feel jealous of the others. I thought 'Good for them'. I don't want to react to them just because they got a job – because it's not right and it's not fair on them.

Some of the others in the group were a pain, picking on me quite a lot. Calling me names I don't like. They called me names like 'spastic' and 'retard' and all that for no reason. Just because they think it's fun to do it. I don't know why they call me it. I said, 'I'm fed up of that word being used.' And I want it way out of people's minds. I want it to go away out of everyday use. Some of them didn't even know it was offensive towards me. They just thought it would be funny to call me it. But there's me thinking I want to hit them but I can't hit them because of what their reactions would be afterwards. In the end I thought 'Right, if it carries on, rise above it.'

I told my tutor about these lads calling me names I don't like and eventually he told the rest of the group. One lad said he would knock me out at work or something, just because they think I'm so annoying, but I'm not even being annoying when I'm doing my own work. They just laughed. They thought I'd never hit them. I just felt angry because they were laughing.

In college I sit next to the support worker. When I was in school I used to always sit with the support worker. When I'm with her, she tells them not to call me names. When she wasn't there, I thought 'I'm not putting up with these lads, I'll see if I can move away from them' but when I was in school they had this seating plan and I had to sit next to them every lesson and I hated it because they were picking on me. They called me 'spastic'. And so basically I've put up with it all the way through school life and college life. I'm completely fed up with it.

When I am going to college in the morning it's like waking up in a different world. I'm in college with the same idiots for the day again and they carry on calling me names. At breaks we are just sitting on a bench. Some of them are smoking their cigarettes, which I find really annoying. Some of them blow it towards me. I think they pick on me because they think it's easier to pick on someone who's got difficulties than someone that's like them – like their own type of group really. I think some of them know about it because of me getting support. They think 'He's disabled, let's pick on him.'

On Saturday these lads started on my mate and started pushing him and chucking bottles at him in town. We hadn't even done anything. We were just there, walking out in the park, and I ran out to phone my Dad to see what he could do about it. The police came. When I go into town with my mate, when I see big lads in town we try and hide from them. I don't know what they are going to be like. I don't know what will happen.

I was in Explorer Scouts but I ended up deciding to quit because I was getting picked on there as well. They said I was hitting them but I wasn't. When these things happen I try and hide it from my Dad. Sometimes my dad's over-protective – like what happened on Saturday when he got the police involved. I think he'll be too over-protective about it. And I'll just like go up to my room and play music dead loud to calm myself down. I like rock music, anything that will just calm me down really. When I'm in a black mood I don't talk much. I don't speak at all sometimes. But I try to stop myself getting into a bad mood. And I don't want to be in a bad mood all the time. It just feels like I've done nothing wrong and I'm getting to the stage where I'm just fed up. I stay in, if I'm in a black mood. I just go in a world of my own. I just play on my X-Box.

I've started looking into getting a job in Halfords stores. I've got an application form. I'm mad on the touring cars. Halfords sponsor the touring car team and that's why I want to go and work for them. I want to be in hospitality at a touring car event or, even better, going to touring cars events with the people at Halfords who I work with. I'd like to get a job there. It would be good for me because it's my interest.

Because I've been picked on, it feels like 'Oh I deserve to be in a better place.' It feels like I've been there all my life. I want a decent place where I don't get picked on all the time. The world I want, well, basically it would have like a go-kart track. It would have loads of touring cars. It would have all the drivers who I know. I do know some of them because I email them, but like they would all be there go-kart racing against me. And I might end up winning or not but we're all relaxed in that world, whereas in this world, where I get picked on, I'm not part of this world at the moment. That's what I want – a relaxed and a calm life.

I'm 17 so I'm getting assessed to get my licence at the moment. So hopefully I can go and drive to the touring car races, take myself off there, go on my own for the weekend, and watch my favourite motor sport and come back for the night. And then that will be ME chilled. If I can drive then that will be my life. I'll think 'No one's gonna pick on me now 'cos they'll think I'm just more independent.'

My brother he picks on me a bit but he doesn't call me these horrible names. I think he just wants to pick on me for a laugh. That's what I struggle with. I don't know if anyone's having a joke with me or being serious. But now I think 'My brother's just having a laugh with me', which he is, though sometimes we just argue, you know what brothers are like. Sometimes my brother will stick up for me.

I think he's at the stage now where he just wants to get on with this own life instead of sticking up for his older brother. But it's just me and him, we just have a laugh sometimes, and play cricket or football with my mate who I know from Scouts. We just play, the three of us. We think that if it's a larger group we'll just get our stuff stolen because of the way they might judge us. Basically I can't bowl the cricket ball like my brother can. I can't kick the ball as good as my brother. I think people might judge us, the way we play football and cricket. I did go-karting and I don't mind going on a track where people don't know me and won't pick on me as much.

Tina's story, after 2007

Andy's confidence initially grew from the 'power' of owning his own story. He showed the transcript to people, as it told the story in a way that he couldn't if he was asked to answer questions there and then. Sharing this story has enabled him to find a 'voice', which has been listened to, and this chain of events has led to his self-confidence soaring as a result of his direct involvement with the local development of self-directed support.

Andy's story made it quite clear that something needed to be done. From my knowledge of the definition of a learning disability, as outlined in DOH (2001) 'Valuing People: a new strategy for learning disability for the 21st century', I was able to find educational psychologists' reports that supported Andy's entitlement to learning disability services and he transferred to the learning disability social work team. Andy had initially been assessed by the district team as meeting eligibility criteria through social isolation at a critical level. I had the confidence to take this action because of the value I placed (as a parent) on the content of Andy's story. It was there in black and white; it was a true reflection of his life at that time.

As a family, we were not picked up by the Connexions transition co-ordinator because

Andy had gone to a mainstream school, so as a family we were already 'outside the box' and unknown to learning disability services.

The 'new' social worker, read the transcript of Andy's life story prior to undertaking his resource allocation system (RAS) questionnaire.

This is where the real value comes from the transcript. The RAS questionnaire is designed to be a self-assessment tool, and this is undertaken by a professional who may well have never met the individual before. I understand that the school transition system now works in such a way that contact is made with a transition co-ordinator when an individual reaches 14, and an RAS is undertaken prior to reaching 18. Whilst it is more likely that young people will be known to their co-ordinator, they will still have to build a new relationship with their social worker once they move into adult services.

I feel that Andy's life story enabled him to make a real impact on his social worker, who worked with him to complete his RAS. I was present during the assessment and I believe that the social worker used the information contained in Andy's story to guide him in answering the questions more 'appropriately'. When you first meet Andy, it is not always evident how much he understands when he's asked a question. He won't tell you that he doesn't understand something. You need to ask him, for example, by saying 'So what does that mean?' He will often reply inappropriately before saying, 'I don't know' or 'I've forgotten'. His use of language can often mask his underlying difficulties, especially when meeting somebody for the first time. This had resulted in him being given the label 'learning disabled'.

To recap, Andy's story was a reality check for me. I could see that the interviewer was concerned about where his life was, at the time when he shared his story, and as a consequence it gave me the confidence to push further for him, by seeking access to learning disability (LD) funding. But, as a result, have I 'given' Andy another label (though we always spoke in terms of his difficulties)? If I have, I don't think it has had a detrimental effect. He would have still been eligible for a direct payment, but without going down the LD route he would not have been able to access self-directed support. I believe that opening up the opportunity to get self-directed support built his confidence further.

Andy's story provided him with a sense of pride; this was his story. Although he had been involved in the earlier statement process in respect of special educational needs, that was not a process led by Andy. Because of the open nature of the interview, I would suggest that he was in some way able to lead the process. Although he was answering the questions, the interview style was capturing verbatim his actual responses, and thereby capturing their significance. He didn't always directly answer the question, but he was enabled to continue, and this approach led to other aspects of his life opening up. For example, how else would we have known what Andy's ideal 'race world' would have been like?

To bring this back to the present, once Andy's story had been captured, his sharing it with new people/professionals entering his life may possibly have enabled a little something of what Andy had to say to enter other people's hearts. Although he no longer uses the story, it remains a baseline against which to reflect upon the significant changes that have since resulted in his life.

Andy's life now entered the self-directed support phase. We received a flyer regarding a Citizen Leadership Academy that was due to run in Manchester in January 2008. Andy was keen to attend. Since his RAS assessment back in July/August, he had been getting a direct payment which he used to purchase four hours' social support a week from a local agency, but he hadn't been involved in developing the support plan process any further while he continued attending the pre-vocational course at college. The only copy of a care plan that we have ever seen from social services is the original one from the district team advising of his eligibility and transfer to learning disability services.

At the Citizen Leadership Academy, Andy met other individuals who were planning and leading the support in their own lives. His life had already changed as a result of the direct payment that he received, but after attending this academy he developed an interest in sharing his messages about bullying and how, by becoming involved in planning your own support, it is possible to lead the changes in your life. Andy felt that this was an important message that he wanted to share with other young people. Attending this event provided the second chance for Andy to develop a voice of his own. This course gave Andy an understanding of In Control (a national charity whose mission is to create a fairer society in which everyone needing additional support has the right, responsibility and freedom to control that support, see www.in-control.org.uk) and the support planning process. He met individuals who were living this life, and as a member of the group he could draw on their experiences to share this message with others.

As a result of attending the academy, the participants were asked to think about what they would do with this training once they returned home.

The four local (to Andy) participants contacted the director of adult social services to offer their expertise and were put in touch with the practice development co-ordinator for self-directed support. As a result of this initial contact, Andy has had the most involvement in delivering the message regarding his experience of the self-directed support process. He has attended developmental support planning training. Through a process of live planning, this enabled him to draw up a rudimentary person-centred plan.

He subsequently worked this up into his own support plan, which he himself submitted directly to his social worker. Andy has led this himself, with only minimal support from me, and I think, if you read his support plan, it reflects the fact that the work is his own. He used an accessible template of seven questions, on which the plan is based, with minimal guidance from me. Other accessible tools have also been provided by the county council.

As a result of this, Andy now regularly attends person-centred planning road shows, where he shares his experience of taking control of his own life.

He is interviewed and paid for his attendance at public events. He wants to save his appearance fees to fund his own business, which he plans to call 'Follow me to getting a life', if he does not get accepted at college. He is currently involved in a publicity campaign for the local authority, depicting the reality of young people developing and leading their own lives; he also attends the county person-centred planning task group.

Changes in Andy's life, 2008

A lot has changed in my life. I can't believe it. Finally I've got my motor sport place at the college. I start in September. So it's going to be one big step forward. For my dad, my mum, my brother, it's obviously going to be hard but we'll get there in the end. It's going to be a year of hard work but it's going to be a good time. I might not come home at weekends now. I'll see how I feel. I'll still have my driving lessons. No one picks on me any more. I'm out there, getting out more with my assistants. They are helping me get my confidence in the community.

I'm doing my talks. I thought they would think 'Well, I'm not going to listen, all he is going to talk about is touring cars', but I've found out they actually do. It's amazing. People are interested now I've had my picture taken with my social worker. It's a poster so it might appear on buses, bus shelters, anywhere.

Last year I didn't talk to people because I got stressed. The improvement! I don't know how it's happened. Last week I talked to a group of twenty or thirty people. I was speaking about how my life's changed since I've had support, direct payment and my individual budget for my support plan. I was dreading it during the week, but when I got up and presented it I thought 'No way, I've got to go and celebrate.'

I'm doing road shows with people my age. We're all getting direct payments. We talk about how to budget, and show our support plans to everyone. We explain what we want to do, what isn't working, what has worked. My individual budget is for a person who takes me out to support me for the amount of hours I want. It gets me out in the community a lot.

I go out with my support workers. I take them out for dinner on a Monday and for a drink on a Thursday. It saves me being stuck in my room. I was in my room a lot but now that's stopped because I'm going out more. When I go to college, I won't have to be stuck in my room and not going out enjoying myself with the student bar and doing other activities. What's the point in just playing X-Box?

Some staff cost £15 per hour and I hate paying that much. One cost me £12.80 per hour so that works better. This guy I go out with now has a good understanding because I took him to touring cars last month so I'm getting there. Oh, I've had so many staff! Some moved on but when it comes to people like dropping out, being stupid, getting drunk and then not turning up the day after they are meant to go out. I had to ring the agency up and say he hasn't attended so he didn't work with me again. It felt really annoying because I thought 'What's the point? I've given up my time and commitment to go out and it's really upsetting.'

When the good guy left to do a new job, I felt really happy for him, but last night when I went to sleep I started really crying my eyes out because he was good mates with me. We are still good mates, no matter what. We are in contact; we go out. Last Tuesday when we went to a really posh Italian restaurant, it was his treat.

I don't get picked on now. I think it's because I've got my personal assistants there. If the people see them with me then they won't pick on me. I'm not scared to go out now. I'll be all right at college.

I sometimes go into town myself now. It's all right. Sometimes it's a bit hectic when I see people in the past who picked on me but I still have the confidence to think 'Don't be scared of them, they're nothing but trouble. If you stay away from them, try and ignore it, or move somewhere else, away from them'. I just walk about town and walk straight past them.

At college I'll be training to be a race-car mechanic. They've got race-cars and they go and enter the races with them. There's a couple of rally cars, there's a formula Ford car and there's a couple of kit cars. I'm really looking forward to it. I'll be having learning support during the day, where I'll be probably having a personal assistant. They'll help me to figure out how to get me from the college campus.

They'll come and help me and then think of how to get me from college to the train station to get home, and then from the train station to the college again. It is going to be kind of a nerve-racking experience because I don't know what days I've got off yet. I've not got my timetable. But I think in the first week in September I'm going to go down to college and see what my room will look like and familiarise myself with it so I know where I'm going and everything.

I can remember getting a copy of my last talk with you [the 2007 interview]. I can remember sending it to my social worker and it changed me now and that's when I read

120

it again. I still read it. If I find it in the house, I get it out and I'll read it. I felt really proud that I'd said it. Look what has changed since then. I think 'Well, it's someone else, it's my twin brother.' I know I haven't got a twin brother but still I say that because it's like the other side of me. It's like this [gesturing] side of myself has done really good and the left side hasn't. It's like me saying I've got a twin brother who's done all this, but it's me really. It's fantastic to say 'I've got a twin brother.' It feels like that last year I was in a bubble. I couldn't escape from all these problems but now I've found out that I've escaped it, it's burst like someone got a pin or something and popped the bubble and let me out. Not sure who popped it! It was probably my support workers, probably my social worker. Most likely I might have got a pin out of my pocket and must have popped it myself.

Andy's postscript

I have lived in Kendal since April 2012. This has caused a lot of things to happen, changing doctors and dental surgery and most of all making new friends and work colleagues. We all get on well. I work voluntarily, helping people with disabilities recycle furniture, and I enjoy it. I now have a paid job working as a cleaner in Asda. I play football for a team who have different disabilities. My life is really good and I am looking forward to the future.

Reflections

The turning point for Andy appears to have been when he got the opportunity to tell his story in his own terms and at his own pace. Andy had previously been involved in a person-centred plan but his own narrative had not emerged. This story proved to be a shock to his parents. Have the people with autism who you support ever had the opportunity to tell their story in their own terms, at their own pace? Have they ever owned a written account of their story that could be used to support them in meetings?

Andy imagined his own 'world bubble', a place where he was safe from bullying and judgement. Do you know what the ideal world would look like for the people you support? Are there any elements of that world you could help them replicate?

Recent success for Andy has included a supporter whose role is to help him integrate into social settings. This involves the supporter simply going to places with Andy as 'a mate'. Does the person with autism you know have such support?

Section 4

Mothers' stories

123

12
A mother's tale
Lois

Lois is a mother of two children with autism. She attended the autism course at the University of Cumbria, and many of the themes in this chapter were first included in one of her assignments. She subsequently lectured on the 'parent perspective'. She thinks that autism runs in her family. Her 'egg mayonnaise on the fur coat of a busybody' story, described below, is one of my favourites!

This chapter is a transcript of a conversation between us. She thinks that she might also have autism but will probably not bother to seek a diagnosis. Her accounts of battles with professionals and day-to-day survival were the subject of her essay. She commonly experiences strangers making comments about her children. Here she describes what happened on a visit to a café:

> "Harry was making quite loud noises and singing 'Away in a Manger', which he had been singing at nursery. The man then started singing along but Harry saw this as an opportunity to sing louder and louder. He would not stop, which then agitated the man, who said things like 'Oh, he probably gets away with everything at home' and 'He's not disciplined.' The people with him were in agreement. I didn't say anything but I could feel myself bubbling inside."

I went on the autism course so that when professionals went waffling on at me, coming out with things that they had obviously read and possibly never put into practice, I could say, 'Oh yes, I've been to university and I've learned about it. But I live it as well.' I just thought it might help in some situations to say that. I don't think it has actually helped that much though! Other parents don't seem to stand up to the teachers; they seem to think that teachers know best. I worry that they will just do things their own way and not tell me. It is a battle.

I have got three birth children. Emma has a diagnosis of Asperger's. My other two birth children do not have a diagnosis. I adopted Harry as a baby and he has a diagnosis of autism. I also adopted John who has a learning difficulty but is not on the spectrum. I am going down a special guardianship route with John.

Harry

When he was eight or nine months old he was doing odd things. He wasn't sitting up and he wasn't holding his head up. He didn't eat. He used to have a bouncy chair made of wire with a cloth cover. He used to sit in there, with his feet and arms going round in circles. I had not noticed it really but my husband pointed it out. I was saying I wanted to adopt him but he was saying, 'You do realise that he is very different.' I just thought it was linked to the fact that his mother had been a drug abuser. Little did I know, he was dealing with drug withdrawal and autism. He didn't really open his eyes until he was four months old. I used to have to clock-watch for when he needed feeding. I had to carry him around over one shoulder all the time. As he got older, he wanted to be carried on the left-hand side. I ended up with a groin injury because of this.

In 2001 I took him to see the paediatrician to get a diagnosis. I noticed a poster on the wall in the waiting room asking if your child did this or that. I told the doctor I had been reading this and she just said, 'If you think he's autistic he's not!' Thank goodness she has retired. She had only just met Harry. The doctor diagnosed 'global developmental delay'.

Before Harry had his diagnosis, he was having physiotherapy. They used to put him into standing frames because he wasn't walking. I always think 'Why intervene?' You know your child better than anyone else. The physiotherapist put in her report that I was obsessed that Harry was autistic. She didn't think he was. I know I have this obsessiveness when I think I'm right. I can't brush it off if I get a comment I don't like. It plays and plays on my mind till I've sorted it out. I never said anything to her after the diagnosis was made, although she said, 'Well, I wouldn't have thought he was.'

It aggravates when people can't talk to you properly. Teachers often talk to you in a patronising manner rather than a normal voice. It's a soft gentle voice as if you are a bit stupid. They phone up for little things. They will ring up to say John has got nappy rash when I am already doing all I can to sort out the problem. They phoned up to tell me that John had a cough. I told them I knew he had a cough and what did they want me to do about it? That then gets their backs up. Do they think I'm just sat here doing nothing?

The school nurse reported me to social services. She said I was unapproachable. Social services told me that if something was said that I didn't like, or didn't agree with, I had to just smile and nod.

Foster children have to go for developmental checks and I used to go to see this paediatrician with James. She had a box of objects to use in assessments. She handed James a spoon, the same as one we have at home. All the years I went with James she had the same boring objects in this box. When I went with Harry, she still had the same things. I remember saying to her, 'Look, you know he's autistic and I know he's autistic. Can you not just diagnose him with that?' She replied, 'I can't do that because it is difficult to undo it, once you have made it. You wouldn't like to be diagnosed with cancer and then someone else turn round and say that it was wrong.' After that I refused to go and see her. I wrote a long list of everything that Harry did and showed it to the GP. I asked what the list meant to him. He said 'autism'. I told him what the paediatrician had said and he referred Harry to a different consultant. This one decided that Harry was on the spectrum. Harry got his diagnosis when he was three.

I wanted the diagnosis for lots of different reasons. If I was out with Harry, he looked so beautiful people would come up to him, and he wouldn't want to interact. People would ask what was wrong with him. I used to have to say, 'He's got global developmental delay.' I felt guilty saying it because I knew it wasn't right. You would get the response, 'Oh well, he looks normal!' I wanted to be able to say to people, 'He's autistic.' It is easier when the child has something visibly different about them but he has such a bonny face.

Harry went to school at about seven; he doesn't like school. I just hope I'm not damaging him by sending him there. We had teething troubles but now he knows how to behave in school; he likes to please. He is perfectly behaved at school but he holds it in. It was after two years that he got to really like his teacher but it was only then that they started to find out about his character and his personality. He's got a brilliant sense of humour; he sings silly songs, making his own words up. I used to tell them this at school but they said they had never heard that.

When I picked him up from school they used to bring him and John out to the car and as soon as the car door had shut, before I'd even driven away, he was shouting obscenities at the teachers. It was as if it had been held in all day and then he was in his own environment with familiar people and then he let it all out. The teachers never saw this. When I told them he could use the 'F' word in context, they wouldn't believe it. I actually recorded it one day on my phone and played it for them; they were shocked! Out of school he does say what he thinks; it just comes out of his mouth. So when I'm driving he will say, 'Mind that 'f'ing car' or 'That was close'. I think he is afraid something will hit him.

The school told us that he had got used to balloons popping but deep down he is just holding the fear down to let out at home. I think they feel that they can get him to overcome his fears of certain things. I don't think you can. You can put strategies in place to help, but still if we see a balloon now he goes hysterical in case it bursts.

Then he moved to high school. I went to a meeting after half term and they said he doesn't like PE. I asked them if he could do some other activity like bike riding or swimming, as they have a hydro-pool. They said they would look into it but they decided they hadn't got the staff to do it. In year 7 he came home with his PE kit in a bag because he had wet himself. He is slow and needs assistance getting dressed. I give him his clothes to put on in the same order every day. I wonder if they are doing it in a different order and it is throwing him. The only time he wet himself before was when some carers changed the routine. Obviously there was some issue at school.

After he was wet I wrote in his school diary that he wouldn't be doing PE. The deputy head phoned and said that she wanted to put him through the whole cycle of stress again (although she wouldn't recognise it as that), and monitor his behaviour through PE. I refused because I thought the best way was to take him out of the situation and get his enthusiasm back for school, then reintroduce PE.

I think she thought I wanted to take him out of PE completely, as she said, 'You've got to give children life opportunities.'

I like to do things on his terms. I explained what I wanted to do but she said, 'I think I've got a plan.' She said the class teacher would phone me after it had been tried but she never did phone. So I didn't send in his PE kit and the teacher phoned me at 10 to 9 and asked why he couldn't do PE. She told me that the lesson takes an hour and a half; they were going to change him in one building, trail across to do the PE lesson, then trail back again to get changed and then do normal lessons. That is too much for any child, let alone someone with autism. She decided they would still do the changing but just keep him in the PE lesson for 10 minutes. They had focused on the wrong bit; the lesson was not the problem.

I wrote back and explained that we had been through all this before and that he was not to do that. She wrote back, saying Harry should not be getting stressed in PE now, there are not many children in the changing room, only two other boys. I had told her it is nothing to do with the amount of people, it is the getting dressed and the to-ing and fro-ing. They had focused on the wrong bit again. I told her that that I did not think the complexities of autism were being understood. She has passed my comments on to the managers. So I'm waiting to be told off now. The class teacher didn't even know I had spoken to the deputy head. There was no communication.

I tend to write things down in his diary if something annoys me. I have to write things exactly how I feel them. The morning after, I re-read it to check it is OK. I used to rip out a page if what I had written seemed wrong but then there was a day missing in their diary. I now write it down on a scrap of paper and then sleep on it. It is still pretty blunt even then.

I had done that a few times and his teacher said that she would run my ideas by the deputy head and see what she said. I told her that if the deputy said she was not going to do it my way then Harry was not doing their plan. Why don't they ask parents? I agreed that he would go to the lesson in his trainers but not get changed. He was to sit out of the lesson but join in when he felt like it. They let him do that.

When he came home he was a different person altogether. He wasn't violent and he wasn't swearing. When I had spoken to him he was able to identify what it was that was bothering him. It was the to-ing and fro-ing and changing. I would like them to do the same thing on Thursday and I am just going to dress him in his PE kit under his uniform. He won't have to change in front of anyone else. They say they are special needs teachers! They are good at their job but I sometimes think that they try to play psychiatrists when it is really something quite simple that is the solution. They have had some training but it is a generic school so there is not much knowledge there.

Recently the school wrote to me and said that they were going to be monitoring his behaviour. I wanted to know what was the issue? It was not his behaviour that was the issue. It was the school that was the problem that caused him to wet himself.

Harry went to a Riding for the Disabled fun day. He doesn't like riding and so he just sat at a table colouring and cutting with no trouble. There was another little boy there and it just seems that Harry is able to attract friends. This boy was obviously clever because he had just passed examinations to get into a private school. He was explaining this to Harry, who was very interested. I wondered whether Harry was in the right place for his education. I wonder whether he would be better in a mainstream school rather than in a special unit. It is something I could discuss with the teachers if they were prepared to listen. They think I wrap him up in cotton wool but I know Harry. I just want to cause him as little stress as possible.

He has got a girlfriend at school. She is on the spectrum. They are both calm and quiet at school, though I don't know what she's like at home. He gets on OK with the other children but I don't think he mixes with them much.

When he's at home he never seems to do anything productive. He tends to walk about a lot, just wandering around. He likes writing and drawing. He will spend hours at the table drawing with a pen. He then spends hours trying to rub it out, even though I tell him it won't rub out. He ends up with bits of rubber all over the table. He then gets frustrated and shouts and swears. He says everything is rubbish and not behaving. He refuses to use a pencil.

Harry has just started in year 8. They've split the group because it is so big. His new teacher is not qualified; she is a teaching assistant. It is a generic school and she has no understanding of autism. She phoned me, saying she knew I had a lot on but Harry needs his nails cutting. He is not the sort of child who would scratch others. Harry doesn't like the word 'cutting' because it is too severe. He prefers 'trimming'. I checked when he came home and they were fine, perhaps the corner of a couple needed a trim.

It is horrible to see him go through what happens when you trim his nails. He can't breathe, he goes hot and sweaty, even the soles of his feet. He is getting a bit better. I felt like I needed to reply and I said, diplomatically, 'I see to all of Harry's personal needs, bathing, dressing and everything else. Do you not think I would notice if his nails needed trimming? You don't need to remind me ever again.' I did bring it up at a review at school. They said she didn't mean any harm, she meant well but even then they had patronising mannerisms and they just never stop talking. They were having a bit of joke between themselves and I laughed along with them. But I was wondering what they found funny because I don't get jokes and I felt excluded. This does nothing for my self-esteem; I felt beneath them. I am not on their wavelength.

Out and about

Harry tends to make comments to people who walk past, saying things like 'Look at that fat lady.' When he was younger it was not so bad, he could get away with it, but now he is 12 it is a problem. It really hit home when he smacked the bottom of a lady who was bending over, using a cash machine, when he was seven. She just glared.

We have been on holiday with him, including going abroad. He doesn't like ferries much, though he loves planes. He does have problems at airports with the queuing and crowds. I had two files; one was a personal file of family and the like, and the other was things we had come across like animals or planes. So if I said we were going on holiday he would go and fetch the files to remind himself.

We used to stay with my ex-mother in law. She had a stallion that was wild! It used to chase us. It used to wander round the land and come up to the door of the house. I was very worried about Harry because he is very impulsive and unpredictable and he was only five at the time. I was worried about how the horse would act if he waved his arms around and shouted. Yet they were best friends! He would follow the horse around and there were no problems. Harry was upset when the horse died

My mum, daughter, Harry and me went to a farm-shop restaurant. Harry was five. There was no one else in the restaurant and so we decided it was safe to have something to eat. We sat in the conservatory. There must have been 50 tables in the place. We looked on the menu for something that Harry would eat. He ordered a mayonnaise sandwich. After we ordered, a middle-aged couple came in with their elderly mother and promptly plonked themselves on the next table to us. This got my daughter agitated and she said, 'All this space in here and they've got to come and sit on our knees!' So I had her to contend with and Harry was making quite loud noises and singing 'Away in a Manger', which he had been singing at nursery. The man then started singing along but Harry saw this as an opportunity to sing louder and louder. He would not stop. This caused the man to get agitated. The man started saying things like 'Oh he probably gets away with everything at home' and 'He's not disciplined.' The people with him were in agreement. I didn't say anything but I could feel myself bubbling inside.

The sandwich arrived and, as Harry picked it up, a big blob of mayonnaise fell out and landed on his chair between his legs. I reached for a serviette to pick it up but Harry beat me to it and threw the blob of mayonnaise and it stuck on the back of this elderly woman's coat. They were oblivious to it but I didn't tell them! I thought 'Payback'! I felt very satisfied. Harry didn't have any intent; he had just thrown it.

I went to the supermarket when Harry was seven. He crawled on the floor, looking at the fans on the freezers. He seemed happy. He was also smelling the butter; not touching, just smelling. He was getting a bit hyper and making noises. An elderly couple came by, pushing a trolley, and I saw the man raising his hand behind Harry, imitating a smack. The man saw me looking but I did not say anything. It may be mischievous but when Harry is getting a bit hyper and people are pulling a face or muttering under their breath I sometimes just leave them to it. I think that if they can't accept someone then I am not going to explain. He is not hurting anybody.

When he was about eight, I took Harry to the theatre to see Mary Poppins with my cousin. We went for a meal first and then, as we were in the lift going down to the theatre, Harry suddenly produced a fork he had taken from the restaurant. We didn't see him take it. Then, as we got the theatre, the security men saw the fork and made me put the fork in my bag. We sat on the end of the aisle and he was really quite good for the first half.

The trick is not to move out of your seat, as this disrupts him, but at the interval my cousin wanted a break. This disrupted Harry. In the second half he started making a noise like an air-raid siren. He kept standing up and shouting and then banging his feet on the floor. People started staring. We probably only had 20 minutes to go but we decided we had better leave. We stood in the aisle, with my cousin and me either side of him, but he wouldn't walk. He wanted to crawl up the steps. People were looking and making comments like 'What's he doing' and 'Can't they shut that child up?' My cousin and I were in stitches, crawling up the stairs with him! We got to the stop of the stairs and saw four big feet. It was the security men again, who said, 'This way please' and escorted us to the lift. Harry was oblivious to it all. He dragged us back to the hotel.

We went out in the car recently. Harry now sits in the front of the car. He loves to laugh at things. The car had to stop at a pelican crossing. Harry spotted a group of youths in a fast-food restaurant and started pointing and laughing at them. One got out of his seat and came to the window, mouthing words at Harry and gesticulating. I was scared of one of them coming out and being aggressive with him.

We had a holiday in a cottage. Harry found that he could move on the leather dining chairs in the accommodation and make a squeaking noise. He found this hilarious and kept it up for the whole mealtime, much to the annoyance of the rest of us. We got round this by taking a chair to his bedroom and asking him to go there if he wanted to squeak.

We went for a week away but I don't know why we bother really! It is doing the same thing but in a different place. You go out for something to eat but as soon as you've finished that's it, coats on and back home. The routine has to be the same and he always wants to rush back to the washing machine. It was hard because John is up at 4 o'clock every morning. When he is at home he can't get out of his bedroom but on holiday he can. He went to disturb Harry and so it was a case of continually taking him back to his bed.

We were walking through the town. Harry doesn't want to hold hands any more so we just have to link arms. This young lad with an enormous afro style came out of a hairdresser's with his mum. You do look and think 'Wow' but Harry says it. He shouted really loudly, 'Look at his hair! Who does he think he is? Does he think he's on X Factor?' I didn't even look, it was just 'quick march'. If there is someone who is fat, he will say, 'Are you having a baby?'

Eating

Harry didn't used to eat very much. For the first seven or eight years, he ate Rocky biscuits, Laughing Cow cheesy bits and Scooby Doo yoghurts. He could eat four yoghurts at one meal. Then the local supermarket told me that they were discontinuing them. I thought 'Oh my God, what am going to feed him now?' They told me that they had some round the back. I told them I would take whatever they had in the warehouse and I bought the lot.

Greggs were our saving grace. Wherever we went, there would be a Greggs with the same sausage roll; we could guarantee it. Because of this, we were able to go to town with a bit more confidence. If we went out to eat, we would take him a yoghourt or Laughing Cow Cheesy Dippers. People would be looking at us and saying 'You are not going to feed that child a yoghourt' with us sat eating a massive steak.

He has changed and now eats as much as a man. He eats almost anything, although he doesn't like milk, not even the smell. He doesn't like Quavers or mashed potato. Every time I make a sandwich for him he reminds me that he doesn't like butter. If we go out to eat he knows exactly what he wants. I don't think he knows when to stop eating now, and he will eat an adult portion of curry. He used to like cheese and onion pie with chips and red beans. They brought it with salad one time and he wasn't happy. I just told him that next time he would have to tell them he didn't want salad. He has got better at being verbal; he tells them now. He is getting more assertive. If they get it wrong he might start to get agitated but I would tell him to explain to them and he would be able to do it.

When he comes home from school he will come into the kitchen to see what is for tea. He will go through everything he doesn't like. He will say, 'Don't put butter on it!' and I will say, 'No Harry, I know.'

'Don't put tomatoes on.'

'No Harry, I know you don't like them.'

If he thinks I'm not listening, I'll get a big poke in the ribs.

Harry's teacher said he won't eat mashed potato. I told her just to call it 'compressed' potato and then he will eat it. He doesn't like the name 'mashed'. I change names to make them sound different. 'Mash' is a sloppy sort of a word but 'compressed' is neat and tidy. Perhaps I see it the same as him! I could write everything like this down for the teachers till I'm blue in the face but they still know best.

Emma

Emma is 25 now.

Emma was a 'perfect' baby, she never demanded anything and you could feed her while she was still asleep! At 18 months old she changed and became really distant. She didn't want to be kissed and cuddled.

She went to mainstream school, where there were major issues. The teacher would leave messages on the answer-phone, telling us about the things Emma had done. She went on to a behavioural programme at the age of eight or nine. She then went to a senior school, where she did not know anybody. She was very disruptive from the start. Teachers were saying that she was very immature. She was kicking water out of puddles at people, and she would insist on keeping her coat on, with the hood up. The teachers said that she had the coat on too tight and it was unhealthy. I always think if it is not hurting anyone else, and it is not hurting her, then there is no problem.

In year 10 she dyed her hair red and black and they said it wasn't part of the uniform. They excluded her so she had to do a year 11 course at college. This was for students who had been disruptive. She did get some GCSEs but not as many as if she had stayed at school.

According to the school, Emma had 'excluded herself'. She was very rebellious and when she was 16 she chose the wrong friends. She was getting into trouble and the police would come round. She was being told what to do by the friends and she would just do it and seemed unable to think about the consequences. She was coming home in the small hours and I would lock her out.

She left home at 16 and got in with the wrong crowd again. She became very nomadic. I used to report her missing to the police and then I would go on what I called 'a mission', knocking on doors where I thought she might be. I used to go out at midnight and if I found where she was staying I would bring her things home. I used to arm myself with a screwdriver just in case I got attacked. She used to end up looking for father figures I think. She went with this older man and he used to beat her.

One time I had to go round to the house with a police escort to get all her stuff out. She was pregnant so I brought her back home. I made a decision not to help her with her son because I knew she had to make a commitment to him. She is so easily distracted. I think people thought I was harsh. I would look after the baby if she wanted to go out with friends. Every relationship she has been in she has ended up being beaten. Partners don't seem to be able to deal with how she acts, how she has what I call a 'shed collapse', a meltdown.

She has three children now and is a brilliant mum but everything else goes by the by – paying bills, sorting things out. I think one of her children may be on the spectrum. That child's dad may be on the spectrum because Emma has told me when they went out and an ambulance went past he would fall on the floor with his fingers in his ears. Emma's child is clever. When Emma went to the toilet he knew which switch in the fuse-box would turn the light off. His language is not very good and he does not sleep very well. I also suspect that Emma's father is on the spectrum. All our children struggle with anything more than a one-to-one conversation.

Me

My partner sometimes laughs at the things I write in Harry's school diary. He says that I can't write that, it's not right! For example, I recently wrote that teachers should be teachers and not try to be psychiatrists. Another time I asked the school to keep John's lunch warm, as he had another appointment. They said they did not have the facilities and I said that they should ask Father Christmas for a new microwave. My partner said that these things were wrong. The school have described me as unapproachable but I think I just speak my mind. When you have two special needs children who can't do it for themselves, there is no point in beating about the bush. Lots of people say that you shouldn't say these things because they offend. I tend to say them anyway. I like to say it as it is.

Another obsession of mine is abuse of disabled parking at school. They have loads of parking, with about 12 disabled parking bays. I pick up Harry when he has after-school dance. Sometimes there are netball and football tournaments going on at the same time. Sometimes parents insist on parking in the disabled bays, and when I get there, there are none left. The bays are near the school entrance. Sometimes when I pick up Harry and John, one is running one way and one the other, and I need to get them into the car as soon as quickly as I can. If the car is there where they can see it, in a parking bay, they tend not to run away.

I have written to the head teacher. He told me he wasn't happy about it either and he would monitor the situation. Nothing has changed though. I checked and, out of 11 cars in the disabled bay, only one had a blue badge and that was mine! I know that one of the cars belonged to the school nurse. Also, Harry likes to get himself in and out of the car, and if we are in a normal parking spot we run the risk of damaging the next car when he opens the door. If we have to go in a normal parking spot I take up two spaces, which I know may annoy other people.

I can't afford for them to get wound up because that makes driving difficult. If Harry gets wound up he starts to stammer and then gives me a poke. I got a new car where they had to sit together in the back but they just ended up fighting. When Harry sits in the front he is constantly pressing the touch-screen to change the CD.

I think my mum's got Asperger Syndrome. I think my mum, Emma and myself are all very similar in the things we do and the way we behave.

I think people on the spectrum attract each other. My best friend is on the spectrum. We have known each other since we were at college. We never stuck to fashion. We both worked as librarians. I could never keep friends and Emma is the same. I think I am a funny person and I thought that I would get invited back by friends but I never did. If things were organised between people at school I never got included. It tends to be me that keeps in contact with people; they never seem to contact me. I don't know why and Emma is the same. She gets a friend and it lasts a short space of time and then it fizzles out. None of my children have friends coming round, although to be honest it is a bit of a Godsend because I would find it difficult to deal with crowds. My mum doesn't have any friends; she lives in a bubble.

I used to have stupid physical tics. They are compulsory, as I have to do them! I've got to feel equal. For example, when I had long hair in a ponytail and it was off-centre I would have to pull the band off. Emma was the same; it happened before a ballet exam and she couldn't do the exam. My socks used to have to be a certain way, above my knee. If one didn't stretch the same as the other I wouldn't wear them. I could sort through a whole stack of socks till I found a pair.

When I was walking to school, I didn't tread on the cracks if I could help it. If I walked on one with my left foot, I then had to walk on one with my right foot, or else I felt lop-sided. If I feel like this I can't concentrate and so if I'm talking to people I'm not listening to them. Afterwards I'm thinking 'God, what have they just said?'

If my boyfriend, Martin, puts his arm round me, that makes me feel lop-sided too. I can't say 'Hug me from the other side' because that's not right, so for the next hour or so I still feel lop-sided. I have to readjust my clothing to try and balance it out. Sometimes it takes all day to get straight again. He'll sometimes see me wriggling and say sorry about making me lop-sided. If I've got a vase of flowers, I can spend ages rearranging them.

I run my mouth on the back of my hand and feel the veins. Then I feel the back of my hand. Harry does the same and yet he has never seen me do it because I do it in secret! My parents used to say, 'Look, she is tired.' I was very young when I started doing it. If I want to do it but can't because, for example, my hairdresser is here, I've got a cape on so I can do it with my fingers. I can feel the veins and bones in the back of my hand. If I am in a public place, I can put my hands up my sleeves and do it. Then sometimes, when it gets too much, I wrap my arms around my head. I put one hand against my mouth, elbow up and the other arm over the top of my head and hold my elbow. I only do that in private or when my family are around. I can't believe I'm telling you this! I have not told anyone else!

Harry likes to smell things and I do too. I am hypersensitive to smell. I also need to touch things. If I go somewhere and it says 'Do not touch' I have to touch it. If we go round the shops, I have to touch things that look textured. Some book covers, for example, are flat but made to look as if they are textured. I have to touch them. These are really compulsions. After I have done them, I feel satisfied. It is comforting.

I also struggle with changes. It is five weeks since I had my bathroom redecorated. This sounds stupid but I am still trying to get over the trauma of the turmoil and upset. The man who did the work has been in contact with me but I can't contact him. With the problems with my children, I have to put everything into it, then I need time to recover. I sometimes have to cancel arrangements with my friend but she understands.

I think I am on the spectrum but I think it is true that girls are better at hiding it. Girls pick up on what is expected of them so they learn from an early age how to cover it up.

James

James is 28 and has never lived anywhere else. He's only been on holiday and to a few festivals by himself. He has never been diagnosed but I suspect he has autism. He lives in his bedroom when he's at home. He is a panel beater. He works hard and is a perfectionist. Because his work is so good, different companies hunt him down.

He struggles with other people at work because everybody doesn't work like he does. They try to make him keep costs down and he's not happy about this. He likes to do things right. He's a very fair person, and there's people who take the best jobs and leave the rubbish ones, which he gets left with. One time he was going in early to do the same to them that they had done to him. I think he gets victimised because he's so quiet. I think people take advantage of him and he sees the best in others. When he sold his bike, he did things on trust and never took a deposit.

Last year he put his work details on the Internet and got an interview to go for a job in Brisbane, Australia. He had three-way interviews on the phone and got the job. He will be going in six weeks. I'm worried because the only way he's ever had to look after himself is to keep his car and motorbike on the road, apart from when I've been on holiday. I worry because he's not a chatty, outgoing and sociable person. Sometimes people struggle to make conversation with him. He is never sociable when people visit the house.

I don't think he has a realistic view of what he can and can't do. I think he will do it but I just have this picture of him wandering around the city centre aimlessly. The company he is going to work for can give him an apartment next to the factory. I don't want him to be stuck in a room over there. I don't want him to be doing over there what he is doing here. I've said to him that he can always come back but he thinks he is putting so much money into doing it that he's going to make it work. He surprised me because when they wanted evidence of his work and he had a good collection of 'before and after' pictures of his work to show them. He works on Volkswagens.

Boyfriend, Martin

I don't know how I managed to find someone who is so tolerant. I am restricted as to where I can go and what I can do. His family has grown up. Although he has raised children, he knew nothing about autism when I first met him. Now he is completely at home with autism. There was a social gathering recently and Martin, John and Harry did not want to go with me. He was quite happy to go shopping and see his mum and took the lads with him.

He's lovely but he makes fun of some of the things I do! I met him on a Wednesday and on the Friday we had a takeaway. This was only the second time he had met me. I sat with my food on my knee and he said, 'I don't want you to take this the wrong way, it's meant in a nice way, but you are a proper geek!' I make him laugh with some of the things I do and say. I never get a joke; he doesn't bother telling me any more. Mind you, he does odd things and I've asked him why. For example, if he's sat with a cigarette, he puts his little finger in front of his eyes. When I asked about it, he told me he was 'lining things up!'

Reflections

Lois attended the autism course to gain a qualification so that, when challenged by qualified professionals, she could say, 'Oh yes, I've been to university and I've learnt about it.' I should add that many of the parents who did attend did so for the same reason; they felt bullied by professionals. We might all ask how we manage our professional knowledge. Could we ever be perceived as bullying? Do we impose our decisions on children with autism when it is against a parent's wish? Even worse, do we agree one thing in front of the parents and then do something else behind their back?

As well as being professionals, we are all members of the public. Lois describes times when members of the public have judged her and her children; it seems that 'permitted' types of behaviour are tightly constrained and limited in public settings. It must take courage to go again into settings where people have been rejecting and judgemental. We have the perfect opportunity to model tolerance in public settings.

I find Lois's ability to keep going quite awe-inspiring. Most of the parents I have met do the same, and yet most have had profound doubts about whether they are doing the right thing. We can all make our respect explicit in our work with parents.

13
A mother's realisation of the importance of transition

Tracy Marie Duffy

Tracy's account formed the basis of her assignment on the autism course at the University of Cumbria. Two things struck me when I read it. First, I was included in the essay as the lecturer who was wrong. It does us all good to be cut down to size! The second was the harsh judgements Tracy made about herself and some of the errors she made. Professional practice might well benefit if health and social care professionals were to engage in such rigorous self-analysis.

Tracy is a mother of a young boy with autism. She describes her struggle to see herself as 'a good mum' during two major life transitions for her young son. She concludes:

"During Adam's time at nursery I learned that I did not know him as well as I thought I did and admitted that I got things wrong, which led to an unsuccessful transition into nursery. However, I learned from and reflected on the mistakes I had made, and with support from the nursery and others involved, such as Adam's new teacher from school, together we implemented positive changes that made Adam's transition into school successful."

I never ever imagined that I would be asked to write my story that will be published in a book just from attending an autism course and completing an essay that was about my five-year-old son, mainly because essay writing has never been my speciality even when I was studying to become an occupational therapist (OT). I feel it is necessary to explain why I decided to attend the autism course. I wanted to increase my knowledge and understanding of autism. I can imagine you, the reader, thinking why would she want to increase her knowledge and understanding of autism? Surely she would have an in-depth knowledge already, being a mum and having done an OT degree?

Well, the truth is, until I completed the autism course, I only had an awareness of what autism is and by this I mean the triad of impairment, sensory sensitivities, pica (the eating of inedible objects), etc. I did not know anything about theory of mind or mind blindness and I am not ashamed to admit this. After all, the assumption that parents are the experts is simply not true, in my opinion. Yes, I know my child, granted. However, I do not know everything about autism. I too am learning about autism, just like other family members, health professionals and teachers who are involved in my son's life.

There are so many stories I could have chosen to write about when it comes to my son Adam and his autism, even though he is only five. Things like the moment when I first noticed that his language was not developing, that he did not play with toys other than to spin wheels or line them up, his sensory differences, his food phobias and so much more. However, I have chosen to write about when Adam was three and starting nursery, as this was a chapter in my life that initially caused me a lot of stress. It led to me doing a lot of personal reflection, which was not easy, so here I go.

I will begin my story with an introduction to Adam and how autism affects him on a daily basis. I can't believe that my beautiful boy is now five. I don't know where the time has gone and so much has happened with Adam in that time. He is fun and a loving boy who has a fantastic sense of humour. He was diagnosed with autistic spectrum disorder (ASD), now known as autistic spectrum condition (ASC) at the age of three. He also has significant speech and language delay, sensory differences, pica and learning delay.

When I think back to when Adam was a baby, as young as six months, there were possible signs that he had an ASC. For example, he was extremely difficult to wean on to solid food and other drinks apart from milk. He would only eat smooth textured foods and appeared to gag or choke when lumpy textures were introduced; the same thing happened with water or juice.

At toddler age, there were many signs that Adam had ASD. He was non-verbal (he only had six single words, which he did not use in context), nor did he demonstrate that he wanted to communicate with others. He had significant social interacting difficulties with other children and unfamiliar adults. He wanted to be on his own and did not like it when others tried to play with him. Toys were and still are played with differently, for example turning cars upside down to constantly spin the wheels, repetitively for hours. He also has special interests or 'obsessions', as I call them, with anything round that he can spin (especially washing machines), lining up objects, transport, sand and water. Surprisingly, at the age of three, he was only just beginning to develop an interest in television.

As well as these social difficulties, interests and fleeting eye contact, he had and still has several hyper and some hypo sensory differences and stimming behaviours (hand flapping, humming and spinning on the spot). These have a significant impact on his ability to engage in activities of daily living and learning. There are too many to discuss in great detail. Therefore, I will discuss the sensory difference that, in my opinion, has the biggest impact on his day-to-day life. Adam's biggest sensory seeking behaviour is his need to constantly chew or bite on non-food items such as clothing; yet he struggles to eat lumpy, moist food and prefers a plain diet. Although I know the reason he chews is to meet his sensory need, I feel guilty about the fact that I find it difficult to comprehend how he can chew and eat non-food items such as sponges, but struggles to eat certain lumpy food textures. Furthermore, all of Adam's difficulties cause him to have high levels of frustration, stress and anxiety. These often lead to challenging behaviour that is sometimes difficult for me and others to manage.

The time was fast approaching to start thinking about nursery for Adam. As his mother, I constantly think about and try to avoid any daily activities that I know will be stressful for Adam, as they can cause him to become anxious and nervous, often leading to meltdowns because he can't cope with the situation. For example, I will avoid crowded, noisy places where possible because this causes a meltdown and sensory overload.

Finding a nursery was something I could not avoid and this filled me with many mixed emotions. I contacted a few nurseries that had been recommended by others before I made any decision. However, my mind was already made up before I had even taken Adam to see the nursery, as it was the only one that said it would be good to bring him with me. All the other nurseries wanted a meeting with me before I brought Adam. When we arrived for a look around, Adam reacted in the way he always did when going into new unfamiliar environments, which was to kick, punch, bite, scream loudly and hold on to me tightly, hiding underneath my coat refusing to let go. After receiving a deep-pressured cuddle from me, he calmed down and went straight outside to go on the play equipment and play with the cars. Then I could not get him to leave, causing another meltdown. I assumed Adam's reaction (not wanting to enter the nursery) was because it was a big, open-plan, bright, noisy and generally over-stimulated environment. This sent his sensory system into overload, causing him to shut down and reach what I call 'full-blown meltdown mode'.

On reflection, I should have prepared Adam for the visit to the nursery but at that time I was unsure of how to do this and planning for any situation was something I did inadequately then. The only reasons I can give for this, which made me feel like an awful mum, was that I was still developing my knowledge and understanding of how autism truly affected Adam. Also, he was non-verbal and we were all unsure of what level of language understanding he had.

After I made my decision about which nursery I was sending Adam to, it was important to prepare all who were involved, especially Adam (as much as I could, after our experience of his initial visit to the nursery) for the transition from home and childminder into nursery.

Part of the preparation was to have a Team Around the Child (TAC) meeting. A TAC is a multidisciplinary team of practitioners, established on a case-by-case basis to support a child, young person or family.

At this meeting, each person took their turn to discuss Adam's strengths and the areas of difficulty he had. Everyone in the meeting had a role to fulfil. For example, the speech and language therapist had to set realistic, achievable child-centred goals, while a nursery staff member gave other nursery staff details about Adam's needs and triggers so they would be aware of anything that might increase his challenging behaviours. We all agreed that I would create an 'All about me' book, as it would initially provide nursery staff with all the important information they needed to know about Adam, including his likes and dislikes. I completed this personal book in the hope that it would help staff to support Adam to settle into nursery.

The day had arrived; Adam had started nursery. I was feeling nervous, tearful and sad, but most of all I was extremely worried about how Adam would cope in a new environment. We had all done as much as we could in terms of planning and preparing for him to start nursery. Unfortunately there were a few things that we could not prepare Adam for – for example, not being able to introduce him to his key worker because there were going to be staff changes, and the children had not been allocated a key worker at the time of the meeting. Also, although I did try to talk to Adam (using simple language with only one to three words) about starting nursery, I have to be honest and say I can't be sure how much he understood, as I did not get any communication from him at all. However, I fully expected to get no response, as he had, and still has, significant language delay.

I was expecting Adam to have some increased challenging, sensory seeking, or repetitive behaviours until he had settled in and become familiar with his nursery environment. But I did not expect, and was completely unprepared for, the level of challenging behaviours that the nursery and I experienced during his first term. The nursery's ethos was for play to be child-led. This was fantastic in principle, and may have worked for other children, but for Adam it was not good, as he relied on adults to encourage him in to engage in play. He would not do this of his own choosing.

At the TAC meeting I had expressed my concerns about this, saying to the teacher present at the meeting, 'Adam will need firm boundaries put in place and will need encouragement from adults to explore different play areas; otherwise he will just do the things he finds interesting, e.g. constantly spin and chew wheels or spin the washing machine.' I was reassured that firm boundaries and adult-led play would be put into place from day one for Adam.

It soon became clear that this had not been done, because within the first week his key worker had reported to me that Adam had taken over the toilets, not letting the other children use them. He had flooded them on one occasion, by turning all the taps on and playing with the water. (Water was and remains another interest of his, even to the present day.) I was concerned about this behaviour, so I asked his key worker about what boundaries had in put in place. Her response was to say that they wanted Adam to settle in, and did not have a problem with him playing with the taps until these two incidents occurred.

I replied that, while I understood that they wanted Adam to settle in, I felt it was important for him to know the rules from day one. Otherwise they would have difficulty stopping him in future, as he would not understand why he couldn't play with taps when it had been allowed before. I knew this because I had done the same in the past with Adam.

These intense, difficult-to-manage, challenging behaviours continued at home and at nursery. There were too many incidents to write about. However, there is one that I will never forget. Adam had bitten two children at nursery and I was informed that he had done this on 'purpose'. I could not believe what had been said. I told them he would not have done it on purpose. His key worker replied, 'He did mean to do it; he bit his friend too for no reason.' I tried to explain, saying that this boy might see Adam as a friend, but Adam might not see him as a friend because social interaction is one of his major difficulties. I can remember feeling so angry and upset to the point that I cried when I got home. I decided to keep Adam off for a week, as I thought it was the right thing to do. I just kept thinking: What have I done wrong? Why was he behaving like this? I could not understand why and felt like I had failed him.

At the time, I understood that Adam had little self-awareness, did not understand emotions and had no empathy towards others. However, I thought these other difficulties were interlinked with his social difficulties. I am not ashamed to admit that I did not know, until I had completed the autism module and read theory by various experts in the field that Adam's increased challenging and repetitive behaviours were also linked to two cognitive theories, theory of mind (ToM) and weak central coherence.

According to Simon Baron-Cohen (an expert on autism), the majority of individuals with autism have difficulty recognising and understanding thoughts and emotions in themselves and others. Reading this made me quite tearful because now I could fully understand why Adam only responded to either really happy or really cross emotions. The latter made me feel like a terrible mother, as I never wanted to get that cross with my son, but it was the only emotion he would respond to, especially in potentially dangerous situations, like running into the road. Furthermore, this theory indicates that individuals with autism also have difficulty in understanding that others have different beliefs from themselves, and often think that others can read their mind. For example, they will think that someone should know that they want a drink, even though they have not asked that person for a drink. I can completely relate to this, especially when Adam was younger and did not make his needs known at all. I would often assume that he was hungry or wanted a drink.

I also read about the theory of weak central coherence. This describes how some individuals with autism only see parts of details, particularly in social situations, where they will extract what is meaningful to them. This is because they have difficulty processing the whole picture. This theory fits Adam like a glove because he will only interact with other children if he is encouraged to by adults, or if they are doing something that interests him, like water play or transport.

For me, these cognitive theories have highlighted some of the reasons why Adam displays challenging behaviour, particularly in new environments and social situations. They have also made me realise that daily life for Adam can be stressful, as there are too many hidden social rules to cope with. This often leads to coping or avoidance behaviours, like biting the boys in his nursery or throwing chairs across the room.

Reflecting back on the conversation with Adam's key worker, I believe it was OK for me to be upset by the comment. However, it was not OK for me to be so angry. I say this because I was still learning about what autism is and how it will affect my son for the rest of his life. So how could I expect the nursery staff to understand autism and its impact on Adam? This was an unfair expectation. If I had known then what I know now (about the reasons why he displays challenging and repetitive behaviours), I might have been able to explain to the nursery staff the reasons behind his challenging behaviour. For example, not understanding the consequences of biting another child may have been because he has weak central coherence, or another reason for biting may have been sensory overload or increased anxiety levels.

In one of the autism lectures I went to, a university lecturer stated 'Parents are the experts.' From my personal experience, I would have to argue against his statement, because in my opinion parents can explain what they observe in their child, but this does not mean that they are experts in the condition their child has. I would argue that we are learning about the condition, just like everybody else, especially as new research is being published all of the time.

I knew that something had to change because things could not continue the way they were at home and nursery so I requested a meeting to discuss a way forward to try and reduce Adam's challenging behaviours. At the meeting, we discussed all the challenging behaviours that he was displaying and the possible triggers for these behaviours. It was agreed that the nursery would apply for funding, as we all felt that Adam would benefit from some much-needed one to one time (he did get five hours per week, which meant one hour per nursery session). I was keen for him to start using objects of reference and the picture exchange communication system (PECS) at nursery, as this was now beginning to work at home and Adam was demonstrating that he was a visual learner and responded well to pictures, rather than spoken language. However, before these agreed changes could be fully implemented, Adam's key worker left due to unforeseen circumstances. I was now feeling even more worried and expecting even more challenging behaviours. However, he did not appear to be affected by this sudden change. I can only assume this was because he had now become familiar with the other staff members at the nursery. The new nursery teacher wanted to know everything about Adam and reassured me that she was going to read all about him that day and observe him as much as she could.

After her first week, she called to arrange a meeting between us. Before the meeting I was feeling very nervous, as everything up to this point had seemed to be going wrong, with no clear explanation as to why. However, after the meeting I left feeling that there were going to be positive changes made, which might help to reduce Adam's challenging behaviours. These planned changes were that Adam was going to have one-to-one support all the time, a structured routine supported with visual aids and encouragement to engage in adult-led activities, including group activities.

In just two weeks it was evident that implementing this structure was the right thing to do. Adam's challenging behaviours had dramatically reduced at nursery and he was like a different boy. Everyone, including myself, was amazed by the change in Adam. For example, he was no longer throwing chairs around and he seemed more settled. Although I knew Adam responded well to firm boundaries, I did get it fundamentally wrong when I thought, as stated earlier in the chapter, that Adam was OK with routine changes. He clearly was not OK with routine changes, and this became evident when a routine was put in place. Reflecting on that moment when I saw that Adam *did* need routine and structure to help him cope with all the unpredictability in his life, I can remember feeling completely devastated and confused by the fact that I thought I knew my son inside and out and it turned out that I didn't. I had failed my son again and again.

Having learned from the mistakes that I had made during Adam's transition to nursery, I was determined not to make the same mistakes when he went to school. During a transition meeting in this process, I insisted that he visited his new school several times before starting in September 2012. His new teacher and I felt this was necessary, as Adam's first visit to the school did not go well. We explained to people present at the meeting that Adam had a full-blown meltdown that lasted the duration of the visit and in the car on the way home, all because he had to come back in to the classroom after having five minutes' play outside.

Everyone who was present at the meeting agreed to the extra visits. These extra visits appeared to have worked, as Adam's transition into school was a success.

As well as continuing to use these strategies, in the future I will consider using social stories. There is evidence to suggest that social stories help individuals like Adam, who have ASD, to understand expectations and social roles, particularly during times of transition and other activities of daily living.

Final thoughts

During Adam's time at nursery, I learned that I did not know him as well as I thought I did and admitted that I got things wrong, which had led to an unsuccessful transition to nursery. However, I learned from and reflected on the mistakes I had made, and with support from the nursery and others involved, such as Adam's new teacher from school, together we implemented positive changes that made Adam's transition into school successful. Finally, I would like to say that it is extremely important that everyone involved in a child's care works together as a team and listens to each other because in my experience this leads to the best outcome for the child, and at the end of the day this is all that matters.

Reflections

Tracy was let down by the nursery that her son attended. A transition plan had been written but the teacher appeared to ignore it and 'know best'.

At one point, Tracy was told her son had 'deliberately' bitten another child, which caused her great distress. Of course, this teacher was also wrong! Tracy reflects deeply on her performance and gives herself a hard time, stating that she felt as though she had failed as a mum. She now feels that she has gained sufficient knowledge to make a better job of being the mother of a son with autism.

As professionals, we might ask ourselves whether our behaviour might ever have caused such distress to a mother. We could question whether we have ever dismissed the views of parents. We could also consider whether our knowledge of autism is broad enough, detailed enough and sufficiently up to date to be of use in supporting families.

14
Life, learning, and getting it wrong
KatyLou Thompson

KatyLou is a mother of twins who are both on the autism spectrum. She attended the autism course at the University of Cumbria, and shared her story with the class. She describes her grief for what could have been for her son, who has both cerebral palsy and autism:

> "What I mean is that his disability raises a lifetime of barriers, of difficulties and heartaches that I as his mum would have given anything to have spared him. I grieve for the things that might have been his: a level playing field for a start, friends, a family of his own, independence, a decent chance of employment, financial and emotional security, a future to build upon not scrabble for, the right and opportunity to make choices, to simply be able to go where he would, when he would, on his own if he wanted, or with people of his choice, just basic things really."

Have you heard the saying, 'You never know what's around the next corner'? Life is so strange sometimes. I never thought when I went out of the house this morning to attend an autism course that I would be coming home ready to write a chapter for a book. I hate writing, really hate it, I mean. But I have a story to tell, so here goes…

Just over 26 years ago, I gave birth to the most beautiful set of twins you've ever seen, George and Edward (Eddie). I know every mum says that but it's always true. They were premature so they spent a few weeks in special baby care, which is such a difficult experience despite the wonderful staff. I vividly remember it to this day.

Sixteen months later, my husband and I were told that our eldest twin, George, had cerebral palsy, although that's a nice way of describing what was actually a horrendous experience. I was devastated. I don't know what my husband felt. I was too sunk in my own grief and shock to notice. But they were still both my beautiful babies and we got through it, but it's all a bit of a blur around that time actually.

It took me a long time to accept disability in my child, especially as his walking difficulty became just one of a set of difficulties. The school years were a totally stressful and miserable time, despite some brilliant support in a system that did not, at that time, really know how to support children with disabilities in mainstream schools. Secondary school was particularly nightmarish and, as I write, I feel nothing but relief that we are past those days.

At the age of 14, however, George was further diagnosed with Asperger Syndrome and the bottom fell out of my world again. I make no apologies for not telling you the details of that dreadful period either. I don't even want to write about how the diagnosis of a second significant disability felt, although I must admit it was like finding the missing piece of the jigsaw that was our son; it was hard. I had never even considered that a person could have two different disabilities; wasn't one enough?

I started my story by saying: Do we ever know what's around the corner? For me, life's like that – full of questions that we can never know the answer to. For instance, when I as a young woman wanted children, did I ever give a moment's thought to what sort of mother I'd make? Did I have any understanding that sometimes it doesn't go to plan? I think 'No' is the answer to both questions.

Over the years, though, I've thought a lot about what type of mum I've been and I think as far as parenting goes I've had a pretty rich, valuable, if also painful, experience. But the greatest reward I've had from parenting, which no pain can ever diminish, is discovering the absolutely gigantic well of love I have for my children, and in the end how fortunate is that?

Having said that, when George was diagnosed with autism, I was still really grieving over the diagnosis of cerebral palsy. I think parents do grieve for their whole lifetime; at least, I think I will. It ebbs and flows as life pushes and pulls. It's not that I grieve for the child I have, but rather I grieve for the child that he could have been and I don't for one minute mean that he is less than he could have been because of his disability. What I mean is that his disability raises a lifetime of barriers, of difficulties and heartaches that I as his mum would have given anything to have spared him. I grieve for the things that might have been his: a level playing field for a start, friends, a family of his own, independence, a decent chance of employment, financial and emotional security, a future to build upon not scrabble for, the right and opportunity to make choices, to simply be able to go where he would, when he would, on his own if he wanted, or with people of his choice, just basic things really. I grieve for the loss of my dreams, of how easy and straightforward his life might have been, and for the loss of my own dream that, one day far in the future I hope, I would be able to leave him contentedly, in the knowledge that he would be safe and happy in his life. It is so hard to dream of improbable events.

Ah, I hear you say, we live in a caring society where we look after the less able members of our communities. Even if that were wholly true (that is, it would be good to believe it was true, for some at least), George's world is his family and we cannot be replaced. His

147

autism means the impact of losing his parents and carers cannot be compared to the loss experienced by the average person with ageing parents. Where then does that leave him for the rest of his life? These are the questions which life with a disabled child brings. These are the questions that relate to the pain we feel, the reason the pain lives on, as we keep searching for our answers.

But, although there is pain, George is the most inspiring person in my life. His courage and determination, character and everything he is, make him so incredibly special to me.

And George is a success story from my point of view. Against all the odds, and I include major battles over the years with the education authority and later with the examinations board AQA, all through solicitors of course, he completed mainstream school with some GCSEs, which I hadn't thought possible at one point, given the complexity of his learning difficulties. After leaving school at 19, he gained some employment and flourished under one manager and shrivelled under another but he didn't give up, he stood his ground and his Asperger Syndrome proved to be an asset as he found his voice and his will to defy a bully.

George simply doesn't see rank or hierarchy. He just sees people and none are better or worse than another, and in finding his voice and the strength to defy his manager he also found a sense of self. How amazing is that? But nowadays, finding another job seems an impossibility; the disadvantages of disability are vast in the employment marketplace. However, he still works. He has a voluntary job, working at reception in a local support centre for those with greater challenges than he has. Again, I would never have thought it possible that George could work as a receptionist but he does and he has just won second place in his organisation's staff awards for volunteers in the Northwest. Incredible, incredible, stuff. I am the proudest of parents. Not everything unexpected around the corner is bad; sometimes gifts await us.

But some events lying in wait around the corner are awful.

Many have said that I should be proud of myself for my parenting of my eldest twin. After all, in my heyday I co-founded and led a local support group for parents of children with disabilities and as a group we heckled ministers, wrote answers to consultations to Green Papers, White papers. You name it – we did it. We put on awareness events, collectively sat on endless committees, steering groups, etc., etc. I supported many other parents after training in emotional and educational support, I spoke at conferences about the experiences of a parent, I would speak anywhere that asked me, I was just so driven to raise awareness, to seek understanding, to make 'it' better, which was impossible, so the next best thing was to make something good come from something so difficult.

With a well-hidden sense of despair, I tried to make a difference. I also had so much to make up for. After all, a late diagnosis of autism carries years of mistakes with it, albeit mistakes made in ignorance. I suppose I feel I tried to do everything as well as I could on every front, life at home, life in support of others, life in conflict with the many powers that be, but it wasn't enough. Not in the cosmic balance of things. You know, you try your best and maybe you'll earn some universal Brownie points and life will be kind for a while. It doesn't work that way unfortunately.

About three years ago, my younger twin, Eddie, was at the age of 23, unofficially but nonetheless properly, diagnosed with Asperger Syndrome or possibly atypical autism. I had two sons with autism after all.

Well, I hear you think, how did you miss that? After all, surely when George was diagnosed with Asperger Syndrome, didn't you immediately set about learning everything there was to learn about autism? Didn't you then set off on the 'we'll work this out together journey' with him? After all, you were a 'professional parent' by this time. Surely you pretty much knew it all, after all that reading. So, with all that experience with George, how could you miss something as massive as autism also in Eddie? And for twenty-odd years, for heaven's sake? Were you asleep? I thought you were close?

I really wish I had even one answer to these questions. Did I love Eddie less than George so I didn't pay attention to him? I don't think so but maybe I didn't see him properly. Maybe I needed to think that he was OK. I cherished his normality, even though I knew he too was slightly different. I think I loved Eddie equally but differently. It was an easier sort of love, less complicated it seemed. I think I valued that too, the simplicity of normal parenting alongside the complexity of different parenting. Maybe I needed Eddie to be without problems, as I really couldn't have borne to see that he had real difficulties of his own and not just the normal 'sibling of a disabled child' stuff. Maybe that would have been too much.

So did I wilfully ignore all the signs that, with hindsight, now seem as large as those overhead motorway ones? I don't think so but maybe the signs weren't relevant because no matter how obvious they were, I simply couldn't read them, so size didn't matter.

But you had the information, I hear you say, the route map, the symbol chart. How did you miss your way? Why didn't you match the signs up, even if you couldn't read them?

I don't know, I really don't know, and that's the important part because now my son, my younger twin, my Eddie, is lost to me. The diagnosis of his Asperger Syndrome happened just before he met a young woman who also has Asperger Syndrome amongst several other difficulties. As a result of this, she is unable to 'do family'. Even though we worked so hard to try and work around the problem, you just can't win every time. So Eddie's choice became simply his partner or his family. He chose the former and six months ago he said goodbye to all of us via email. In his message, he said:

> I am different and I know that that has made me difficult for just about everyone I have ever met … So I'm sorry and I accept the consequences of my actions. I'd rather let you [meaning all of us, me, my husband, George, his grandparents] begin the healing process…
> Goodbye, and all the best to all of you.

If I had needed clearer proof of his autism, could I have asked for more?

Only someone with autism could think that you can simply email your mum, and think that walking out of our lives via email, will help the 'healing process to begin', and very nicely wish us all the best, as if his loss from our lives was like the equivalent loss of a barely known sixth-removed cousin going to live in Australia. I can't tell you, even though I knew he had been thinking about it before, what a shock it was at 10.30pm on a Sunday evening in December to receive that email, when I'd been talking to him not ten minutes before (thinking 'This is hard work but we're getting somewhere and if we keep trying it'll work out in the end because if you really love your children you can slay any dragon for them, heal any hurt, build any bridge'). I hadn't thought it was possible it could really happen because we were such a close family. Not a perfect one, by any means. Our family life had been tough for many reasons but we had always stood together, dealt with stuff together. But we couldn't cope with someone else's autism as well. We messed up.

I couldn't tell my husband or George for days and when I did his dad could not believe that he could simply abandon us without even saying goodbye to him in person. His grandparents, who had also been very close to him, were devastated and really, six months on, we're all still dazed. No negotiation, no chance of working things out, just goodbye, a wall of silence and the space he left behind.

So did I see that coming? I'd like to say 'No' but I can't because as soon as I finally grasped the fact that he really did have autism it was too late. He had already met and immediately committed to the young woman with whom I sincerely hope he still lives and is happy with, because the possibilities of where and how he is if things haven't worked out for him are unthinkable and those straws really would break this donkey's back. As understanding finally dawned in me that his difficulties in previous relationships and difference generally were the result of his autism, so too did the awful awareness grow of his vulnerability and, ultimately, fragility. My fears, which led to the exploration of his possible inclusion on the autistic spectrum, have been borne out.

And worse, I don't believe he will come back, ever, in any circumstances. He might perhaps if he were less rigid, less committed to a path once set, less autistic. So yes, I suppose I did see that one coming but I tried to deny it. And then, despite my best efforts to head it off, disaster was still lying in our road, not even out of view round the bend. But we couldn't avoid it, there were no ways around it and we're still feeling the effects of the collision. And the collision makes me realise that I've written about the successes and my pride in George but none of that about Eddie so I just want to tell you there is all that too for Eddie, but at this time it is just so hard to think about any of that for him because all I can think about is that he's gone.

The rest doesn't matter and I haven't got my head together about how to remember him because there are so many conversations about the past in the light of his diagnosis that we haven't had, because he met his partner and he became someone different, virtually straight away. There are just more questions on questions. Is it usual for a young man with Asperger Syndrome to jump in head-first and immediately become someone else? If it is, how does that work? If it isn't, does that mean there's more chance of him coming back, or less? There's endless questioning and wondering, sometimes with some hope, sometimes with none.

So, what of us left behind, my husband, myself and George? Can we survive the loss of someone who was one corner of our family square such a short time ago? I didn't think so at first. Sometimes I think the answer is still no, but then I look at George and see that, even though he is struggling with this so much, he is simply carrying on at the same time. He hasn't lain down and given up; that's been more my line. But this estrangement is so difficult for him to understand and I don't know how to help him. There are no books, there's no research I can find on separation in autism under these circumstances. How do I explain to someone who has difficulty in understanding relationships that his twin has not meant to 'betray' him, when actually it sort of does feel that way, even though it isn't? If I am struggling to deal with it, how can I support my son? 'What can't be cured must be endured' but I haven't told you half of what George has had to endure already in his young life. Why is there always more?

It seems that learning is sort of like climbing a mountain wearing a blindfold. I have learned such a lot, how to live with pain and grief (well, not always live, just survive mostly), and I know we've had incredible gifts as well. Yet, even with all the knowledge and understanding and experience I have gained over the years, which logically should mean at some point I might actually know what I'm doing in this life, the truth is that knowledge means nothing as I blindly feel my way round the next crevice, round the next bend. I'm not even sure this mountain path is going upwards anymore.

The only thing I still know for sure is that I will always love my family (however they are, wherever they are, with me, or apart) and George knows that. I just wish Eddie knew it too. Maybe if he'd been able to receive or understand that, he'd still be part of our lives. And I know it is really impossible to guess or prepare for what's around the next corner. But you can't stand still, that isn't a choice, so I'm just going to keep on trudging. I'll ask my questions along the way, and one day I might find a clue as to what it's all about so that one day I might stop getting it wrong.

Postscript

A couple of months later…

Fate plays little games, amongst the larger ones. A few months ago, before I had begun the autism course, my husband, after listening to *Desert Island Discs* on the radio, brought up a podcast of the programme on the computer so I too could listen to it. He knew I would be interested, as the person being interviewed was Uta Frith, someone I had never heard of but whose work with children and adults with autism had received great acclaim. I listened with interest to her life story and her renowned work as a pioneering professor of neuroscience but the part I remember most was her empathic understanding of the challenges of being a parent of a child with autism. I was moved. In fact, I felt she spoke directly to us as parents with compassion. The message I heard (although of course this is a personal interpretation) was to recognise our struggles and to stop blaming ourselves. That was what I remember. I was so glad my husband had provided me with the opportunity to hear the programme; it's not something I would normally listen to.

So when I had finished the autism course and was working on my assignment, an essay analysing my parental experience of autism, I saw Uta Frith's book, *Autism: Explaining the Enigma*, on the library shelf and naturally brought it home to read. I found it an excellent book and would recommend it to anyone who wishes to understand the subject, and again her voice of compassion is clearly heard throughout.

However, I don't know if you can imagine how I felt when I came to a section explaining how twin studies have provided some of the evidence supporting a genetic basis theory for a possible cause of autism. As a parent of twins, this idea is not new to me, and as a cynical parent of twins I feel twin studies can always be counted on to prove something if it is needed in any field. Sorry, but scientific use of twins isn't something that appeals to me; whilst understanding their apparent usefulness in the scientific world, as a parent, it feels that there is something distasteful about it. This is a purely personal view, I'm afraid. I think it has something to do with the felt echoes of what was done to twins in the name of science in the last world war. Even though I know logically that the days of eugenics are in the past, and today we have the humanely practised study of genetics, I still fear for future generations about what the study of genetics may one day result in. After all, societies don't always move forwards.

However, my parental misgivings about twin studies aside, I then discovered something – initially with shock, then anger and great upset. In talking about twins where both have autism as 'concordant' and where one doesn't as 'non-concordant' (as in mine, I had thought before Eddie's diagnosis), Uta Frith wrote:

> However, the authors went one step further: many of the brothers in the non-concordant pairs of identical twins did in fact have a milder form of autistic disorder…
> In fact, the autistic features of these less affected brothers became more apparent as they got older. Using broader criteria, which allowed for milder forms of autism, the concordance in identical twins was now as high as ninety per cent.

So Eddie had had a 90 per cent chance of having autism, according to the information in a book printed in 1989, written by one of the leaders in the field, when Eddie was two years old, from studies collected ten years before he was born. Now I fully understand that Asperger Syndrome and/or the autistic spectrum in still regarded as relatively new to the world at large. I have to tell myself that is the reason why the psychiatrist who supported us with George from the age of three to thirteen didn't see fit to tell us, his parents, that she had diagnosed him with Asperger Syndrome some time before she finally retired, leaving us to find out in our first session with the new psychiatrist.

At the time, I refused to believe it until it was verified by an expert second opinion. The reason why I refused to believe it was that, although I knew in my heart it was true, I could not believe someone whom I had absolute trust in, and who was my chief support through some extremely difficult years, would not tell me my son had autism if she had diagnosed him with it. Why didn't she? The only reason I can think of was that she didn't know enough about it, although even that is hard to believe, as I do know of a young man she did actually diagnose with Asperger Syndrome when George was five, so it isn't true to say she didn't know of it at all. Perhaps this is another of those questions without answers…

And here's another… What about the psychologist we saw as a family, only seven or eight years ago, who told me we were as a family 'enmeshed'? The reason we saw him was due not only to our ongoing difficulties with George's behaviour but to Eddie's inability to accept George's diagnosis and to adapt his own behaviour, as we all needed to lessen George's stress. I could not understand why Eddie was unable to understand his twin's difficulties when he was intellectually very able and not unkind by nature. The psychologist obviously couldn't either, as he told Eddie that basically it was tough but he did need to make changes for his twin.

I am absolutely aghast, now that I know this knowledge of twins and autism existed, that this psychologist was not only oblivious to Eddie's 'milder, becoming more apparent, autism' but was so insensitive as to only direct Eddie's behaviour without at least trying to look beyond, to find the obvious cause for it. Yes, you could say I wasn't seeing it, so why should he? Well for a start, I expected a professional to have an expertise in the field that I didn't have, which would have included reading up on twins with autism if he were treating a twin with autism. I expected a professional to try to work out the dynamics of our family before making snap judgements and being easily and quickly directive. I expected help and a sensitivity, which we certainly didn't get. I didn't expect a professional to let us down again.

This is yet another conversation that I can't have with Eddie, now he's gone. I wish I could tell him now how sorry I am that I didn't listen to him when he told me how angry he felt after he saw this psychologist. I still thought he was being immature. To repeat the words from my first piece, how wrong could I be?

I cannot tell you how angry I am feeling again, at knowing that things could have been so different. I know that hindsight is not a wonderful thing and I know that my anger is still part of my grieving. I know it's not going to help to blame professionals for what they did or didn't do. And yet reading the work of Uta Frith, and at the same time feeling so let down by some people who have no idea of the negative impact they've had on our lives, brings home to me what has been my whole experience where professionals are concerned, whether they be from medical, educational, or social backgrounds. The ones that do least harm if they don't know much, through to those who make a huge and so appreciated difference, are the ones like Uta, who try to understand what it's like to be in a parent's shoes, and even more importantly talk to parents on equal terms, not as experts doling out expertise, but simply people helping people, no matter how wonderfully knowledgeable they are. But the ones who will to me be forever memorable for how they failed us, are no doubt continuing to look down on the rest of us from the ivory towers of their very questionable expertise.

Reflections

KatyLou is clearly very angry about the 'help' she has received from so many professionals. As professionals, most of us will have been on the receiving end of such anger and it will not always be personal. We are professionals working in an organisation that will probably have let the parents down on many past occasions. We represent that organisation. Are you able to empathise with parents' anger? Are you able to communicate your understanding? Can you respond to the parent's needs and not allow a defensive attitude to get in the way?

KatyLou has serious fears for the future. Services have been poor while she is alive; what will happen to her son when she dies? She awaits the next shock to 'come round the corner'. As a professional, do you have the trust of the parents you work with? Are you even seen as one of the shocks 'waiting to come round the corner'? My own acid test is 'Would this service be good enough for my own child if I were no longer around?' Sadly, my own conclusion is that the services I know would not even come close. It can be hard to work in a system that we feel does not really do the job it purports to do.

15
A concrete thinker's journey to Wonderland...
Archita Basu

Archita is the mother of Bob, who has autism. In this essay, written for the autism course at the University of Cumbria, she describes a very specific event from Bob's life at school. He was required to read and discuss the Roald Dahl story *Lamb to the Slaughter*, in which a woman murders her husband. The husband was about to leave her and so she killed him, but she concealed the murder weapon in an ingenious way and managed to trick the police. The superficially 'black and white' nature of murder is given a typically challenging twist by Dahl in this story. Bob found this difficult to comprehend, as he has a tendency to concrete thinking.

Archita is an English teacher and her style of writing is very different from most other contributors to this book. She suggests that:

> "Lamb to the Slaughter bares the heart and soul of autism and sheds revealing light into the nooks and crevices of difficulties experienced by someone with autism. Understanding perspective taking, irony, paradoxes, alibis, metaphors, sarcasm, narrator's voice, the fast paced action, are minefields for children on the autism spectrum – the story by Dahl presents mammoth challenges in decoding inherent levels of complexity."

Here is a short summary of the plot of Dahl's story:

> Mary Maloney, a pregnant young woman, waits for her husband Patrick to come home from work. He is a detective in the local police. When he arrives, Mary notices that he is strangely aloof and assumes that he has had trouble at work. Patrick confesses that he intends to leave her.

> Mary is shocked at the news. Seemingly in a trance, she fetches a large leg of lamb from the freezer to cook for their dinner. Patrick tells Mary to stop the routine and not make him dinner. She snaps and kills him by bludgeoning him in the back of the head with the frozen leg of lamb. In order to conceal her crime, Mary cooks the murder weapon, the leg of lamb. Then, after practising a cheerful routine, she heads out to the store to buy some vegetables for her

roast. When she gets back, she enters the room where she killed her husband and calls the police.

The police arrive and come to the conclusion that Patrick was killed with a sledgehammer. They search for the murder weapon with no luck obviously. Mary offers the policemen dinner, including the cooked murder weapon. During the meal the police discuss the possibility of the murder weapon being right under their noses. Mary laughs slyly to herself at the irony.

In this chapter, Archita writes about the way the school enabled Bob to make sense of the woman's motives for carrying out the murder and deceiving the police, despite the difficulties in understanding presented by his autism. Archita writes as a mother, a teacher and someone with a novelist's eye.

How am I to make a deserving start? I cannot hold back from questioning myself over and over again. Is the task irremediably beyond me? For what is a human being but everything that a human being is: the sunrise and the sunset and all the shades of colour in between? How shall I begin to describe an exceptionally bright, kind-hearted and quirky 13-year-old lad with the double label of autism and dyspraxia? Try as I might, the autism label does not convey the soaring sincerity of his atypically transparent grin.

And yet, one thing remains certain. One cannot help but feel overwhelmed by the spontaneous kindness and steadfast friendliness that Bob inspires amongst his classmates and teachers alike. A case in point, the success of his mainstream class of Circle of Friends initiative, in terms of support, constancy and the sheer number of schoolmates eager to actively participate in every weekly meeting, is testament to Bob's indefatigable spirit and optimism.

Fond of scientific and mathematical topics, Bob nonetheless devotes the same degree of effort to all those other subjects that continue to pose a daily challenge to his learning experience; not least those, like PE and English, which strain his motor and language skills to breaking point. Is this uncanny perseverance, enviable constancy and relentless hard work, and not his autism, what really sets him apart from us all? Is this what truly makes him special?

The ability to take somebody else's perspective is referred to by (autism researcher) Simon Baron-Cohen as theory of mind (ToM). It is a vital milestone in a neurotypical child's development. This ability elevates the progress of the pragmatic side of communication and language and is indeed key to comprehension of a story or narrative. The enigma of autism is visible in Bob's struggle to comprehend the thoughts, feelings, beliefs and behaviour of people around him. It is what Baron-Cohen referred to as 'mindblindness'; he struggles to grasp the social and emotional nuances of the world around him – something that other children apparently do intuitively but for him is a serious cognitive challenge. Navigating a complex literary text for Bob might be seen as akin to us neurotypicals driving in the dark remote mountains of Peru without a map and without much help; it could indeed be an unsettling unpredictable experience!

In more ways than one, when first approaching author Roald Dahl's short story *Lamb to the Slaughter* as part of his mainstream year 8 English lesson reading task, Bob could have been described (not inaccurately) as Patrick, the protagonist's unsuspecting husband – that inadvertent 'lamb' setting himself up for 'a reading bloodbath'. To put it blatantly, it rapidly became clear that he found himself on a very surreal and utterly unknown journey to Wonderland; one very much like Alice's own bizarre journey in that timeless children's classic. The analogy seems justified and pertinent.

Firstly Bob, a 13-year-old teenager on the autism spectrum, was visibly showing difficulties in engaging in with the storyline independently, as was expected. Likewise, he struggled to reflect on the writer's presentation of ideas and issues with the measure of depth the story implicitly required. Moreover, Bob appeared dazed and puzzled by the author's crafting of characters' complex viewpoints, assumptions, attitudes and behaviours, let alone the overall impact of the plot. Appreciation of a story is guided by the reader's understanding of a character's motivation, feelings and emotions and how these feelings temper the character's reactions – a child with autism's blinkered comprehension of abstract feelings, which are elusive by nature, acts as an impediment to this important aspect of literacy.

For many children with autism, reading could be merely relegated to factual memorisation of words and letters. They could perhaps derive more meaning and enjoyment from the repetitive, predictable visual arrangement of letters, rather than participating in the emotional journey with the characters in the text. Significant expressive and receptive language difficulties have a detrimental impact on their understanding and inferencing of text and consequently result in delayed processing. They are typically concrete thinkers and these core differences in thought processes make it difficult for them to comprehend the abstract nature of books and the embedded characters. Challenges in perspective taking and relating to others mean that they may find it difficult to appreciate and infer the inner motivations and relationships of characters. Restricted vocabulary can also interfere with their ability to infer meaning and form personal connections with the text.

Undeniably, amongst the plethora of skills children learn during their school years, the ability to comprehend what they read undoubtedly represents the single most relevant skill they have to master before their coming of age. However and precisely because knowledge as such relies so heavily upon this particular communication channel, one very crucial question needs to be asked beforehand: what is to be done when the prerequisites for reading are themselves impaired by such a pervasive 'disability' as autism? Effectively, while this skill could take a sizeable amount of effort for the non-disabled pupil, children on the autism spectrum (AS), on the other hand could be described as being confronted with the challenge of a lifetime.

Let us summarise the story briefly. A pregnant, meticulously methodical Mrs Maloney quite dramatically sums up what might happen when fallible beings are placed in a corner by life's unpredictable twists. In a nutshell, the only certainty in her life, her husband, has grown progressively indifferent and almost unbearably distant. She stoically continues to make every possible effort to please the man she professes to love and adore – and the reader remains oblivious as to how wrong things are bound to go…

Within a few paragraphs then, the story confronts us with a highly dysfunctional scenario – one that forces the reader's higher order thinking skills to stay supremely sharp constantly. However, without the right set of social interaction skills, the reader will find it difficult to understand Mary Maloney's dramatic reaction to Patrick's sudden decision to abandon her. In effect, because the way an individual forms social relations and establishes intimacy and warmth with their immediate circle remains unintelligible without these social skills, Bob could not but frown upon her homicidal reaction. Even when asked to ponder how he would have reacted, Bob remained puzzled, as he found himself utterly incapable of relating to or sympathising with the 'apocalypse' scenario that flooded Mary Maloney's mind. As far as he was concerned, an everlasting and implacable condemnation was the only judgement she deserved. This clearly reflects the supposedly 'black and white' thinking styles of people on the autism spectrum, where no shades of grey can lurk on the horizon.

Word by word, the reader is expected to visualise Mary Maloney's tense body language turning her into a wild predator under attack, her overwhelmed facial expression becoming paler and paler as the inevitable abandonment flashes before her eyes, and her broken tone of voice upon hearing Patrick's uncaring revelation. It is well accepted that children on the autism spectrum routinely struggle to decipher non-verbal communication in real life; here, the dual disadvantage was that Bob had to rely on the words used by Dahl to describe Mary's extreme emotions and complex non-verbal cues in order to gain an insight into her tortured state of mind. Taking all this into account, homicidal impulses, though never justifiable, can certainly be explained without either vilifying or advocating for the protagonist.

However, Bob's impaired understanding of non-verbal cues constrained his understanding of Mary's complex character and thwarted his ability to understand her perspective. The simplicity of Dahl's short story belies its complexity – not a single word is wasted in the story. It was this meticulous attention to every word in the story that appeared to tax Bob. He seemed to be able to understand the words in an isolated manner, but struggled to link them to the larger picture. Effectively, Bob concerned himself with purely physical traits, while largely ignoring mental characteristics.

All in all, as the murder mystery story draws to a close, the reader is likely to reach the final full stop with a distinctly distasteful mixture of fundamentally opposite and almost irreconcilable emotions. Still, as Bob had difficulty in identifying and understanding the emotional expressions of others (as well as their own emotional triggers), he found making sense of the shades of grey that define the character's dilemma, and transition between good and bad when forced into a corner, remarkably challenging. No doubt about it, lack of self-knowledge stands in the way of effective perspective taking; after all, how are we to be aware of others if we fail to be aware of ourselves?

Current research has shown that literal-concrete thinkers, known as 'systemisers', facing the challenge of fictional-abstract decoding, can be assisted in their journey to make sense of that decoding. The key, it has been proposed, lies in the use of visual organisers and connective strategies that harvest prior knowledge, past experience and harness a child with autism's fascinations and motivations. Earlier, the analogy of driving without a map in remote Peru was used to exemplify Bob's difficulties in understanding literary pieces; what if we had a friendly navigator speaking our local tongue sitting beside us, guiding us joyfully towards our destination? Or if we had well-illustrated maps with vital signposts highlighting the journey route? Without a shadow of a doubt, that would make our life much easier and the journey in desolate Peru would be more appealing. For Bob, visual strategies are the friendly maps that help him to comprehend the words on a page. Dr Mesibov, of Treatment and Education of Autistic and related Communication Handicapped Children (TEACCH), explained this very well in a training workshop in 2012. To paraphrase what he said, verbal words and gestures disappear into thin air, leaving no trace for children with autism, whereas visuals can be revisited time and time again – they are concrete, durable and endure more and are therefore more valuable for children on the spectrum. He also used the analogy of auditory information disappearing into thin air 'like smoke'.

By listing the positive, negative and 'grey' traits in a visual organiser, using diagrams of clouds, Bob (who is fascinated by meteorological phenomena) was exposed to the reason why Mary Maloney was simultaneously capable of both good and evil when being 'between a rock and a hard place'. Moreover, the flowchart graphic organiser helped Bob understand the 'what if' reasoning type of questions. For instance, what would have happened if Mrs

Maloney had admitted to the crime (versus not confessing), with the intention of saving her unborn child from being taken away and becoming an orphan? This aided in developing his metacognitive skills by compelling him to question his own thinking. The visual of the hot air balloon, again taken from his favourite repertoire of aerial transport, enabled him to look beyond the physical plane while judging people and paying attention to mental traits and the complex chemistry of emotions, thoughts, words and behaviour.

One of Bob's favourite visual aids was the Volcano graphic organiser, which plotted the fast-moving storyline against the changes in the character's emotions. He appeared to be enthralled by the sight of the volcano spewing magma, symbolising the protagonist's turmoil of emotions. The visuals made the surreal dilemma tangible and visible. Bob's personal favourite was the real orange outside–inside organiser, which enabled him to attempt to grasp the complex task of inferring meaning from language and move beyond the literalness of his thinking. As he said, it made him think about 'what was really meant' (the orange core) and distinguish it from 'what was literally evident or said' (the orange skin).

The reader will indeed wonder if it was worthwhile for an impressionable vulnerable young teenager on the spectrum to attempt to navigate the murky waters of Dahl's angst-ridden short story, with a tantalising twist at the end that would stretch the imagination of ordinary mortals. Mary, the pregnant protagonist, is so obviously in love with Patrick, the father of her unborn child, who she murders with a frozen leg of lamb in a rage when he reveals his decision to abandon her. Her whole life seemingly in tatters, her mind collapses, she kills and then in an effort to save her unborn child clinically proceeds to arrange an alibi that fools his impeccably attired and impossibly clever policeman colleagues. One can't help but marvel at her ingenuity in contriving such a perfect plan – she cooks the murder weapon and invites the policeman to consume it, thereby destroying the only viable evidence and sealing the case for posterity.

Lamb to the Slaughter bares the heart and soul of autism and sheds revealing light into the nooks and crevices of the difficulties experienced by someone with autism. Understanding perspective taking, irony, paradoxes, alibis, metaphors, sarcasm, narrator's voice, the fast paced action, are minefields for children on the autism spectrum – the story by Dahl presents mammoth challenges in decoding inherent levels of complexity. However, all hope is not lost as we have witnessed first-hand how the visual organisers gallantly came to the rescue of autism, and indeed signalled the first glimmer of hope and dawn on the dark horizons. It was a relief and a revelation that Bob was ultimately able to rest his case that Mary Maloney's act of murder was not appropriate, but under the gut-wrenchingly difficult circumstances the alibi and the destruction of the murder weapon potentially saved an innocent unborn child's life.

161

Reflections

You might remember the television series based on Roald Dahl's stories, *Tales of the Unexpected*. The stories were known for their unexpected twists and turns, and often portrayed the darker side of human nature. Morality was often skewed or nuanced in these tales. These stories were very popular in the 1980s, but – having read Archita's account – I think it was probably only the neurotypical population who enjoyed them.

For people with autism who think 'in black and white' and like clear rules of social behaviour, these stories could appear unfathomable. Bob was facing a world in which the curriculum, common culture and his neurotypical classmates all presented him with something that did not make sense. The morality and feelings described were like a foreign language to him.

How might we help Bob to understand and function in our dark world of nuanced morality? What counts as entertainment for neurotypicals might be a serious challenge to reality for the person with autism.

Section 5
Sisters, churches and nurses

16
A sibling's tale
Amber Leigh

Amber is the sister of two people on the autism spectrum. Her story describes the day-to-day chaos of living in a large family with autism. It also details the unfolding horror of serious abuse in a school and its impact on the family. Amber found the telling of this story to be a cathartic experience. It formed the basis of her essay for the autism module at the University of Cumbria. The effects of all these events on everyday family life were profound:

> "My father strongly felt that Sarah should go into care, as she was making life difficult for the rest of the family. My mother loved Sarah and felt that it was her duty to take care of her daughter but found it really hard to accept that she was getting too much for her to handle. My mother also felt that after what had happened at Scotforth House she could not trust anyone with Sarah again. These arguments were especially bad at around Christmastime, when all the excitement would get too much for Sarah. As a consequence, I do not have very positive or warm, fond memories of Christmas. It simply meant that there was even more pressure on my mother to create a happy, festive, family atmosphere, which would be disrupted at some point by Sarah."

Everybody can say that their childhood was different because all parents are unique and bring up their children in their own way. Parenthood is complicated and difficult, and we all make mistakes every day and hopefully learn from them. People have different ideas as to what is beneficial for their children and what disadvantages them. My childhood was not only different but difficult, not as a result of abuse, poverty or neglect but because I have an autistic brother and sister.

When I reflect upon my childhood, I remember my father constantly saying: 'We are all living on tenterhooks.' I understood that the phrase implied that we were all living in a constant state of agitation and at the time thought that it meant we were hanging on hooks that were 'tender'. Therefore our family was under the threat of falling, as the hooks could not hold the weight much longer. In fact a 'tenter' was a frame used for drying and stretching cloth after it had been woven and washed to remove oils and dirt that remained from the fleece. The tenterhooks were the metal hooks that fixed the cloth to the frame. Our family was, like the woven wool, stretched to its limits by the constant threat of chaos, as the slightest little thing would trigger a 'screaming fit' from my sister Sarah who has severe autism.

If I am entirely honest, the term 'autism' has very negative implications for me and my non-autistic siblings James and Vicky, as we see it as the 'thing' that robbed us of a happy childhood. I am the eldest of five children. The second child, Matthew, has autism with severe learning disabilities and so does the youngest, Sarah.

I was born in November 1968; 16 months later Matthew was born in March 1970; and 15 months after that James was born in June 1971. Vicky came along in January 1976, and Sarah was born in December 1979.

Family life was restricted and slightly more difficult as a consequence of Matthew's autism, but Sarah's autism and our lack of expertise made any hope of a normal family life seem impossible. I still feel resentful that my childhood and teenage years were so stressed and tense. I was stuck in a house with funny noises, tantrums and obsessive repetitive behaviours, distressed screaming and over-excitement. I feel that I missed out on the quality attention of mother/daughter and father/daughter relationships.

My father would frequently say that our family members were the 'real experts' in autism after 'living with a Sarah and a Matthew'. However, I do not agree with this, as our family life was living proof that we were not experts and that we did not understand the nature of autism. And our lack of expertise meant that the threat of Sarah's 'screaming fits' controlled our existence.

I can never remember a time without autism even though I never heard the word used until I was about eight or nine, when Matthew started to attend Scotforth House Autistic centre in Lancaster. I can recall watching him as a very young child and feeling confused by his strange behaviour. He would crawl all over the room at top speed and would enjoy flicking switches, and flushing the toilet repeatedly. I also recall that he used to have an obsession with robots. I remember my mother asking me to dress him when I was about four or five, and he was only one year younger. I recall feeling resentful about this, as I could dress myself at that age, and I am ashamed to say I would inform him of this and call him 'stupid'.

I was aware that he was different but was completely confused as to what this difference was, as it was never explained to me. I also recall that my mother seemed to spend a lot of time feeding Matthew, who had trouble swallowing food without choking. Mealtimes were an ordeal for my mother, as I was a very fussy eater and she was very insistent that I ate a healthy

165

meal and I recall being awkward and stubborn whilst she had to contend with a new baby and Matthew. I remember that I resented the fact that I had to eat minced beef, potatoes, cabbage and carrot, whilst he had his favourite foods all the time: 'eggiwoo' (which was Matthew's name for scrambled egg, and the name adopted by the family) or mashed banana. As a child, I actually felt very puzzled about why Matthew was so different and other children at my infant school (which I attended from 1973 to 1976) would ask me: 'What is the matter with him?'

I never knew the answer and would feel embarrassed. I was bullied between the ages of five and seven at my first primary school and was teased for having a 'stupid' brother and told that I therefore had 'germs'. I believed that Matthew was a 'spaz', as that is what the bullies called him. I never brought the subject up with my family, as Mum was always too busy with Matthew and the baby and Dad was always at work.

I too displayed difficult behaviours and was reprimanded for being naughty. I occasionally used to hide in the school car park all day and threw my dinner money in the bin, as I did not want to stay at school at lunchtime. Today teachers would see my behaviour as a sign that I was having problems but back then they thought I was simply being naughty.

My parents always planned on having a large family, as my mother is very maternal and loves children. My father was an only child, whose father left him as a newborn baby, and he never had a good relationship with either his own mother or his step-father. He always felt resented by them and 'not part of the equation'. They never spent any quality time with him when he was a child and he was left to his own devices. As a consequence of this, he wanted to have a lot of children (a 'football team') and be the kind of father that he would have loved to have had. He felt that he needed another son to compensate for Matthew so that James could have a brother, who was a companion. He also felt that, as he loved sport, at this time especially football, a son would be ideal. My father helped run a football team in the local village and decided that another son would be the perfect addition to our family. After Vicky was born in 1976, my parents moved to a larger house and even fostered children 'short term' for a while. And when the time was right they had another baby – not the son they had hoped for but what appeared to be a healthy baby girl, Sarah.

Mum knew from Sarah's birth in 1980 that something was 'not quite right' because she failed to look up at her as she fed. She also screamed constantly from when she was a new baby, failed to develop normal speech, showed no interest in interactive play or pointing to objects of interest. Doctors told Mum that she was 'paranoid' as she already had one disabled son and the chance of her having another autistic child was thousands to one! But eventually the suspicions of my very experienced mother of five were confirmed and Sarah was diagnosed at the age of three in 1983.

Whilst Sarah was being assessed, I remember that things were really tense at home. I was going through puberty and my parents were arguing a lot. Doctors were telling my mother that Sarah was just developing a little bit slower and that her screaming would ease eventually. My mother was exhausted. My father had also bought a new business, extended his loans and was working long hours to ensure that the business was a success.

I remember that my parents insisted on having her assessed and I recall praying really hard for her to be OK. My parents had insisted that I went to church every week, along with my siblings, and I attended the local church secondary school. I had been taught about faith and the power of persistence in prayer and at that young age I still believed in it. I truly believed that if I prayed hard enough Sarah would not be diagnosed as having autism and her behaviour would soon improve and she would catch up developmentally. I did not believe that a loving God would give a good family two disabled children. On hearing that Sarah did have autism, I had my first faith crisis as I began to question for the first time how a benevolent and omnipotent God could allow such suffering. I could see how wars, famine and other evils could be blamed on humanity but this issue and my unanswered prayers, despite my faith, made me question what I believed. I felt deceived.

My father also had trouble accepting the diagnosis. He held the doctor who had been calling my mother 'paranoid' up by the throat and threatened him; he may have even hit him. I do know that my father left the family home for a while and went to live in 'his office' – a house he owned near his business. I think he was having trouble accepting the fact that he had fathered not one disabled child but two. This may have made him question his own masculinity. My father is a man who likes to feel in control and he was unable to control Sarah's behaviour, her autism or her learning disabilities. I believe that my father was embarrassed that he had two autistic children, as he would often tell people that he only had three children, as he did not want to 'get into the autistic thing'.

My parents decided, after Sarah was diagnosed with autism, that it would be unwise to have any more children, as two children with autism was enough and they did not want to risk having another. My mother was sterilised, and deep down this upset her greatly, as she would have dearly loved more children and my father still felt that he had a lot to offer another son. My parents decided to apply for the long-term fostering of a boy, and a young man named Tom came to live with us for a period of time. It did not work out and when he left us it was quite obvious that our family could not consider fostering any more, as Sarah was becoming increasingly difficult.

During term time, Sarah would often scream all morning and be 'difficult' in the evening, which meant that there was no time for us to relax. I used to lock myself away in my bedroom.

This was harder for James, as he shared a room with Matthew. During the school holidays, it was hard, as Sarah was around all the time.

A typical day in our house would begin with Sarah waking up and demanding to watch television. The threat of screaming occurred almost every morning at breakfast and she would breathe heavily, chanting 'Wackaday, wackaday.' (This was a Saturday morning children's television show that Sarah never actually watched; it was simply an indicator that there was no school.) On a bad day the table would be swiped clean, and crockery, food and drinks would fall to the floor and my mother would panic as Sarah bruised her legs on the wooden benches as she kicked.

Sarah's screaming fits were like toddler tantrums on a much bigger scale and their causes were often a mystery to us. Sarah was always large for her age and would build up to these fits with heavy breathing and we knew that inevitably the screaming would come and could last for minutes or hours. It was loud; she would throw herself on the floor, kicking her legs, smashing anything in her way.

The police turned up several times at our detached house, as people were concerned that something terrible was happening. My father even had an extension built onto our house, which included a soundproof bedroom for Sarah to go to when she screamed. Unfortunately when Sarah had a tantrum it was rarely in this room and it was impossible to move Sarah up the stairs or anywhere, for that matter, once she had started to have a meltdown.

Sarah used to struggle in supermarkets and would often build up to a tantrum. The music, sounds of people chattering, tills, sounds of the fridges, smells of fish, bread, chicken, crowds of people, tempting foods and videos on display, fluorescent lights and changing temperatures must have been like a sadistic torture chamber for her. But we did not realise this at the time. When she was about four she had a tantrum in Asda and it took my mother and me 45 minutes to get her out of the store and back to the car. During the entire event, the security guard and a crowd of people peered over us, making us feel very intimidated and inadequate, without offering assistance. We never took Sarah shopping again. Instead I was expected to sit in the car with Sarah whilst my mother did her weekly shop, a task I found very boring, until I was trusted to stay at home and take care of Sarah there. As a result, I still to this day enjoy shopping in supermarkets and consider it a treat.

With Sarah, trips to the dentist, doctor, having her hair cut or simply driving in the car often led to tantrums. I recall that I seldom asked to go on evening trips, as I knew I would have to ask my mother for a lift and taking Sarah could lead to a tantrum. If there was somewhere I really wanted to go, I would ask my friends' parents for a lift, which they were always happy to give me, but I would feel embarrassed asking.

Taking Sarah out to places meant there was an increased risk of a tantrum. Crossing roads or walking long distances was difficult, as a tantrum on a road or in a public place was not only humiliating but dangerous. Sarah also had a mind of her own and would go in the direction that suited her, and redirecting her was not easy. We were unable to park in designated disabled parking spots, as we did not have a 'disabled badge'. My parents applied for a disabled badge; not mobility allowance or money, just the badge, and were refused it because Sarah is ambulant. My parents felt that if she had been in a wheelchair the dangers would have been considerably less. As a result of this, my father took Sarah to County Hall in Preston, where the disabled badge applications were sent, and asked the man in charge if he could please return Sarah to the car in the car park. After he had experienced what it was like to walk with Sarah, who did not have a tantrum but refused to be cooperative, my parents were given a badge.

Sarah would usually wake at the same time as my mother, as they often shared the same bed. Sarah would insist on mum sharing her bed at bedtime and my mother and Sarah would have to stroke each other's eyebrows in order to relax Sarah so that she could sleep. My mother was sometimes able to come downstairs once Sarah was asleep in order to do the ironing, but if Sarah woke again then my mother would have to return to her bed, probably for the rest of the night.

Sarah usually went upstairs with my mother for a bath at about 8pm and would be in bed by about 8.30. Sarah was a very light sleeper and it did not take much to wake her – a creaky floorboard, music playing or a phone call could do it. I recall having to tell my friends as a teenager, in the days before mobile phones and the Internet, not to phone after 8pm in the evenings. Frequently my friends would forget this and call on the landline to ask about homework or chat about boyfriends or other 'girlie' things. I would then get into trouble, especially if Sarah awoke, and would get a lecture off my father, who would demand to know what was so important. I would be unable to converse with my friends, who on occasions believed I was being rude or snappy when I cut short the conversations.

When my mother and Sarah got up in the morning, there would be a big build-up to a tantrum, which usually occurred eventually. On a good morning in the school holidays, when Sarah realised that there was no school, things were not quite as stressful but a nice relaxed lie-in was almost impossible. Sarah and my mother would get up at around 6am and my mother would spend the entire day concentrating on Sarah and trying to prevent a screaming fit. Sarah's moods were always the priority and if we wanted to watch something on television it was unlikely that we would be able to, as Sarah would want to watch *Grease* or *Puddle Lane*.

Matthew would be wandering around talking to himself. He would usually be reprimanding himself for having broken his latest cassette player. Every birthday and Christmas he would get a new cassette recorder, which he would play with inappropriately. He would put in a cassette and just fast-forward or rewind it so that it would make strange noises until it broke. When he left home, this obsession progressed to more expensive pieces of equipment such as televisions. These would be broken by, for example, water being poured into the back. When visiting him once at the home where he now lives in the Wirral, his bedroom resembled something of a gadget morgue, as broken electrical carcasses filled every shelf.

Mealtimes were always an ordeal because at breakfast Sarah would usually be building up to a screaming fit or having one, until she became aware that there was no school. Matthew used to struggle with swallowing food as a baby and used to choke a lot. Consequently my mother would be concentrating very hard on trying to keep Sarah calm and on watching Matthew eat, as she had developed a phobia that he would choke and die.

When my father was at the table he would want to converse about the things he considered important and insist on silence from the rest of us, which added to the tension. When my father was not present, my brother James would amuse himself by teasing Vicky and me by flicking the contents of his nostrils onto our food. This boyish humour was something that disgusted Vicky and me but would provide James with some amusement in a tense family situation. Vicky and I would complain to my mother, who would not really concentrate on what we had to say, as she was so totally absorbed in Sarah and Matthew. As it was Vicky and I complaining and attempting to take her attention away from our autistic siblings, it would be us, rather than James, who got reprimanded.

Even now if my mother goes out for a meal with Matthew and he chooses a dish with fish or chunky meat, she will refuse to allow him to have it, and encourages him to have a cottage pie, macaroni cheese or lasagne instead. Matthew has been able to chew and swallow most foods since he was about 10 years old but the fear of him choking is something that has never left my mother. As a result, she now denies him his freedom of choice and his face does drop when this occurs.

Having a conversation with my mother was really difficult because when Sarah or Matthew were in the house she would constantly seem distracted and would not really listen to what we were saying. It was unthinkable to even consider asking my mother to help with homework, as she always seemed tired and too busy. When she was not busy with Sarah, she was trying hard to keep on top of all her washing, housework and ironing.

Unlike most teenagers, James and I used to love school and it is no surprise that both of us received a prize for 100% attendance when we finished compulsory education at 16. I always used to leave the house in the morning with a sick feeling in my stomach, as I could hear Sarah screaming or threatening to. It was hardly a good way to start the day. At school I used to receive a lot of praise, as I worked quite hard and wanted to do well and I could chat to my friends. Unlike most school children, I never really looked forward to the holidays and often dreaded going home. I remember walking home with James and our driveway was quite a steep hill, with tall trees and shrubbery on either side concealing the parking areas. Walking up the hill, James and I would be saying, 'Hope Dad is out.' We would be happy if his car was not there. This was because the atmosphere was tenser when my father was around because Sarah's tantrums would lead to my parents arguing. The arguing was far worse than the screaming fits.

My father always used to refer to Sarah's tantrums as 'screaming fits', whilst my mother referred to them more politely. She used to say Sarah 'creates'. Sarah's screaming fits may have been a result of our home life causing sensory overload or heightened sensory awareness. Dad would insist on James, Vicky and I playing the piano for an hour each evening. We had three downstairs rooms, two of which contained pianos. Often, two of us would be practising scales and learning new pieces at the same time. Matthew could have been in the same room as Sarah with the television on, and he'd have been making siren noises to himself whilst flicking the light switches, and Sarah's heavy breathing would start.

The lack of structure in our home must have been difficult for Sarah. Mealtimes would change to suit after-school activities, and unexpected visits from friends or phone calls would either distress or over-excite her. Sarah liked things organised and in their place, and large families produce clutter. She'd often take the newspaper off whoever was reading it and put it away, or take pens off us and put them into the pencil case. We had to become structured and all our actions and words seemed to be influenced by how they would affect Sarah. We would spell out certain words such as 'bath', 'school' or 'sweets'.

Dad would take my 'normal siblings' out of the house to escape the home environment but presented them with different pressures as he pushed them to succeed at tennis. My Dad often told us that we were 'the lucky ones' and we were expected to compensate for Sarah and Matthew's autism by achieving at school and at sport. As a result, we grew up under constant pressure to succeed. I also felt an obligation to be 'Mum's little helper'.

Mum and I resented the fact that Dad focused on my 'normal siblings', giving no attention to Matthew and Sarah. By his own admission, he found it hard to take care of them, especially Sarah, and as my mother was unprepared to put Sarah into care, he did not see why they both had to suffer.

We 'normal children' felt under a lot of pressure never to get into trouble or express normal teenage worries, as Dad would say, 'Do not bring me any of your problems; we have enough with Sarah and Matthew.' We were denied the freedom to play out, ride bikes, go horse-riding or anything else that could lead to an accident, as they 'already had two disabled children and did not want another.' We had to attend autistic sports clubs, youth groups and coffee evenings, whilst the other siblings in their teens were allowed to stay at home!

It was difficult bringing our friends home because we found our complex circumstances embarrassing. Sarah could scream, burp or smear faeces on the carpets or act in other socially unacceptable ways. In his teens, Matthew would enjoy the attention of women and discovered that if he cried he got a cuddle. He did this at church with the mothers and with my teenage friends, who thought it 'sweet' that my younger brother wanted a cuddle. However, he began doing it to my younger sister's friends, who were very uncomfortable with the 'creepy' behaviour from her 'weird' brother.

I would sometimes, in my mid-teens, take Matthew into town and I remember once how he wanted me to buy him a new cassette player, which I could not afford to buy. He cried and I felt really embarrassed as people looked in our direction, as I thought they might have suspected me of doing something mean to him.

On another occasion in town, Matthew needed the toilet and I took him to some public conveniences. I sent him into the Men's and I went into the Ladies and asked him to wait outside for me. I was as quick as I could be but when I went outside Matthew was not there. I waited a while and when he did not reappear I began to get concerned. I nervously went into the Men's toilets and called him, feeling embarrassed by the presence of men urinating. I checked every cubicle and was horrified to discover that he was not there. I was in a state of panic and did not know what to do and was petrified of telling my parents. I decided that I had better go to the police station. Then, as I began to walk away from the public conveniences, I saw Matthew approaching. Relieved, I greeted him and asked where he had been and he answered: 'I only went to McDonalds toilets. I did not want to use those ones. They were dirty.'

Matthew also went through a period when he was encouraged by his head teacher to use public transport in order to find his own way to and from school. He started off doing this really well but unfortunately a friend of mine saw him being teased and hit by a group of boys from the grammar school. Matthew had said nothing of this.

To make matters worse, the boys knew Matthew and played in the village football team that my father ran voluntarily and financed. In fact one of the boys was the son of my father's friend and fellow coach. This man was a keen sportsman and a very successful pharmacist. My father informed this man of his son's behaviour and genuinely expected some support and disapproval of the bullying. Instead the man said: 'Well, what do you expect when you put a boy like that on the front line? You stupid man!' This led to a falling out and disharmony in the football team and, most sadly of all, Matthew, who was doing so well at using the buses, had his short episode of independence taken from him and had to go back to taking the school taxi with Sarah.

Matthew also has a habit of letting his imagination get the better of him. He used to believe that we had a monster living in the garden that he called 'The Geek'. He would also enjoy ringing the police and telling them that there was a burglar in the house, or he would call the fire brigade and say that there was a fire. This would lead to unexpected visits from the emergency services. Whilst at a college in Blackburn, Matthew went onto a very busy main road, more than once, and began to direct the traffic.

Mathew is sociable and has friends, with whom he can converse and have fun. He enjoys his food and at the home in the Wirral both he and a friend were putting on a lot of weight so they were put onto a healthy eating plan. The staff were confused when neither Matthew nor his friend seemed to be losing any weight. It turned out that they were the first in the dinner queue every mealtime, and had figured out that when the kitchen staff serving the food swapped round they could go and collect a second meal!

Matthew can also express his opinions quite strongly. For instance, when Sarah was given a place at the same home where Matthew lives, he made it very clear that he did not want her there. She very nearly lost her place as a result of his objections. He complained about her screaming and how she would ruin his life. However when it was explained to him that she would be living in a house a good distance away from him, and that he would not see her, eat with her or have to socialise with her in any way, he finally agreed that Sarah could live there too.

Sarah was unconcerned about how appropriate her behaviour was in public. She used to like to touch elderly ladies in shops and call them 'Betty, Nancy' (two elderly aunts). She didn't mind screaming and throwing herself into a full-blown tantrum in public, nor did she mind breaking wind and laughing. When trying to speak to Sarah, you would never get eye contact and she showed no interest in people's emotions nor did she realise that we could feel pain.

We also suspect that Sarah was responsible for the death of Tabitha, our pet cat. Tabitha was struggling to breathe and the vet said that it looked like she had been squeezed. Sarah would often pick her up and squeeze her too tightly when she tried to get away but usually someone would intervene. As a result, the vet had to be called at midnight on Christmas Eve to put the cat out of her misery. Sarah never showed any grief; nor did she seem to understand the sense of loss that the rest of the family felt.

Sarah never made friends at school and she clearly struggled to express her emotions through anything other than screaming or hysterical laughter. Sarah never demonstrated any sense of how to play but did like doing puzzles and shape sorters with my mother's encouragement. As she got older, she enjoyed watching the film *Grease* on video, repeatedly. When it reached her favourite scene, where a character burps, she would rewind it and replay it over and over, obsessively, whilst laughing.

Sarah has very limited speech and yet appeared to understand what we were saying and could follow films of her choice. Her spoken language was limited to single words and echolalia. She would usually just wander around, tapping us all on the head, saying, 'Sarah, Sarah, my Sarah, Sarah'. Or she would burp, laugh and say, 'Pardon me, Sarah, pardon me' until one of us, usually my mother, would say, 'Yes, pardon you, Sarah' and she would stop. She was able to read books at key stage I level but could not speak in sentences unless reading aloud. She often read words incorrectly as if she was picturing the word with a picture: 'lady' instead of 'mum', or 'Miffy' (family pet) instead of 'cat'.

In 1985 she went through a period where she was afraid to use the toilet and would only use one of the four toilets in our home. If someone was using that particular bathroom, she would urinate or soil the carpet and smear it. If we tried to take her to another toilet, she'd shout: 'No, no, hedgehog, no'. We wondered if she was afraid of the toilet brushes, as they may have resembled hedgehogs, but removing them made no difference. Some months later she called a picture of a crocodile a 'hedgehog' but we never got to the bottom of the problem, which did, however, stop when we moved house.

During this time I was once, at the age of 15, 'babysitting' whilst my mother went to Asda. Sarah needed to go to the toilet and James was having a bath in the bathroom that she used, despite the fact that he could have used another. I asked him to get out and he refused. I tried pleading with him and asked him to just wrap a towel around his waist and let Sarah use the toilet. As she dropped her pants, I had a choice. I could either allow her to empty her bowels onto the carpet, which she would then stand in, smear and spread across the house, or I could let her use my hands as a potty. If I chose the first option then I would have had the job of cleaning up Sarah and the soiled carpets, with her in a distressed state because ironically she did not like mess. As this option would have taken a long time and put Sarah in a bad mood, I decided that the second option was quicker and easier to deal with, much to my disgust. I can laugh about this now but at the time I was not happy with James, who found the whole incident highly amusing.

During my childhood, we rarely had days out and once Sarah was born we never had a family holiday because it was impossible to take Sarah anywhere without a great deal of stress. When we did eventually receive help in the form of respite, my mum was often too tired to do anything but rest. However, respite was important for the whole family because we struggled with autism on a daily basis and my father had to fight really hard for the little bit of respite we did eventually receive.

It was hard watching Mum constantly trying to prevent meltdowns after having been up all night with Sarah. As well as this, she was also perpetually cooking, cleaning and managing to keep the large family home clean and tidy, never getting behind with her washing. I do not know how she did it. It was also unpleasant as a teenager to be aware that our parents' marriage was not the secure loving relationship that we'd have liked. For many years, my mother often spent the nights in bed with Sarah and most of her time was taken up with her. This and Sarah's screaming often led to arguments, and resentment was building up on both sides.

Before we managed to get any entitlement to respite, my father decided that we definitely needed help, and in 1984 he and my mother hired a nanny to help with Sarah so that my mother could cook, shop and do other household jobs. As well as this, my father hoped that he and my mother could spend some time together, and the rest of the family could have a few days out. Unfortunately this did not go according to plan, as the nanny struggled with Sarah's behaviour and ended up doing the housework and cooking, which she neither enjoyed nor was very good at. During this time we did manage a few days out, until the nanny left us, as she had been offered another job.

We never received help from extended family members, due to the stigma of having a disabled child. My paternal grandmother turned up at Matthew's school, demanding that the headmaster allow her to take Matthew out of the 'nutter school'. My maternal grandmother also requested that we never visit them in London, as she thought my aunt and uncle would never marry if people knew there were 'problems in the family'.

I remember as a child at Christmas waiting for my grandparents to arrive as promised, two years on the trot. They never showed up and when my father told them not to bother coming again, they didn't. We would have benefited greatly during our childhood if we could have gone to visit grandparents occasionally and have that special relationship grandparents and grandchildren have. It would have been lovely to have had somewhere to go to escape the chaos at home and to have had an outside family member we could have talked to and confided in.

My mother always felt a need to know what had caused her children to have autism. She often blamed complications at birth. When I married I became concerned that when we started a family I might have an autistic child. I did not want to bring an autistic child with learning difficulties into the world. My husband, who I had been with since I was 15, had experienced a taste of what life was like living with autism. He told me that, although he could cope with a child 'like Matthew', there was no way he would live with a child 'like Sarah'.

These were harsh words but I did agree that if there was a chance of me having an autistic child then we would risk having one child and no more.

We were reassured after receiving genetic counselling in 1991 at Manchester Hospital, prior to starting my family, that it is genetic and both parents need to carry the 'faulty gene'. We were told that unfortunately this gene cannot be identified but if we both carried it there would be a 1:4 chance of producing a child with autism. The counsellor told us that the chances of my husband and I sharing the same 'faulty gene' and having an autistic child were the same as anyone else's. I now have four sons and one daughter, and my sister has a son and a daughter. We are very lucky, as not only do the children not have autism but they are all healthy, attractive and reasonably bright. I am aware that many parents do have happy, beautiful, bright, healthy autistic children but I am expressing relief and feel fortunate that my children are not autistic, following a childhood of negative experiences. I cannot believe that a child who screamed as much as Sarah did could have been living a happy existence, and nor did the rest of the family.

It has also been noted that autistic traits can be seen in close family members of autistic people. Up until recently I had always thought that autism was a condition that caused learning disabilities. I have only recently learned that people who are 'normal' or 'high functioning' can also have autism. I have considered how my father can become very fixated on certain subjects, never sees the point of view or feelings of others, likes everything organised and in its correct place. Mum is obsessed with things being clean and tidy. Vicky has serious obsessive compulsive disorder (OCD) that prevents her from living a normal life and revolves around obsessive rituals and numbers. James has obsessive thoughts about numbers, has a photographic memory and is a compulsive gambler.

The Scotforth House School scandal hit the headlines in the late 1980s. On discovering that Sarah and Matthew had been amongst those abused, Dad became very angry and obsessed with getting justice. Mornings at our home had been unbearable for many years as a consequence of Sarah not wishing to go to school.

In June 1988, a group called the Parents of Scotforth House Abused Children (POSHAC) began to make complaints and insist on disciplinary action, police investigations and inquiries into not only the abuse that had occurred over a substantial period of time but the lack of action taken when complaints had been made. This led to the head teacher resigning, two nursery nurses being dismissed at a disciplinary procedure in 1989, an inquiry led by Janet Smith QC in 1992, and eventually the school's closure.

Dad became totally engrossed in the case for several years. He talked about little else, was constantly on the phone to the police, press, council officers, MPs, other parents, the

National Autistic Society solicitors, etc. I was dragged along to meetings, court cases, inquiries, etc. Despite our belief that two teachers were guilty of abuse, they were found 'not guilty'. We believed that one of them was probably responsible for Sarah's bruising after an incident in PE, and Matthew claims that the other force-fed him vomit. Other autistic youngsters had also made allegations.

On reading the report, it would seem that my father began a hate campaign against these characters, harassing them, ensuring they were named in the press, threatening them and making nuisance phone calls. Although I share his frustration and his belief that these teachers were guilty, I think his obsessive behaviour, which I suspect could be 'autistic' in nature, was inappropriate, and its effect on the family was overwhelming. The impact of all this on my mother led to depression and strong feelings of guilt. The Scotforth House abuse case was overwhelming and exhausting, not only for our family but for others too.

The abuse consisted of children doing academic work constantly all day from 9am until 3.15pm. During this period, children were not allowed a break or free play, as the head teacher believed that it interfered with valuable academic time. They only had 20 minutes in which to eat their lunch. This led to children, many of whom had problems with choking and swallowing, being force-fed. If they vomited as a result, they were forced to eat it. Desserts and main courses were mixed together for speed and the head teacher said that one child had 'so little brain it doesn't matter'. Children were roughly handled, shouted at, had their hair pulled, were restrained whilst drinks they disliked were forced down their throats, were verbally abused, and were smacked for not reading words correctly or being unable to answer questions.

Sarah was probably one of the main victims of the abuse, as she was a difficult child to handle. She was smacked, had a jug full of water thrown over her during a tantrum, hit to force her up the steps of a slide, pushed in a changing room, dragged into a swimming pool by her ankles, forced to swim across the pool with her head submerged under the water, despite the fact that she was screaming, choking and gasping for breath. Sarah once came home covered in bruises and my mother was told that this occurred on a climbing frame during a PE lesson. Witnesses claim that a teacher hit Sarah against the bars several times and witnesses to the bruising saw hand-shaped marks on her buttocks. This allegation was never proven.

These are only the incidents that were witnessed. There may well be hundreds more that we will never know about. Student nurses, supply teachers, nursery nurses, parents and speech and language specialists had made several complaints to the correct educational officials but they were never acted upon. The inquiry identified the inadequacies of the education officials at Lancashire County Council and the unacceptable teaching practices that had occurred.

The worst thing about our family life was not just the threat of Sarah screaming but the domino effect that her meltdowns had. My father would often lose his temper, not at Sarah but at my mother. My mother would blame almost anyone or anything for Sarah's tantrums, which often meant that we would get the blame – unfairly. It was a common occurrence for my mother to ask me to keep Sarah occupied in the living room whilst she cooked tea. Sarah would then decide to try and leave the living room. If I allowed Sarah to leave, my mother would get angry with me because Sarah would not allow her to prepare the meal, and hot pans and ovens were an obvious danger. If I prevented Sarah from leaving the living room, she would scream really loudly and then my father would shout at me for allowing her to scream, as he may have been on the phone, or having a migraine. Either way, I could not win. In fact, in all honesty, I often felt a lot of resentment towards Sarah and frequently wished my parents had never had another child.

My father strongly felt that Sarah should go into care, as she was making life difficult for the rest of the family. My mother loved Sarah and felt that it was her duty to take care of her daughter, but found it really hard to accept that she was getting too much for her to handle. My mother also felt that, after what had happened at Scotforth House, she could not trust anyone with Sarah again. These arguments were especially bad at Christmastime, when all the excitement would get too much for Sarah. As a consequence, I do not have very positive or warm, fond memories of Christmas. It simply meant that there was even more pressure on my mother to create a happy, festive, family atmosphere, which would be disrupted at some point by Sarah.

After the abuse at Scotforth House, the supply teacher who had informed the parents of the abuse occurring at the school taught Sarah at home. Sarah was very fond of this lady, who provided Sarah with home tuition for a while and then supported her as she was integrated into a new high school.

Eventually, after an incident at a swimming pool, my sister's teacher began to question her ability to control Sarah – after Sarah almost drowned her whilst playing roughly in the swimming pool. At around the same time, Sarah attacked my mother during a screaming fit whilst she was driving and almost caused an accident. It was finally decided that, at the age of 13, Sarah, who at this stage was twice the size of my mother, should go to boarding school in Sunderland.

Living with autism has brought the rest of us feelings of sadness, pressure, jealousy, embarrassment, resentment and guilt. It also brought us unreasonable responsibilities, which made us grow up fast. I do, however, feel that these experiences have helped make me the person that I am today. After I left home to go to university, life changed a great deal for me and I stopped suffering from migraines.

I struggled with going home, after living away. I then made the choice to move in with my future husband and I stopped at his house during university break times. I felt that, as long as Sarah and Matthew were in good hands, that was enough for me. I needed a few years away from autism and to experience life in a normal family unit. However, whilst I was doing my PGCE at St Martin's College, I knew that eventually I would end up in special education, as that is what life had prepared me for.

Things could have been easier with more respite, counselling and supportive social workers experienced in autism. A positive attitude from Dad, and shared parental responsibility for all the children in our family, would have eased resentment; and less pressure on us to compensate for Sarah and Matthew's autism would have made us feel less stretched. Today we are not a close family, as we feel we have let our parents down. Physical affection from my mother is something none of us non-autistic children can recall. My parents are still together and are enjoying their seven non-autistic grandchildren, whilst Sarah and Matthew are now settled at the home in the Wirral and Sarah's screaming fits have decreased with medication.

Reflections

For me, Amber's tale is the most shocking story in this book. Her sister and brother were beaten, nearly drowned and made to eat their own vomit, and this abuse was carried out at a 'specialist school'. Then the education authority attempted to cover it all up. A whistle-blower proved to be the means by which the family broke through the closed ranks. As professionals, do we have the courage to be whistle-blowers?

Amber's story describes extreme abuse but most of the abuse described in this book is more nuanced and subtle. It is, nonetheless, abuse and harmful to the person with autism and we should be prepared to report this too.

This chapter clearly describes the devastating effects of abuse on the whole family. This should remind us that we do not just work with the person with autism; we work in a family context that may well contain other, similar, deep-seated problems.

17
Welcoming difference: An act of faith
Caroline Henthorne

This chapter is a little different from most of the others in this book. It has been written by someone with autism, who interviewed other people living with autism about their experience of accessing worship. Such access is an issue for people with autism, of all ages, and their carers. So how welcoming are churches? What barriers to access need to be removed? As she puts it:

> "Since the advent of the Disability Discrimination Act, churches, as public buildings, have had to make themselves accessible. This makes a great deal of sense. We cannot know whether '…there is any just cause or impediment why these two persons should not be joined in holy matrimony…' if poor access keeps those in the know shut out."

She describes the experience of a mother who takes her autistic son to church:

> "When asked at church, how she is, Natalie's reply, 'Well we made it here', is all she can manage to say. Natalie is focused on coping with managing Salvador in the moment and can't comment on whether she is free on Thursday for a coffee. So people don't see that she has had a week of having clumps of her hair pulled out, and being bitten, by Salvador. She can't stop and talk about how she is, and has no time away from supervising her children to receive prayer."

Let's see how the church responded to the access needs of both Natalie and Salvador.

Welcome and worship

Since the advent of the Disability Discrimination Act, churches, as public buildings, have had to make themselves accessible. This makes a great deal of sense. We cannot know whether '…there is any just cause or impediment why these two persons should not be joined in holy matrimony…' if poor access keeps those in the know shut out.

The trouble is, if you were to design an accessible building you wouldn't design anything like an old church. Old churches were designed to make people feel unworthy to be there. They have a cross-shaped ground plan. The architect's plans, if we had them, would show a gigantic crucified figure lying on the ground with his head pointing East. While symbolically rich, this layout lumbers churches with a seating area, in, if you will, the 'legs and torso' of the building, which is made up of a large number of short rows: rather like the top deck of a bus. So few people have a front-row seat. Meanwhile, the action is taking place at the altar, some distance from the congregation, in what we could call the 'head' of the building. When these churches were built, it was considered appropriate for ordinary people to be at a distance from God. The congregation weren't supposed to have a clear view of what was happening at the altar.

Churches have had to address the question of access and have discovered that it's a question of faith. Making everyone welcome in the house of God is changing the way churches worship. How churches welcome people shows how they understand God's love. When people experience welcome at church, this in turn allows their understanding of God's love to grow.

Autistic people present the Church with a challenge. The usual ways of welcoming people don't work for autistic people – like chatting over coffee after the service, which an autistic person might find means having to put on an act. It's tempting to assume that the autistic person needs to learn to act normally, and church is a safe place to practise. But this falls into the trap of trying to fix people who are different. We haven't welcomed what we try to change. We feel welcome when we are accepted as we are, not when we feel we must pretend to be like everyone else.

Here's a case study of someone we'll call Natalie Barnes. Not the nativity in the barn which kick-started the whole shebang, but a woman with an autistic son we'll call Salvador (not the Messiah). Is there a space for them in their local church?

Natalie takes Salvador to a Church of England church in the low Anglican tradition. (The Church of England spans the part of the Christian tradition that has Catholicism on one side and post-Reformation denominations like Baptists on the other. Low churches are nearer to the Baptist end of this spectrum.) Natalie and Salvador's church is a typical example of a very common type of church. There's probably a church like theirs just down the road from where you live.

Let us assume that the church in question is called St Basil's. It was discovered by 'the powers that be' that Basil was deserving of sanctification when it came to light that these days Donald Sinclair, the man who ran the Gleneagles Hotel, on which a certain Mr Fawlty's establishment was based, would have been recognised as having a place on the autistic spectrum, and not simply written off by the Python team as the rudest man they had ever met. Basil, it turns out, was a misunderstood man who actually had a genius for making people welcome.

At church

St Basil's has a congregation of about 300 people who attend one of two Sunday services. This pattern of worship is typical of many churches, with the morning service catering for families and offering Sunday School classes, while the evening service has an adult congregation.

There are a handful of autistic children at the morning service, with Salvador being the noisiest and most active. Of the half a dozen disabled adults who attend the evening service, one or two are autistic.

I join Natalie, Salvador and the rest of the family at a morning service on an ordinary Sunday in September. We enter by a side door in the north transept. The transepts are the 'arms' of the cross-shaped building and the door could be said to be the 'right hand' of the church. This entrance leads to a lobby, where we leave the pushchair, which has transported Salvador's younger brother to church. The lobby also has toilets and a children's play area. We leave the lobby and walk through to the church.

Part of the north transept in the church is a small area with seating, which is enclosed behind and on both sides. The seating faces the part of the church where the pulpit is located. It is possible, while seated in the north transept, to see the person who is speaking, while the rest of the congregation, which is seated in the legs and torso of the church, remain hidden from view. I see clear advantages in placing ourselves in this part of the church, but Natalie has a tinge of regret. She has snuck in by a side door and hasn't said hello to anyone.

Sitting here is, however, an improvement on following Salvador's preference for exploring the balcony. The balcony does have the advantage of being separate from the part of the church in which most of the congregation is seated, but is not a suitable place for children to play. Not only could Salvador fall from the balcony (he has no sense of danger), this is also where the sound desk is located. Salvador's noise makes it hard for the technician to work. It took a couple of months for Natalie to train Salvador to accept not sitting in the balcony.

The morning service begins with singing and prayers. Natalie spends this part of the service chasing Salvador around the building. She does this with her eyes fixed on Salvador, deliberately not looking at anyone else. She feels that Salvador's behaviour, and her parenting, is being watched and tutted over. She might be receiving sympathetic glances but does not look up to check.

When it is time for Sunday School, Natalie takes her children to their classes. Salvador has just turned four. Natalie has agreed with the teacher to keep him in the pre-school class of two to four-year-olds even though he is about to start school (in a unit with autism support). Salvador isn't ready for activities like finding the word 'Nebuchadnezzar' in a puzzle grid. The teacher of the pre-school group happens to be a reception teacher in a mainstream school, who has some experience of teaching autistic children. She plans her classes so she can cater for Salvador, and at the end of each class gives Natalie feedback on how Salvador has responded to the activities. For example, Salvador won't join in a song with the rest of the class, but will turn the music off by playing with the buttons on the CD player. So he watches a music video on a laptop, with one-to-one support.

Each month there is an all-ages morning service, where the children don't have Sunday School, and the whole congregation worships together. This is a short service of 45 minutes, made up of songs with actions, a simple talk which can be understood by primary school aged children, and a short and simple time of prayer. None of this content makes sense to Salvador, who dashes around the church while Natalie chases him.

Natalie told me that she finds it hard that other people just watch her struggle to manage Salvador. They are tolerant of his behaviour but do nothing to help. No one knows how Salvador might respond to someone he doesn't know restraining him, but no one has asked the simple question, 'What can I do?' There is no special skill required to manage Natalie's other children, while Natalie keeps Salvador safe. Instead Natalie receives comments like, 'It's so encouraging that you made the effort to be here' – as if her struggle is there to motivate others on their journey of faith.

Natalie's response to difference and faith

After church, in Natalie's living room, she tells me more about her experience of being a church member with a different child. We began by discussing how Natalie's attitudes to difference developed alongside her faith.

We only woke up to autism in the UK in the 1980s, but it's always been with us, and we have now reached the second generation in which it's been recognised. Autism runs in families as part of a cluster of differences in the way the brain processes information, such as Tourette's Syndrome, dyspraxia and so on. All these conditions can be described as forms of neuro-diversity.

Both Natalie and her son have neuro-diverse conditions. Natalie tells me how she came to accept her own difference, dyslexia. When Natalie was a child, society was even less disability-friendly than it is today. Natalie was failed by the school system, which did not understand her needs, and also by her parents and their church, for whom her thinking difference was something to be cured, rather than celebrated.

As a primary school child, Natalie's parents took her to a Christian healing event in a neighbouring city. She was too young to understand why she had been taken there and remembers the event as something that was done to her, rather than something she was able to make sense of and take part in. In an arena that seated thousands, Natalie was asked to go to the stage at the front of the meeting hall to read aloud from the Bible, to demonstrate whether she had been healed. Her parents went along with this request, so there was no whisper from her mummy, saying, 'You don't have to do this if you don't want to,' or, 'It's OK, I'll come with you.'

These days, prayer is sometimes offered in a more private setting, but in the 1980s prayer was a spectator sport. (I say private, although I have witnessed prayer offered in a transept, during a service, as loud music was played nearby, from the place where the arms cross the body of the church.) The desperate holding on to faith of the post-war years was replaced in the 1980s with wondering how the church fitted into a multicultural society. A sense of confidence in the God of miracles was a popular import, fresh in from the USA.

As a child in the meeting hall, Natalie just felt abandoned by her parents. She left the meeting not cured but emotionally wounded. She had no words to express this so her wound remained invisible to her parents. It was not until she was an adult that she confronted them about the incident. It should be noted that autism runs in families and was not identified in Natalie's parents' generation. We can't know whether their actions stemmed from social conformity, religious conviction, or their own possible social naivety.

The very fact that Natalie's parents had taken her to the healing event left another wound – the idea that there was 'Something wrong with me, and it cannot be fixed'.

Struggling through school, anxious and frustrated, the adolescent Natalie, convinced she was worth less than other people, became very depressed. Teachers with no understanding of her learning needs would casually call her lazy, when she had spent hours on homework that should only have taken minutes. This created a further barrier to learning, and years later still undermined her self-esteem. She remembers an evening from her adolescent life, the feeling of disorientation on finding herself seated at her kitchen table, unable to remember the part of her walk home from school after the bridge she had found herself staring over, wondering what it would feel like to jump off.

It took someone else who had a thinking difference to point out that her negative view of her difference was self-hatred, because how we think is who we are, and the positives about ourselves are part of that difference too.

After leaving school and entering adult education, Natalie encountered a different attitude to learning. A disability learning tutor at college showed Natalie that she could learn if taught a different way, and that there was nothing broken about her: it was society that was broken in not accepting her.

By this time in her life, Natalie's poor self-esteem had led to lifestyle choices that conflicted with the values of her faith, and caused her to blame herself. She had a destructive use of substances, and was involved with emotionally troubled men. Natalie chose to change her lifestyle but her emotional healing came much later. Natalie had a sense that if she laid her issues to rest she would be failing to bear witness to her story. She now feels that she can be at peace with herself, with her past informing her understanding of difference, but not causing her pain in the present.

Faith, difference and parenting

Now Natalie is the parent of a different child. She has a supportive husband and extended family, all fellow church members. But none of these people have expertise in autism or an understanding of difference and faith.

Natalie was adamant that Salvador would have his needs met at school. His autism diagnosis was actively sought and merely confirmed Natalie's suspicions. Yet Natalie's response was grief. She felt that all the opportunities any mother would wish for her child were behind doors that had been slammed shut. Natalie needed to take stock. She doesn't know what Salvador's future will be, but is sure God made no mistake in making him the way he is.

Before Salvador was diagnosed, there were people in the congregation at St Basil's who couldn't understand why Natalie and her husband weren't giving Salvador more discipline. Natalie knew that intervening in Salvador's disruptive behaviour to take him outside would lead to a tantrum, which would be even more disruptive. Natalie wasn't teaching Salvador values so much as watching a pot heat up to boiling point.

When Salvador's autism was diagnosed, Natalie then had to decide how to tell the congregation. Natalie was able to be confident in discussing the diagnosis. She knew what issues needed to be raised to include Salvador. She had herself taught Sunday School, and had experience of working with autistic children before having her own family. She was also sure that her family had a right to be in church, which was not dependent on her children's behaviour.

Natalie chose to tell people she was close to and the staff team, and asked them to pass on the news, so that she didn't have the job of telling everyone and having to do so in front of Salvador and his siblings. She felt that this worked well.

185

However, Natalie says that only a handful of people have moved their thinking beyond Salvador's presence being tolerated to seeing that he and every other member of her family has spiritual needs, including needs arising from having Salvador in the family.

Natalie often copes by arriving late for church and taking her children straight to Sunday School. This cuts out the task of chasing Salvador around the church during the first part of the service. It is not unusual for Natalie to stay with Salvador in Sunday School. There often aren't enough volunteers to cope with him being left in the class (despite a considerable effort having been made to find such volunteers), certainly not regular volunteers, and Salvador cannot be left with someone different each week. On the weeks when Natalie's husband stays with Salvador in his Sunday School class, Natalie takes her turn teaching Sunday School for the classes to which her other children belong. This leaves few Sundays when Natalie hears a sermon.

After Sunday School Natalie avoids further chasing of Salvador around the church by going straight home with her children. So Natalie is cut off from being part of the church herself. She cannot go to an evening service, as this would mean leaving all the children at home with her husband at the time of day when the children are put to bed. Natalie is trapped in this isolation because there are very few people who can babysit her children: handling Salvador is a task for the experienced.

Even when Natalie does hear the occasional sermon (never a whole series on a topic), the teaching at St Basil's addresses issues of the Christian faith in general. Natalie must look elsewhere for resources on difference and faith. Natalie's own learning needs make accessing such resources as there are somewhat tricky. She manages to get to the occasional conference, but as she struggles to parent Salvador effectively and bring him up in faith, she herself is spiritually starving.

When asked at church, how she is, Natalie's reply 'Well we made it here', is all she can manage to say. Natalie is focused on coping with managing Salvador in the moment and can't comment on whether she is free on Thursday for a coffee. So people don't see that she has had a week of having clumps of her hair pulled out, and being bitten, by Salvador. She can't stop and talk about how she is, and has no time away from supervising her children to receive prayer.

Searching for good practice

Where does inclusion good practice come from? Natalie has found herself cast in the role of expert, when she herself is coming to terms with what it means to parent Salvador, whose diagnosis was confirmed only a few months ago. The rest of the community can't know what she doesn't tell them. Natalie must take the initiative and communicate Salvador's needs, as well as her own.

Yet if Natalie were to grow in her expertise, this could be a hollow victory. Across town another family have been trapped in the role of experts. Margaret and Ed are parents to an autistic teenager, Dan. (These are not their real names.) Margaret is an occupational therapist and has professional experience of working with autistic people. Their church employs her husband Ed. They are seen as expert by their church – they are Dan's parents, the autism professionals, the experienced church workers. But Ed has found himself unsure how to play his role in church. What he does as a paid church worker, as a member of the congregation, and as a parent, overlap, with the boundaries unclear to other church members. People are willing to support a family in their congregation with a disabled child, but not help someone do work the church is paying him to do.

Meanwhile, Margaret knows that Ed is on the receiving end of comments about Dan, which are unconnected to his role. These are comments which, had they been made to a family without a leadership role, she would not have heard second-hand.

Disability at St Basil's

Natalie and Salvador are not the only different people at St Basil's. Before we left morning service, Natalie introduced me to Sybil, St Basil's disability coordinator. Sybil told me more about how St Basil's welcomes disabled people. (Sybil is not her real name.)

When Sybil arrived at St Basil's 14 years ago, the Disability Discrimination Act was just about to come into effect. At that time, St Basil's was planning to refurbish their church hall, where the Sunday School class rooms are located. Sybil needed to encourage the church to include step-free access in their plan. The hall was used by parents with pushchairs every week but access wasn't part of the church's thinking.

Sybil started changing attitudes by training the volunteers who greet people as they arrive at services, so that they took an inclusive approach. Sybil is keen for the welcome disabled people receive at St Basil's to be different from the attitude they encounter elsewhere. Inevitably some of the disabled people who are part of the church have had troubled home lives and have poor self-worth. Sybil is keen for the church to be a place where disabled people are involved and where it is recognised that they have something to offer.

Sybil listed activities people could get involved in: being on the team that welcomes people to services – as new people know what it's like to be new; being in a small midweek group where you can get to know others instead of feeling lost in a church with several hundred members; doing the soup run; being in the music group or Christmas choir; working the sound desk; or cleaning. She could certainly keep someone busy.

St Basil's has a midweek group for learning-disabled people. The group is somewhere members have grown in faith. Sybil spoke about a man who came along as the friend of another group member. He arrived wondering what it was all about, commenting that, 'It's not nice what they did to Jesus.' The group helped him to explore faith and after a while he asked for baptism. Now he expects God to act in his life and asks for prayer when he has hospital appointments.

The group is not pitched at the right level for every learning-disabled person, so St Basil's has offered some 'more able' people one-to-one teaching, alongside membership of a mainstream midweek group, which Sybil tells me has worked fairly well.

What other churches do

Natalie also wants me to understand what is happening for disabled people in other churches in her town. After lunch she takes me to the monthly meeting of the Jesus For Me Project (not the project's real name). About five years ago, some parents of children at the town's special needs secondary school (including some parents of autistic children) realised that at the various churches they were part of, they all faced the same issue: their children were welcome but were not being helped to grow in faith. Each child was practically unique in their congregation in terms of their learning needs, so these parents set up a monthly gathering with accessible worship for their children and a support group for themselves.

The project has brought people together from different churches, including some local churches that do not usually join in inter-church activities. The types of church represented are Catholic, Church of England, Baptist and House Church. Working together has been pragmatic, with differences between group members set aside. However, some issues of faith have had to be addressed.

Natalie tells me that for some it is important that Communion (bread and wine representing Jesus's body) is only offered to those who understand the ritual. (This leaves learning-disabled people out in the cold, while the rest of the population assumes that having a few more IQ points means they can fully grasp the mysteries of faith.) The Jesus For Me project has not offered its members communion; they have had sharing meals instead. Another issue was that volunteers from different churches needed to be briefed on when prayer for healing was appropriate.

As the meeting begins, I watch the half a dozen group members settle into the meeting with a choice of two group activities: a craft and a game.

Then there is a story from the Bible. For this adult group, the group facilitator has adapted a Montessori style of Sunday School teaching called Godly Play, which was developed in the

188

USA by Jerome Berryman. This technique presents a story using visual aids, in a manner that encourages deep reflection on simple ideas.

The story is followed by a non-verbal prayer activity: placing a star on a picture of the sky to express thankfulness for creation. Care is taken to ensure that facilitating involvement does not coerce anyone into participating.

The group then worships through songs, with Makaton signs and sung lyrics used together. I'm told that the signing adds a dimension to participation but is not an access need, and that signing is not used in the churches of which group members are a part. Some of the songs were written by Prospects, a national Christian organisation for learning-disabled people. These songs were designed to be signed.

The group also uses other songs that are familiar to members from their church experience. Using familiar songs removes the need for group members to follow words in a book or on a screen. Some attempt is made to avoid songs that are wordy or express obscure concepts. Even so, I witness the group using a song that poetically describes God as keeping snow in storehouses. (There is a thin drizzle outside, about which lyrics are yet to be penned.)

Lastly, the group has an opportunity to share news about what is happening in their lives and the members are offered refreshments. As refreshments are served, the facilitator tells me that the meeting's activities are planned in response to group members' preferences.

I speak to some of the parents. Agnes tells me about her autistic daughter Brigid, who is not verbal. (These are not their real names.) Agnes has been taking Brigid, now a young adult, to Mass each week since she was a baby, so Brigid is an accepted member of the local Catholic church. (Mass is the Catholic word for a Communion service and this is the usual weekly service in Catholic churches.)

When Brigid was a child, Agnes used to take books to church to keep her quiet. These days Brigid does what everyone else does, standing when they stand and sitting when they sit. She doesn't understand why she is standing or sitting at different points in the service, but isn't causing a problem. Agnes is sure that Brigid wants to be in church; one week, when she and her husband were too ill to take her, Brigid kept looking at the clock expectantly at the time they usually set off. The family attends sung Mass each week. Agnes describes Brigid smiling and dancing to the music. Agnes says that Brigid loves music but there is something more in church; Brigid responds with her whole body.

Agnes went through the usual response to being a parent of a disabled child, wondering, 'Why me?' She now sees the world from a different perspective: clearer on what really matters. She also values Brigid's company. Brigid's smiles are not social convention; they are simply a gift. Agnes would like people to see what Brigid has to offer. Brigid's support worker

189

has commented on how Brigid is a delight to be around. She calmly enjoys what she is doing; she can take three-quarters of an hour to eat a sandwich and enjoy every mouthful.

But Brigid is quite isolated. She is the only disabled person in her church, accepted but without peers. At Jesus For Me meetings, she is with other people like herself. Agnes describes Brigid as not relating to others the way non-autistic people do, but nevertheless showing pleasure in being with others. Jesus For Me meetings are somewhere where Brigid isn't vulnerable or intimidated; they're a safe place to be with others. As they approach the venue each month, Brigid recognises where she is and smiles.

Another parent, Ed, talks to me about his teenage son, Dan (the same Ed and Dan as mentioned earlier, with pseudonyms still in place). Dan has complex needs, with attention deficiency featuring alongside his autism and learning disability. For some years, Ed and his wife Margaret taught Sunday School, adapting the content to include Dan. But as Dan reached his teenage years, the class for his age group was no longer suitable for him. For a time, there was another autistic child in the church and the two of them could be taught together, but this depended on the availability of enough Sunday School volunteers.

The church valued learning-disabled people and had a number of midweek social projects that attracted them. The church's café employed some learning-disabled people and staff prayers were accessible. But Sunday mornings were a different story. The worship was unsuitable for Dan. It began with two minutes' silence, which Dan could not keep. Other aspects of the worship were too loud for him. The Lord's Prayer was said out loud by the congregation as a whole and Dan was overwhelmed by everyone talking at once.

Ed and Margaret tried a different Baptist church with Dan and had a very different experience. Ed puts the difference down to demographics. His old church had a congregation of retired people, whereas the new church is made up of members with a wider age range.

At the new church the atmosphere is relaxed, with coffee available throughout the service. People tell Ed and Margaret off for trying to keep Dan quiet and no one minds that Dan loves to drum his fingers on his chair, picking his seat on the basis of the chair's tonal qualities.

In theory the new church shouldn't work for an autistic person. It's rather chaotic. Different people are responsible for the various tasks each week. This is because the church has a transient congregation made up of people who are in town on a short-term basis, like students. Ed thinks this means the congregation is alert to the importance of involving people as soon as they walk through the door, and this welcome worked for his family.

The church offered one-to-one Sunday School for Dan, but he prefers to stay with the adults for the sermon, sometimes playing with the pre-schoolers and their Lego as the sermon is preached. Ed and Margaret are able to teach Sunday School elsewhere in the building, knowing that someone is keeping an eye on Dan. The church meets in a modern building that has a space Dan can use to chill out. But he can also just wander off.

However, the content of the sermon is not relevant to Dan. The sermons are pitched at non-disabled adults. Ed also worries that the preaching is inexpert. It is done by members of the congregation taking turns. Often sermons are preached by people with no training, who have not been Christians for long. Any attempt at accessible teaching for Dan would be provided by these inexperienced volunteers.

Ed has thought carefully about how to offer spiritual teaching to Dan. He is aware that Dan can mimic what happens at church without understanding what he is doing. At home Dan uses the exuberant tone which characterises how people pray at his church. But what he says shows that he is just mimicking others. This stands in contrast to Dan's uncomplicated expectation that daily trials can be prayed about – a simple expectation which challenges Ed to have a more active faith.

When Ed and Margaret have taken Dan to an annual Christian conference, where a special education programme is available, Dan opts for this programme every time. Ed observes that Dan likes to be with others who are like him. Accessible teaching, if put in place at church, would mean one-to-one work, and Ed knows that Dan needs to be with peers.

While Ed feels that the new church is a welcoming place for Dan, where he can experience God's acceptance of everyone, the Jesus For Me Project offers Dan something his church can't: teaching about God that he can access. Ed and Margaret supplement this at home between monthly meetings.

With the Jesus For Me project, the challenge for Ed is to let go and trust others to lead. He's picked up the pieces of other people's mistakes too many times. But Ed knows he has to let go. Ed is aware that Dan has always had parents who have been in leadership roles in church. Dan has mimicked Ed's social script, making sure he says goodbye to everyone present. At the Jesus For Me project, the parents leave their children to have their meeting unobserved. This means that Dan has what all teenagers need, a place where he is not his father's son but his own person.

During the meeting, Ed attends the parents' support group, which he describes as a group of very different characters, who also have very different stances on both theology and church practice. Nevertheless the group has big plans. They aim to create a Christian community for learning-disabled adults of all ages: providing a place of acceptance and belonging; meeting people's social needs; helping learning-disabled people grow in faith; addressing housing needs; and providing meaningful daily activities. But individuals in various churches (not church congregations or leaders) set up the project. It has not become part of the vision of the churches to which its members belong. Finding regular volunteers has been challenging.

The teenagers the project first served are now young adults. They have plans of their own and have taken a step towards independence, with several members having joined different churches from those of their parents.

A local House church (see page 193) has a separate session for learning-disabled people (mainly teenagers), which takes the place of hearing the sermon. This type of church has proved popular with Jesus For Me's young adults.

What next?

After the meeting, I say goodbye to Natalie. She has shown me what difference and faith mean in her life, for her family, in her church and in her town.

The next section contains my thoughts on how to prepare ourselves as support workers to engage with our local churches, to ensure that when we bring an autistic person to church, the church is ready to welcome them. This section is based on personal experience, not research.

What you need to know

Types of church

Sadly there is no type of church that is a ready-made fit for autistic people. Most churches will respond to the needs of people in their congregation. This leads to others with similar needs joining that congregation. At any point, one particular church in a town might be the church that is being the most innovative in terms of disability inclusion. It's a case of nomadic demographic critical mass. Initiatives come and go. All churches rely on volunteers and have limited funds.

That said, there are certain access issues that occur at certain types of church. Catholic, Church of England and Methodist churches use a form of worship called a liturgy. This means that there are set words for the different parts of the service, like prayers; rather than people praying with whatever words come to mind. The wording for the service cannot simply be learned by heart. Each week, the wording is slightly different, reflecting the point we are at in the year. The liturgical year begins in the run-up to Christmas, with reflection on Jesus's birth. It follows the life of Jesus through to Easter with reflection on Jesus's adult life, death and resurrection; and goes on to cover the purpose of the church over the summer months.

It has been commented to me, that repetition with variation is a helpful practice for some autistic people. Through the year, an established pattern responds to the passing of time, with enough familiarity offered to give a context to what is new. However, finding out in advance what precise wording will be used each week is challenging. Each paragraph of the Church of England's service book is numbered to allow it to be slotted in on appropriate weeks. The result is a tome of non-sequential numbered sections that looks as if it was written at Bletchley Park – in order to treat the next prayer as an item of classified military intelligence. Most churches print the wording they are using that week on a handout available on the day. You may need to ask if you need this information in advance.

You may also wish to note which weeks are Communion services, as these services present a social challenge. The Church of England Communion service has the congregation ritually shake each other's hands as a symbol of living in peace with each other. This means that, long after taking a seat and greeting, or not greeting, those among whom you are seated, those around you will offer you their hands to shake. Within the space of two minutes, half a dozen different hands may be offered. Those offering their hands may or may not acknowledge you further, at coffee time after the service. This can be both overwhelming and mystifying for an autistic person.

The wafers used in Catholic and Church of England churches for Communion are usually gluten-free. However, some churches in these traditions and most churches in other traditions use actual bread. Many churches offer an alcohol-free option at Communion. Feel free to ask about this.

Body language is key to accessing Communion in the Church of England. Stance needs to be clear. Kneeling with hands outstretched leads to being given the bread and wine. Kneeling with hands lowered leads to receiving a blessing.

Catholic and Church of England churches are the types most likely to present autistic people with the sensory challenge of incense. (Incense is used in those Church of England churches described as high Anglican, which are close to the Catholic tradition in their practice.) Incense can be overpowering to people who are sensitive to scent. In Church of England churches, it may help to choose seats at the back of the church, away from the central aisle, so that the person you support is not near the places where incense is used.

Other sensory issues can occur in many types of church. Some autistic people like to sit away from the organ, as these instruments are designed to fill a church with sound and can do so quite suddenly.

Stained-glass windows are popular in many types of church and they can create moving patches of coloured light. This is not helpful for reading service sheets, but fun.

Some people at the Jesus For Me Project are part of a House Church. House Churches started in the 1970s as an alternative to other types of church. This type of church takes its name from the fact that early groups met in members' houses. House Churches now meet in bigger venues, like cinemas and school halls. Some venues lend themselves to inclusive worship more readily than others.

There are some inclusion issues that occur at House churches. These issues are not unique to House churches but arise from practices that are typical of this type of church. While somewhat more established than in the early days, House churches can still be characterised by authoritarian leadership, insensitive handling of people, and shouty preaching, which promotes a simplistic and overly literal view of the Bible that can be oppressive in its attitude to some sectors of society, and misguided about issues like healing. It has been known for some members to go as far as advocating exorcism for autistic people.

House churches can also be typified by noisy worship involving singing, clapping, waving hands in the air and dancing. You may have to protect the person you support from criticism for not joining in noisy worship. For example, members may ask someone sitting quietly if they are OK, as if sitting quietly was a very odd thing to do. Or, more worryingly, they may suggest that someone needs to be less inhibited, has an attitude problem and is failing to please God, or even needs to repent of not wanting to join in. House churches have one emotion – this is joy and it's compulsory.

Support workers need to be aware that some ideas presented by churches (of all types) are unhelpful to autistic people. Telling people what to think, and do, does not help autistic people who are inclined to take what they are told at face value and obsess over rules.

No church was designed for autistic people. Those with quiet reflective styles of worship can be somewhat mystical. Sadly, this tends to be the case in the new, so-called alternative worship communities, also known as the emerging church. In this type of church, prayer can be an intuitive emotional activity with ideas expressed in metaphor. This is a shame, as these groups might otherwise appeal to autistic people. They are usually small groups, where people work at building meaningful relationships. They also use styles of worships that appeal to all the senses, involve a choice of activity, and where people can engage in activities at their own pace.

Christian attitudes

At any type of church, you can encounter unhelpful attitudes to faith and disability. Here's a 'map' to help guide you through this minefield.

Blame

We've squashed the idea that parents are to blame for causing autism by withholding love. We withstand the condemning looks of those who think we shouldn't have had children if we knew autism ran in our family. We stand up to those who condemn us for not giving our children enough discipline. We withstand the comments of those who think we are neglectful because our autistic child is not on the (fill in the name of the latest trendy solution) programme, and also of those who, on the other hand, condemn us as pushy, because we fight for our child's educational support. But the Church finds other things to blame us for. The real problem is, apparently, our lack of faith in a cure or the fact that our character needs development – God is testing us; that's if we're not being punished through our disabled child because God is displeased with us.

You recognise the advantages of blame game. Because it's all your fault, the rest of society doesn't have to help you. Let's take things up a level. In church we can blame ourselves and each other, and this lets God himself off the hook of having to do anything. Suffering can't be God's fault – it's too scary.

The church is more comfortable telling individuals to repent than welcoming difference. But if the church joins in the blame game, it fails to take a stand with disabled people for social justice. You may need to point out that the person you support is not the problem. You may need to assure the person you support that they do not need to blame themselves.

Words and pictures

When the Reformation arrived, images were out, and the word of God in our own language was in. Statues in churches were defaced and broken. This was bad news for visual learners, as all the visual aids were smashed up. On the plus side, it did create an uncluttered visual environment.

Our culture stills bears the legacy of the Reformation. As soon as someone can read fluently, they are no longer thought to need books with pictures; learning is through words. So educated adults become fearful of galleries, and feel sure that their response to the pictures will be inadequate. They mutter that art is something for people who don't have proper jobs.

Churches are beginning to look at how all our senses can be involved in worship. If the person you support needs a certain type of sensory experience in order to participate in church, you may need to ask for this to be made available.

Doctrine and images

So the reformation arrived, and images were out. The making of images of God was said to break one of the Ten Commandments. But what's never been disputed is that God's image is all around us, in our fellow human beings; women and men created in God's image.

Many see disabled people as 'cracked mirrors', unable to truly reflect God's image, and so not fully human. I am absolutely sure, however, that God is just like me: autistic. How could the universe be formed and sustained without nerdy-scientist God having counted all the molecules and put them to work in the right order?

We all do this; we make God in our own image. So when we meet someone who is 'not like me', we assume that they can't possibly be like God. This is an emotional response dressed up as a doctrinal issue.

This emotional response is writ large when it comes to autistic people. Christianity is social, a belief system which asserts that it is good to be nice to people. Non-autistics feel rejected by the autistic person who isn't being 'nice', so the autistic person is rejected in return. People can accept intellectually that difference is OK, but they don't feel comfortable with someone who behaves differently. You may hear ideas expressed such as, 'How can you be a Christian if you can't love people?' – meaning 'I feel snubbed by you.'

You might need to point out that if someone can't see God in the person you support, there is something wrong with the way they are looking. (Yes, this does all get rather 'Emperor's New Clothes'.)

Healing

I'm actually in favour of prayer for healing, if conducted sensibly. What disabled person doesn't have a lifetime of exclusion and hurt to address? But…

Neuro-diversity is to be celebrated. People who don't think like the majority of the population have much to offer. Neuro-diverse people also need to be seen as disabled, so that our struggles are recognised and addressed. So what we are saying is that we are disabled but not broken.

The church is getting its head around accepting disability and not making people feel they have to be cured before they can belong. But the church's default response to disability is to seek a cure. Offering an autistic person a cure is offering to turn them into someone else. It's like offering to cure womanhood or black skin. People are disadvantaged by these things but it isn't the essence of an individual person that needs to be fixed, but a broken society.

If there is a sermon on Jesus healing people, or prayer for healing is offered, be ready to keep the person you support from feeling that they ought to be cured or have been forgotten by God if they are not cured.

Social aspects of church

Let's assume the people at the church to which you have taken the person you support are genuinely friendly. There are still some pitfalls to be aware of.

Churches often host social events such as bring and share meals. You may need to help the person you support understand what they need to bring and how to participate. These events can mean eating lunch with a couple of hundred people, including noisy children. They can also be confusing if the person you support has certain foods they avoid. Make sure the person you support doesn't feel obliged to attend social events that won't be helpful for them.

You might need to help the person you support navigate relationships at church. People in leadership roles can be very friendly when in role. But they may not necessarily say hello if bumped into outside the church context.

People may be encouraged to invite others to church. Ensure the person you support can make sense of this, and does not make themselves a target for abuse. They do not have to invite the person they meet at the bus stop on the way home, mistaking this person for a friend.

Sermons on family values make no reference to how people can form relationships; these skills are taken as read. Marriage might be a Christian value but coffee time after the service isn't a speed-dating event. Churches typically have more female members than male. If you support a man to attend church, be aware that there may be several single women in the congregation. They will all be nice and say hello to the person you are supporting, and be far too polite to say directly that they do not want to date him. Be ready to help people be clear, by pointing out that direct communication is not rude, and that leaving someone thinking you might be interested, when you are not, is actually unkind.

Young women can be intimidated by someone who communicates differently; they may not have the experience to be assertive. St Basil's included a middle-aged autistic man who repeatedly shook young women's hands, which some young women found awkward. The church needed to ensure everyone felt at home. As the man's hand shaking was also an issue in other settings, it was addressed by his key worker. You may need to step in as a professional to support church members in addressing social issues that arise for the person you support.

Practical measures you can take

Planning your first visit to church

Find someone the autistic person is comfortable with, and have that person take them to church as often as shift patterns allow. This will enable a strong working relationship to be built with the church. Once identified, this supporter should go alone to a service at the

197

church to which they will accompany the autistic person, to see how a typical person is welcomed. If a church is unwelcoming, the supporter should try somewhere else.

Before taking the autistic person to a service, phone the church. (Most churches have websites with contact details.) Ask who you can to talk to about disability access and then ask them to describe a typical service. You need to know roughly how long it will be, get an outline of the content, find out what parts (if any) are formal, whether the general tone is relaxed or formal, and what kind of language is used. In liturgy, Bible readings and hymns, for example, old-fashioned 'thees' and 'thous' can be a barrier to access. You should also ask how people are normally welcomed into the church. The person you support might be able to go to a newcomers' supper, or might need some other type of introduction.

You should also find out how the person you support can be a full member of the church and have a say in church affairs. You may need to point out that, with the right facilitation, people who communicate differently can share their views.

Plan your first visit. You also need to find out how best to get to the church. Is there a calm way to arrive – easily accessible parking spaces, for example.

And subsequently can the person you support be independent, once they have settled into the church? Are lifts to and from church available?

You may wish to ask for someone to meet you the first time you bring the person you support to a service and show you where the toilets are and where to get a drink.

When you attend with the person you support, ensure that a welcome is extended to them. Some church members may be more at ease trying to convert you than talking to someone who communicates differently. You can simply point out that you are there to facilitate the involvement of the person you are supporting.

It may also be helpful to bring something familiar to the autistic person, like a weighted blanket, to help them adapt to a new environment.

What shouldn't you do?

If a leaflet comes through your door helpfully telling you the times of the service at your local church, then as sure as the stable in Bethlehem has no room for Rudolf, Christmas is on its way. Place the leaflet in the recycling bin, with the flyer telling you that two delicious eggnog-topped pizzas can be had for the price of one. Church will still be there when the Christmas rush is sleeping off its hangover.

Never visit a church for the first time to attend a carol service. Carol services are run by those members of a congregation who have not gone away for Christmas (the B Team), for the benefit of people who do not normally attend church, or at least not that church:

the pews being filled by other churches' A Teams, who have escaped their responsibilities elsewhere in the country. Carol services cannot offer you a typical experience of your local church, and no one you ask will know what in the name of all that's holly is going on.

People who keep rotas are eagled-eyed at spotting new talent. You and the person you support don't have to join any rotas or committees. You are both entitled to have your needs met, not run around trying to either find inclusion solutions or run jumble sales.

You and the person you support are also under no obligation to donate money to church projects. People may be strongly encouraged to make donations by preachers, but the person you support most likely lives on benefits and should not feel they have to contribute, when they can barely afford their rent. You may need to assure the person you support of this. Nor should you feel that the organisation you work for should enter a partnership arrangement with a church.

Resources

Sometimes churches will look to you to help find inclusion solutions. So far there has been more work on access to church for learning-disabled people than for autistic people, but autism is beginning to be addressed, including access for autistic people who are not also learning disabled. This is a brief list of organisations with expertise to share:

- 'Churches Together in [enter the name of your town]': Churches in your area will have a committee that facilitates working together. If a church near you doesn't have any autism experience, they might be able to learn from other churches nearby.

- Denominational headquarters: Every type of church has leadership at a national level. For example, Ann Memmott advises the Church of England on autism inclusion. Her advice has been published on the Internet by Oxfordshire diocese.

- National bodies looking at disability inclusion in church: Some groups work across different types of church; some have their roots in a particular type of church. Attitudes to disability vary:
  - Livability – covers all disabilities.
  - Through the Roof – covers all disabilities (use the UK spelling of 'through' to avoid getting the website of a similar organisation doing work in the USA).
  - L'Arche – a Christian communal living group that welcomes learning-disabled people. Experienced in making worship accessible. Some non-residential work for learning-disabled people in pilgrimages and 'Faith and Light' groups. L'Arche was started in France by Catholics. It works with learning-disabled people of all faiths, and always has.
  - Prospects – produces Christian resources for learning-disabled people.

- Conferences bring together all the people tackling inclusion in churches throughout the country and showcase good practice.
  - Greenbelt worship, led by Lambeth L'Arche, the 2013 conference had a panel discussion on autism and the church
  - New Wine: Has a special needs programme that Dan (not his real name) likes.

Conclusion

I'm sure you've walked past churches and seen a sign saying, 'All Welcome'. This is not simply hospitality; it is a socially subversive statement. By welcoming people who are different, we make room in our heads for a different, deeper understanding of the God who welcomes us all.

I hope that when you go to church you shake it up a bit. I hope that your own hand is shaken.

Reflections

Some of the accounts in this book describe autism-unfriendly settings that are largely beyond our control as health and social care professionals. In situations where government policy, local policy, budget cuts, constant change and marketisation may render the services less than autism-friendly, there may be little we can do to change things, other than make careful use of our vote at election time.

However, Caroline describes the problems encountered in a local church, which is unusual in being an institution where the individual members may be able to exercise significant control. In a church, the congregation themselves can, perhaps, engineer a greater degree of social acceptance and tolerance. Furthermore, the Church is an institution that claims to be based on these principles.

We might reflect on the places where we work and socialise. Even if we can do little about the macro-organisational factors, we may be able to affect the micro-features. Our classrooms, supported living units, face-to-face interactions and public front can all be manipulated and adapted. We should be wary of letting 'macro' problems dissipate the energy we need to address issues on the 'micro' level. Sometimes small changes can make a big difference, and can help turn exclusion into inclusion.

18
Reflections of a nurse
Austin Dorrity

Austin is a learning disability nurse who has struggled to take on board what it means to work with people who have autism. He looks back on the way he worked with some regret. He is honest about his attempts to incorporate his personal narrative into his professional narrative:

> "I had my reputation to think of. I did not want my colleagues to think of me as incompetent and I did not want to show any weakness whatsoever. I wonder how many professionals have found themselves in this position? It could be argued that organisational and professional cultures that do not allow for transparency, or for people to say that something is outside their competence, are contributing to the appalling standards of health and social care experienced by individuals on the autism spectrum in the world today."

This chapter is based on his submission to the autism course at the University of Cumbria. As frequently happens, his learning caused him to reflect on his past practice.

As a volunteer and as a registered learning disability nurse, I have worked with and supported individuals on the autism spectrum for nearly 30 years. This chapter follows my journey to date, recognising events, situations and interactions that have significantly informed my self-awareness, my career and most importantly how I can influence positive outcomes for individuals with autism.

As a young child, I remember feeling scared when I was in the company of people who appeared different to me. My parents always told me that I should not stare at people who appeared different. This resulted in my not looking at them at all and probably ignoring them completely. I believe this added to my fear.

At the age of ten, I was asked if I would help support a group of teenagers with autism on a swimming trip. I said yes, as I did not really feel I could say no, but I was absolutely terrified. The people in the group were older than me; they were bigger than me and I did not know how to behave in their company. This was probably the first time I witnessed what professionals call 'challenging behaviour' or 'expressive communication'. Although I was petrified, I felt the most important thing at the time was not to show my fear. I can look back now and recognise how I avoided the people who were doing what I perceived as strange repetitive behaviours and or loud vocalisations. Instead I focused my attention on the individuals who were quieter, more placid and who I possibly viewed as being more like myself.

Further on in this chapter, I will discuss and explore these feelings of 'fear', as I recognise now that it is only through reflecting on my past emotions and actions that I have been able to increase my self-awareness and inform my practice approach and developmental needs. Over the years, I have recognised fear in other people who are working with individuals who are 'challenging'. I have recognised how they have avoided interactions, hidden their fear and moved their attention to someone less challenging. I believe that this is one of the fundamental reasons why people with autism often experience inequalities in health and social care and widespread discrimination.

Sam

As a teenager, a number of my close friends were volunteers for a charity that supported young people with autism on holidays and days out. I was approached and asked if I would also like to volunteer. Although the memories of my emotions some years earlier with the swimming group came flooding back, I said yes and agreed to volunteer on a week-long holiday. If I am honest, the reason I agreed was not so much about supporting people with autism on the holiday. It was more about socialising and spending time with some of my friends, doing something different. I would never have admitted this at the time, but I am sure I was not the only person with this agenda.

I met the young boy who I had been given the responsibility of supporting for the week. We got on the coach and arrived at our destination, which was a large purpose-built centre in the Yorkshire dales. My anxieties were amplified by the fact that I had been given very little information about the nine-year-old lad, who I will call Sam. Sam did not seem to want to have anything to do with me. He wanted to sit on his own. I kept trying to look at him and talk to him. He didn't like this and he would often start screaming and putting his head into his hands. I found this very distressing, although my main fear at this time was that other, more experienced volunteers would judge me as being incompetent and useless. The more I tried with Sam, the worse it seemed to aggravate him.

I wonder now how many other people have been in a similar situation to the one I found myself in with Sam. I made sure that I did not ask anyone else for help, as this would have shown a weakness in my abilities, and I did not want to be perceived by others as being unable to manage the situation. I can recall a number of occasions during my nursing practice where I have witnessed other people in a similar situation; and their reluctance to hold their hand up and ask for help has often resulted in individuals with autism being wrongly treated, sometimes quite brutally, and very often ignored and left in a state of high anxiety and distress. Unfortunately in these situations, the individuals have often displayed challenging behaviour, which resulted in them being restrained physically and then with medication.

There is a part of me that blames the fact that I was given very limited information on how best to support Sam. However, I recognise that my immaturity, lack of understanding and knowledge, and my fear, were the main contributing factors to my inability to support him effectively and fairly. This makes me acknowledge some of the deficits in services set up to support individuals with autism, as we often have limited information to draw on, support workers are often young and inexperienced, and most importantly they are in such employment as a stop gap and not necessarily as a part of the career.

When I reflect back on the time I spent trying to support Sam, aside from my fears and immaturity, a major barrier was that I did not know Sam. I did not know any of his likes and wishes, what caused him distress and how he liked to be supported when he was highly agitated. Person-centred planning is something that is often talked about, and there are often examples of attempts to implement person-centred planning within the masses of unruly paperwork and documents that seem to surround individuals with autism who are reliant on support from others. I would suggest that these attempts tend to be very limited, due to ignorance or presumptions being made about the person due to discrimination.

Whilst I knew very little about Sam, any effort I made to try and make life easier for him involved me trying things to see what his reactions would be, and probably causing him more distress and confusion through these trial and error methods. I thought if I knew how to maximise shared, two-way communication between Sam and myself, then I would be far more likely to understand the world as he saw it and therefore the things that caused him distress and anxiety. In my innocence, I knew little about communication and probably gave up as soon as I realised that there was very limited verbal communication between myself and Sam. I believe this was a fundamental error. Once I realised Sam had no interest in me, I gave up; I obviously did not know the first thing about autism. Yet I would suggest that it is common within a lot of services for people with autism that support workers do not explore the full range of communication approaches and technologies that are available nowadays.

If I had been able to establish a shared means of communication with Sam, his experience of the holiday could have been made less distressing but I believe I still would not have been able to gather the information I needed, as I did not know what I was looking for. This is why I believe person-centred approaches are limited by the support worker, carer or professional's lack of knowledge; you need to know what you are looking for!

Sam avoiding eye contact with me put up a barrier to communication, and I made unfounded presumptions, which added to the poor support he was receiving from me. Not being able to recognise that Sam experienced and saw the world in a completely different way from me made it impossible for me to connect with his feelings, fears and pain. I can now identify a number of stimuli that led to Sam becoming distressed and anxious: crowded noisy areas like the dining room; the window in the coach where the sun flickered irregularly as we drove through the trees; and the most distressing, which was his starchy pyjamas against his skin.

I knew nothing about autism. I had never heard about sensory difference so I did not stand a chance of even attempting to identify the stimuli that were causing Sam such pain and distress. In my ignorance I attributed his behaviours to him being badly brought up, spoilt and homesick; or I was being prejudiced and discriminatory, not intentionally but through sheer lack of knowledge and understanding.

I now realise that I was not very good at supporting Sam, and I believe that there are a number of people supporting individuals with autism, day in and day out, who are in the same position as I was in with Sam many years ago.

Some years later, I embarked upon my nursing career, three years of university training and exposure to a variety of different practice placements. Upon qualifying as a registered learning disability nurse, I secured a job within a community team, and a number of individuals I was working with had a diagnosis of autism. Unfortunately, by this time I had picked up a bit more knowledge and experience of working with individuals with autism and believed I knew a lot more than I actually did. My little bit of knowledge had the potential to be a lot more harmful than none at all.

People were looking to me as a healthcare professional for help and advice when supporting individuals with autism and I would impart bits of limited knowledge. They hung on my every word and I was in a very powerful yet dangerous position. My reluctance to hold my hand up and say that I was fearful, or that I did not know what to do when I was supporting Sam years previously, had multiplied in my new career. I had my reputation to think of. I did not want my colleagues to think of me as incompetent and I did not want to show any weakness whatsoever. I wonder how many professionals have found themselves in this position? It could be argued that organisational and professional cultures that do not allow for transparency, or for people to say that something is outside their competence, are contributing to the appalling standards of health and social care experienced by individuals on the autism spectrum in the world today.

Paul

Seven reports of self-injurious behaviours (two of which resulted in hospitalisation), three physical assaults on staff, and reports of screaming and destruction of property – this was clearly a man who was very distressed! As the supporting service was struggling to cope with this young man, who I will refer to as Paul, a referral was made to the team I was working in, and I picked up the case. The reason for the referral was that they needed professional help to address the issues highlighted above.

Paul has a moderate learning disability but did not have an autism diagnosis. Concentrating on the issues highlighted, my approach to this complex situation was to complete a functional assessment and analysis of the 'challenging behaviours' reported in the referral as part of a positive behavioural support approach. The positive behavioural support model approach was then, and still is, regarded as best practice when working with an individual whose behaviours are challenging to themselves and others. I felt competent in my approach, and as a healthcare professional I had gained a great deal of experience in using the assessment tool used in the functional assessment process.

Gathering relevant and appropriate information for the assessment proved very difficult. I can now recognise that Paul's support team were at 'burnout' stage, and I believe that they viewed Paul as a problem, as opposed to a very distressed human being who was struggling with many aspects of his life. I felt as if I had a mountain to climb at this stage, as the attitudes of others to Paul were so negative. I knew there was a massive barrier to them embracing a positive behavioural support approach.

On reflection, there were probably similarities to how I had felt years previously when I had volunteered to support Sam. In trying to gain further in-depth current and historical knowledge and understanding of Paul and his life, I was met with extremely scant and negative data from his support staff such as 'he is just evil', 'nothing we can do with him because he has always been the same', 'he should be locked up' and 'I won't be seen out with him cos you can't trust what he might do'. Paul's support team just wanted the problem to go away and were not open to other positive approaches. I understand now why there was such a high turnover of staff within the organisation, and this lack of consistency in Paul's life will have contributed significantly to his distress.

An assessment tool is only a useful medium to gather information if the person using it knows what they are looking for, or what they want to find out. This is something I have realised over time. Unfortunately you do not know what you do not know, and may therefore be unable to gather the necessary data. I was gathering information on potential triggers to Paul's behaviours within his environment. But because Paul did not have an autism diagnosis, I naively did not make any links between his behaviours and issues often associated with autism.

To me, this is a clear example of how I, as a health professional, made an assumption; just because Paul did not have a diagnosis of autism, it did not mean that he did not have autism. We know that there are a high proportion of people with autism without a diagnosis; and we also know that this proportion is even higher for people with a learning disability. I knew this; I learned it during my nurse training; and I had read a number of articles and case studies that highlighted the issues of undiagnosed autism and challenging behaviour. Yet in Paul's case I did not make the connection. I wonder if my inability to think outside the box and take a more holistic approach to my assessment work with Paul was heavily influenced by what I was being told by others. I was told that Paul did not have a diagnosis of autism but perhaps what I actually heard and took from this was that Paul did not have autism. I wonder how many other times I and other professionals have misinterpreted key information in this way.

Many recent inquiries into failings in health and social care have identified issues of communication. Yes, I believe there are reasons why we struggle to communicate, and there are often many barriers in our way, but very often I feel we don't know what information we are looking for and therefore don't ask the important questions. Through not knowing what information we need in order to support someone appropriately, we can often make unfounded assumptions about what we feel would be right for the person, based on our own neurotypical lives and values. How disempowering must this be for a human being who knows what they want to communicate when we do not have the skills and insight to hear their voice.

Regrettably, I can now see that the assessments I carried out and the data I gathered in order to gain a greater understanding of Paul's 'challenging behaviours' were not fit for purpose. My approaches were intrusive by nature, and probably quite impersonal. Through this imposition, I was asking a lot of the wrong questions and I am in no doubt that I will have caused further distress to Paul.

If I were to go back in time, it would not matter if Paul had a diagnosis of autism or not. I would not assume he had autism and I would not assume he did not. I would simply take a holistic approach, with an open mind, and explore all avenues. It is highly likely that much of Paul's distress could have been attributed to how people approached him, his environment, or sensory difference. It is also possible that there were a number of factors contributing to his distress and 'challenging behaviours', perhaps including some underlying unmet physical and mental health problems. In many cases, carers and professionals can become overwhelmed by the complexities of someone's presenting needs and attribute everything to their diagnosis, such as autism. We call this 'diagnostic overshadowing'. To me, it is simply an inability to see the individual as a person, with their own unique thoughts, feelings and needs.

At the time when I was working with Paul, I had a little knowledge of autism and probably made a lot of assumptions, such as 'all people with autism need routine', or 'people with autism struggle to relate to others and socialise'. My little bit of knowledge proved dangerous, as others looked to me for advice and guidance, but my ability to objectively identify Paul's individual unique needs was overshadowed by my generalised and limited knowledge and understanding of autism. I also acknowledge that the long drawn-out assessment process, which failed to achieve positive outcomes, probably strengthened the views held by others about Paul, and made the service and support staff more resistant to future professional interventions.

I remember at the time I felt very critical of the members of Paul's support team and of the commissioned service. I saw them as prejudiced, inhumane and lazy, when they were struggling to support Paul. Now I recognise that the reason for this was that they did not understand his needs and the triggers to his behaviour; therefore they did not have the appropriate knowledge and skills to do their jobs properly. This was not intentional on their part; they were not bad people. Deep down, they wanted to be able to minimise Paul's distress, and support him to achieve a valued and meaningful life. I had the same aspirations and I was also unable to achieve this because of my lack of knowledge and understanding. I thought I knew a lot more than I actually did. I also wanted others to believe that I knew more than they did in order to protect my professional identity.

I see 'protection of professional identity' as a very dangerous trait in myself and in others who are in the privileged and powerful position of supporting people with autism. What is it in us that cannot let others see our weaknesses and why do we go to such great lengths to mask our fears and portray false confidence? Earlier on I talked about my failings as an inexperienced volunteer in meeting the needs of a young boy with autism and how I hid my fears and inadequacies, because I thought the worst thing would be for others to see me as incompetent. I recognise the same responses in Paul's support team and in my own practice as a healthcare professional.

Sarah

A number of years on from my experiences with Paul, I started a new job within an educational setting. My role was as a team leader for the healthcare provision. Reflection has become an essential part of my day-to-day practice and my professional development, and the next story describes a horrific situation that I was able to influence to ensure positive outcomes for an individual with autism, who I will refer to as Sarah. I recognise now that it was only through deep reflection on my past experiences and honesty with myself that I was able to alter such damaging and dangerous practices.

Sarah was 19 years old at the time; she had a moderate learning disability, autism and type I diabetes. It was the first week in my new job. I was still settling in and getting to know people and gain an understanding of the requirements of my role as a nurse within the organisation. My door crashed open and a very red-faced, angry-looking teacher dragged Sarah into the healthcare room. Sarah was screaming and hitting out to try and release herself from the teacher's grasp, making the teacher more determined to hold her.

Sarah was positioned against the work surface in the corner to ensure that she would not run off. 'Look at me, look at me,' the teacher said. 'Look at me, will you? Are you going to have your bloods tested or are you going to be a naughty little girl?' I could not believe what I was hearing and how the teacher was treating this poor person. It became apparent that I was now supposed to go over and perform a finger-prick test in order to ascertain Sarah's blood sugar levels so we could appropriately manage her diabetes. I did nothing. I was horrified and in complete shock. This poor student was clearly petrified. She was shaking, screaming and fighting to get away.

My refusal to play a part in this degrading attempt at a 'health intervention' caused contempt, which was further amplified when I shared my disgust and concerns with the others. It was still my first week, and most of the staff were not talking to me. They did not trust me, as they viewed me as a troublemaker, and we were not getting any data on Sarah's blood sugars, leaving her in a position which was potentially dangerous to her health – not a good start! I felt unsettled, frustrated and powerless.

College was clearly not a positive experience for Sarah. She would arrive on a minibus in the morning and would refuse to get off until she was eventually dragged off the bus and into the building. This seemed to set a precedent for the whole day. Sarah was talked at aggressively, at a very fast pace, using abstract concepts. She was not afforded the courtesy of time to process the information and to respond, before she was hit with another question, louder, faster and even more obscure than the previous one. Someone at some stage obviously thought that attending college would be meaningful and appropriate for Sarah, or perhaps it was just the only option at a time of financial cutbacks in social care.

We talk about empowerment, choice, respect, rights and independence as being the principles underpinning services for people with autism. I could see no evidence of any of this for Sarah, yet she had a person-centred plan – ironic!

Just as in the situation with Paul, those whose job it was to support Sarah viewed her as a problem. I was able to identify this from my reflections on previous experiences. I would suggest that there was some 'overshadowing' here. People knew of her diagnosis of autism and therefore made generalised assumptions about her ability to communicate with and socially interact with others. If people also viewed Sarah's 'challenging behaviour' as part of her autism then they probably felt that there was nothing at all they could do about it, apart from trying to contain and control her as much as possible. Fortunately, and I attribute this to my ability to reflect on previous experiences, I did not see Sarah as presenting with challenging behaviour; in fact, quite the opposite. I saw Sarah reacting and responding to the appalling actions of others, which were challenging to her.

It was important that I recognised that I had two responsibilities: one to ensure that there was appropriate and ethical support for Sarah; and the other, with the wider staff team, to model to them more appropriate approaches. I had a massive task on my hands, to turn things around for Sarah, and at this stage my every effort and movement was being scrutinised and shunned by other staff members in their bid for me to fail. This sounds quite negative but I now believe that they were only doing what I had done previously with Sam and Paul, which was protecting their professional identity. If I succeeded where they had failed, they believed they would be perceived as incompetent.

All too often in the past, and I am sure it has been the same for others, I have come across a problem and I have wanted to just fix it overnight. I know now that this rarely works; and if by chance it does, the likelihood of any changes being sustained is minimal. I have learned through reflection that you need to understand what the problem is at present, identify an aim or ideal and chip away at achieving it, whilst motivating and enabling others in the process. I recognise that this approach is less threatening to others, as it does not directly undermine their approaches; instead it gives shared ownership of a new direction and way of working.

At the start of the process I did not inform others of my intentions, as I knew I would be met with hostility and my efforts would be sabotaged. I started off by making time to talk to Sarah and open opportunities for two-way communication. Sarah was reluctant at first, and it took a considerable amount of perseverance on my behalf for her to respond to my invitation to communicate. I gave careful consideration to my approach. I did not force eye contact, as I had identified that this was something that distressed Sarah. I was also careful not to invade her personal space or overload her with questions and demands. I chose my words carefully and avoided the use of abstract concepts. Over time, our relationship developed, Sarah learned more about me and my role; and I was able to gain a huge amount of understanding about her, her feelings, her fears and some of her perceptions.

Part of my aim with Sarah was to find a more humane, legally viable and ethical way of monitoring her blood sugars, as it was becoming increasingly apparent that her diabetes was being poorly managed and this was having a detrimental effect on her life. By developing communication channels between myself and Sarah, I was able to establish a clearer understanding of her cognitive abilities and her ability to process and retain information.

It had been apparent when I first met Sarah that she was not consenting to having her blood sugars tested. We talked at length about her health and, whilst Sarah could not grasp the physiological complexities associated with unstable diabetes, she knew what it felt like when she felt poorly and she was able to understand the link between checking her blood and preventing her feeling poorly. I call this part of any intervention the 'enabling capacity stage', and it can require a host of different approaches to communication. These are essential in empowering people to gain control of their own health and all aspects of their lives.

Key members of the support staff team within the college had started to emulate some of the approaches I was using with Sarah. They used some of the words I was using; they were standing back and not pushing their own need for eye contact; and I could see that their relationships with Sarah were developing in a positive way. I remember feeling delighted with the progress Sarah and myself had made. I knew we still had a long way to go but the attitudes of others were slowly starting to shift. Sarah was now viewed as a human being, with the same unique needs as anyone else, as opposed to simply being a problem causing everyone frustration.

Sarah now arrived by minibus in the mornings and she was greeted by a member of her support team. They would say, 'Good morning, Sarah.'

Sarah would say 'Hello.'

Sarah would then be asked how she was and if she wanted to get off the bus. This was very empowering for Sarah, and set a precedent that gave her control over the rest of the day.

Once in college, Sarah would come by herself to my room. She would stand in the doorway and shout 'Hello.' I would turn and smile at her and ask her if she wanted to come in. She knew she had the choice not to if she did not want to. I would ask Sarah who I was and she would say that I was a nurse. We would have a chat and I would ask her why it was a good idea to have her bloods checked. Sarah would explain that it was to help keep her happy and healthy, and to stop her from becoming poorly. I would then ask Sarah if she wanted me to test her bloods. Usually she said she wanted me to, and other times she would say 'Not yet'. Sarah knew that I would never force her to have her finger pricked to test her bloods, and she knew she had control over the situation.

Other people in the college started seeing Sarah in a different light. Those perceptions I had witnessed in my first week (where people viewed her as a naughty problem child) had faded away. People now saw Sarah as a confident young woman, who was in control of key aspects of her life. Sarah's physical health also improved and I feel that by means of us taking a truly person-centred humanistic approach she did become 'happier and healthier'.

I have taken some pleasure in reflecting on my experience of working with people with autism to date, although memories of some situations make me cringe and think: 'Did I really do that?' Being transparent about my own practice has brought its own rewards, and to that extent I have found it quite liberating. If I can be critical of my own practice, then I am more likely to allow others to be critical of how I practise without feeling threatened. A greater sense of self-awareness should provide solid foundations for personal and professional development.

Exploring my own behaviour has allowed me to gain a greater understanding of how and why others behave in certain ways when they are met with unfamiliar and uncomfortable situations. If I was avoiding situations and not holding my hand up for help and support, then why should I expect others to?

I now know that those who are in the privileged position of providing support for people with autism need appropriate guidance, support and training. In my present position, I need to ensure that I remain approachable to others and that I do not judge them for their lack of competence or experience. As a professional in a position of power, you become a role model to others. It can be very easy to abuse this power by not listening to others or by minimising any problems. I have come to realise that in-depth knowledge of autism is not an essential requirement when supporting a person with autism. If you have a genuine desire and drive to improve the life experiences of others, through genuine honest reflection you will seek to find the knowledge and approaches that are uniquely required by each and every individual you have the privilege to support.

Reflections

Austin is very honest in reflecting on how wrong his practice has been in the past. This is a challenge to us all. We might identify times when we got things right in the past. We might also identify times when we got things wrong, and think carefully about how such mistakes might be avoided in the future. Are our interventions mostly positive in outcome and, even better, improving?

Section 6
Conclusion

19 Reflections on these stories

19
Reflections on these stories

During the years of my involvement with the world of autism, I have heard many accounts from people with direct experience of living with autism. These stories have touched me in a profound way. Understanding developments in theoretical autism knowledge is clearly essential to anyone working in the field, but there is another facet to understanding, rooted in reflection on the nuances of living with autism. For me, this learning has been the richer of the two. The accounts selected for this book have all resonated deeply with me. They have lingered and re-emerged in quiet moments. They have refused to go away. They have challenged my neurotypical misconceptions about autism. They have challenged my notions of professional practice. They have challenged my superficial knowledge of what it is like to live with autism and other people's response to it.

I offer these brief personal reflections on the themes that suggest themselves to me. You, the reader, will probably have your own reflections to make, and it may prove interesting to compare our perspectives.

All-pervading

My main impression from reading these accounts is that the issues of living with autism are overwhelming. The challenging environments, professional interactions, disruption to life and exclusion are life companions – the 'drip drip, nag, nag' of problems is there every day for the people whose stories are contained in this book. Every hour, every day and for the rest of your life, autism is a key feature. When the experiences are negative, then the negativity and challenge become all-pervading. Richard was overwhelmed by impenetrable administrative systems, to the point of going into meltdown. Cornish was overwhelmed with sensation on his first day at school, due to his sensory difference.

Cornish describes the anticipation of each day of his school life as being as fear-inducing as it was for the passengers on the second plane to hit the Twin Towers on 9/11. He expected to die of fright! Andy describes being picked on by the same individuals all through school and then on the college course he attended. The same individuals were also in the Scouts, and even when he went to town those same individuals were waiting. The only escape from those who persecuted him was his bedroom. School overwhelmed Samuel and Christopher.

For Amber Leigh, the fact of autism existing in the family defined her entire childhood. Her relationship with her parents, her home life, her life at school and her sibling relationships were all forged in that same fire. KatyLou feels as if she is in a nightmare each day, full of guilt, with the future extremely uncertain. She describes a sense of helplessness, waiting for whatever unpleasant surprise is round the corner. Her son faces overwhelming problems now, but what happens when she dies?

When the problems are all-pervading, it can be very difficult to know what to do about them. KatyLou feels helpless and unable to control the future. Andy has no idea how to stop the lads bullying him. Cornish describes being just swept along in the tide of events, with 'horror awaiting'. Julia Clifford is well aware of the problem she has understanding what others want, and she has to face this lack of understanding every time she is with others. Similarly, Christopher does not know what others expect of him. Thomas had no idea of how to meet the social expectations of the university drinking society. Samuel and Christopher do not know how to fit in with their peers.

The everyday can become virtually impossible. Gay found it impossible to attend the mother and toddler group because of the amount of eye contact. Lois finds it difficult to simply visit town with her children; holidays are extremely challenging too. Getting on with people at work and socially is a big problem for Thomas. Caroline describes the difficulty of attending church as a family. Andy, KatyLou and Cornish have all had their dreams crushed by their experiences and see no way out.

When we neurotypical professionals enter the lives of people with autism, we 'visit'. This visit takes place from a place of neurotypical safety and afterwards we return to it. We are visiting a world in which the autistic person struggles all day and every day – for a whole lifetime. We dip in and out, but for that person there is no escape. On one level, this is an obvious point, but it begs the question of whether we act in a way that suggests that we *do* understand. Austin observed professional staff behaving as if they really did not understand this at all. He also has the insight to acknowledge that he has been guilty of this too.

One of the key lessons for me is that sensory difference is not just an inconvenience; in certain environments it can be totally debilitating, as it is so overwhelming. When someone is constantly plagued by background noise, it is easy to imagine that we professionals are just one more bit of background noise. However, we are often a bit of background noise with the unusual power to punish, control and intervene. If this is the case, we need to intervene in a state of heightened consciousness, considering the *real* impact that we have on the lives of others.

Cornish and Christopher have no idea what others expect of them. As professionals, are we just adding to that sense of confusion about expectations?

Negative impact of services

In most of the accounts in this book, a consistent theme emerges: We practitioners, and the agencies who employ us, are a big problem at times. So many of the stories describe a lack of empathy from professionals.

Many of the stories describe impenetrable systems. Richard struggled to navigate employment support systems; Cornish, Thomas, Christopher, Samuel and Andy struggled to make sense of what was required in educational systems.

KatyLou, Lois, Tina and Tracy describe individual practitioners who were not helpful or did not have the knowledge to be 'experts'. Tracy had to cope with the distress of seeing her son go into meltdown because the nursery did not implement a routine.

Sometimes the impact of services can be so negative as to constitute abuse. We have all become familiar with the depressing parade of abuse reported in children's homes, learning disability services and elderly 'care' homes. Gross examples, such as sexual abuse, violence and starvation/dehydration, are easily understood as abuse; presumably few people would disagree with this label. The abuse suffered by Amber Leigh's siblings falls into this category. Being made to eat one's own vomit would, one hopes, be seen as vicious abuse by most people. Cornish being slapped by a teacher is now seen as abuse, although teachers hitting children was countenanced at the time.

However, some of the practice that was experienced as abuse is more hidden and nuanced. Cornish and Thomas left school with post-traumatic stress syndrome and have received counselling to help them cope with life. Presumably their teachers had little idea of the effect of their practice. The new generation of school leavers, Christopher and Samuel, describe what they experienced as abuse. It is easy to assume that any slight felt by people with autism is due to their own sensitivities. We neurotypicals might suggest that the slight is unintended, trivial or even a joke. Christopher and Samuel offer good examples of this. However, the slight is perceived and it is therefore real. It is important that we do not impose neurotypical standards. This situation could be likened to the kind of comments that were made by men before sexual harassment was acknowledged as a real issue: 'Don't be so sensitive, love. I was only joking.'

The abuse suffered by people with autism, and the number of professionals who are perpetrators of that abuse, is a shocking aspect of these stories. Although these accounts include some barely credible examples of abuse, for legal reasons it has not been possible to include two accounts that demonstrate the most severe abuse.

Resilience

I find the resilience of these writers inspirational: Christopher, Cornish, Andy, Thomas and Richard attempting to gain access to work and education despite setbacks and abuse; Lois, KatyLou and Gay struggling with the already difficult task of raising their families; Lois knowingly adopting a child with special needs, having already experienced the reality of life with autism. I am not sure I would have had the resilience and stamina to fight as they have done – against what must have seemed like overwhelming odds. Christopher and Samuel have attempted to negotiate higher education despite big problems in statutory education; Richard is still pursuing work; Andy has stuck with it and built a life for himself that includes marriage. Cornish came back into education despite the abuse and trauma he experienced at school. I remember him shaking with fear when he attended the autism course; yet he has gone on to lecture on autism.

Several of the authors in the book, as well as those of the chapters I could not include, describe lives fraught with problems and yet they have chosen to put themselves in a position of advocacy for others in a similar situation. The sad thing is that so often they need to play this role of advocate as a support against unhelpful services or professionals.

People with autism have to be resilient to survive but at the same time can show a lack of resilience when it comes to certain issues. For example, Richard struggled with the day-to-day insanity of public services. Many readers will recognise the frustration of working for statutory services, with their apparent lack of logic, political directives, unclear purpose and lack of focus, but perhaps neurotypicals find it slightly easier to cope with these issues.

Richness

I find the world of autism intriguing. Having the privilege of peeking into this parallel universe feels like an opportunity to take an oblique look at myself. The people I have met in the course of this work, many of whom have contributed to this book, have enriched my life in ways that I would not have been able to imagine before I engaged with autism. It would not be overstating the case to say that my work with Cornish, Thomas, Andy, Julia and Lois has radically altered the way I think and behave.

Archita, Tracy and KatyLou describe the gifts their children have brought them. Those of us who are parents know the all-consuming nature of this role, which brings a rich return that we may not have anticipated before having children. Perhaps being a parent of someone with autism can be a deeper version of this experience?

Amber Leigh told her story to colleagues on an autism course. These colleagues told me of the deep respect they felt for Amber Leigh, as most were not aware of her past. She has since gone on to raise a family, using rich lessons learned from her own upbringing.

Accommodation

Gay's life is a prime example of successful accommodation. Having a partner who gives her space to be autistic has been sufficient to sustain a long-term marriage. Lois describes how important it is that her boyfriend accommodates the differences she and her children display in their behaviour. She thinks she is lucky to have found him.

These two successful examples are both in the realm of personal relationships. Similarly, all the parents describe accommodating their children's differences as being the only way to survive. However, it is a completely different picture when we consider accommodation in services. Most of the authors describe problems arising from lack of accommodation in this context. Systems quite simply do not make reasonable adjustments. Richard was not accommodated in work or job seeking. Julia Clifford does not think that neurotypicals are very ready to forgive her autistic transgressions. Schools had major problems in accommodating Thomas, Cornish and Lois's children. Tracy's son was not initially accommodated but then, with some simple changes, a successful outcome was achieved. Christopher, Samuel and Andy found that higher and further education struggled to accommodate their differences. Cornish challenged me to accommodate him both as a student and a lecturer in higher education. Similarly, Thomas, Julia and Lois have been colleagues and, again, only *they* can say how successful we were. One day I will pluck up the courage to ask!

Caroline describes how even the church, an organisation with an avowed intent to accept all comers, struggles to accommodate people with autism. She is going on to research this issue.

Gay describes how people do not accommodate her fear of eye contact when she attends meetings, for example. Having been present at some of these meetings myself, I realise I may have been part of this problem for her. It is very easy to slip into the default neurotypical need for eye contact when talking to someone. I have been told that my eye contact can be quite intimidating for some neurotypicals! When talking to Gay, I have found myself looking at her eyes, and have had to make a conscious effort to break that contact.

Anger and resentment

Many of the writers feel anger and resentment about some aspects of their lives. Some of this anger runs very deep and has persisted over many ears. Professionals and services are often the cause of anger. KatyLou feels deep resentment about poor advice she has been given by 'experts'. Cornish is very angry towards his teachers and the educational system. Samuel is angry with school, teachers and fellow students. Christopher is angry with those who label him. Julia is angry with people who have been unkind to her. Lois, Samuel and Julia are angry at being patronised. Thomas, Andy, Samuel and Christopher are angry at being rejected, at times in very cruel ways. KatyLou and Amber Leigh describe ways in which their families were rejected for 'containing' autism.

Amber Leigh is angry towards her parents and siblings, and guilty about feeling this way about her family. KatyLou feels grief at the loss of her dreams for her sons. Cornish feels grief for the loss of a life. Amber Leigh has grief for a lost childhood.

The implication for professionals is that, when engaging with individuals and families, we are visiting a setting that is already infused with anger. If that anger is towards services, then (as agents of the 'guilty' organisation) we can be seen as legitimate targets for that anger and grief. Anger is not rational, and we might expect distrust and dislike. Professionals are just the last in a sequence of those who have let them down. It is not (necessarily) personal. The positive aspect of this is that when professionals *do* get it right, they can become very significant figures. Andy, Julia, KatyLou and Lois all report getting important, positive support.

Isolation and exclusion

Isolation and exclusion are problems at some point for most of the writers in this book, and yet not wanting to be included is a wish at other times. Julia and Cornish see themselves as separate and do not demonstrate a great wish to be included. They are happy with their own company.

We professionals often strive towards integration and inclusion but perhaps we miss some of the nuance here! It could be that the inclusion being sought is access to work

219

or education, for example, and not always to social engagement. Most of the authors report social engagement that includes bullying, ridicule, judgement or rejection.

Perhaps social inclusion is important, without there necessarily being integration or relationships. Thomas has told stories about his work experiences as a software designer, where he was happy to be left alone to get on with his work and not have to engage with the office banter and politics. Cornish describes the nightmare of playtime on his first day at school. He and Thomas say that integration in school left them with post-traumatic stress disorder. Andy hid in his bedroom playing on his Xbox and listening to rock music. He dreamed of finding 'another place', a world featuring touring cars that he was skilled at driving and where people did not judge him. Cornish looked back to his early childhood, when he was happy in his 'bubble'. It was crude attempts to include him that led to harm. Inclusion can feel like a trap. Cornish felt trapped at school for ten years; Amber Leigh felt trapped in the family home. On the other hand, being excluded can feel like a trap; Andy felt trapped in his room.

Cornish has challenged groups of professionals to explain why they are so committed to inclusion. We neurotypicals value inclusion very highly and seldom appear to ask ourselves why. We don't appear to like loners much. I find it interesting to watch news reports unfolding after horrific crimes. By the second day, it is usually reported that the perpetrator is 'a loner', and neighbours will say things like 'he kept himself to himself'.

Sometimes people will want to make social links. Thomas has often attempted to gain access to social groups. Despite not having autism, Amber Leigh feels alone in the family. She also feels isolated and separated from her peers – she is the one with the 'stupid' brother. Samuel felt isolated from his peers because he did not 'get' their jokes.

A common feature of the accounts in this book is the extraordinary effort people have to put in just to pass muster. This leaves me with an overwhelming respect for the effort people have to make to meet neurotypical expectations. These expectations are complex and irrational, and the authors tell us how poor we are at accommodating their differences. How often do people with autism end up as victims of bullying, despite making their best efforts to meet our neurotypical standards?

Sense of self

People with autism are frequently subject to labelling and assessment. The consequences of this can be devastating to one's sense of self. Gay describes being assessed as 'having an absolute lack of warmth'. I would imagine this to be a damaging label to be given. It is also one that makes no real sense. The use of the term 'absolute' suggests something scientific, something we can measure; we might talk of a temperature of 'absolute zero', for example. 'Lack of warmth' suggests to me a snake or a lizard! A person's 'warmth' is subjective and probably partly determined by the other person in the transaction. We might wonder what the professional writing this report thought they were doing. For me, telling someone that they have 'an absolute lack of warmth' borders on abuse. To do it from a position of power, as a professional, can be seen as abuse of power. As professionals, we need to be careful in our choice of words, and conscious of the impact these might have on a person's sense of self.

Christopher eloquently describes the pain of having the label and feeling trapped by it. For Christopher, it is the simple fact of having a label, and not the particular choice of words used, that is the problem. It is difficult to know what might have been done to make this any better for Christopher; perhaps the most we can do as professionals is be mindful of these possibilities. Meanwhile, both the Julias found the label helpful in understanding who they are.

These stories contain a lot of negative self-images. Julia Clifford thinks she must have been a 'horrible child', when in fact all she is telling us is how her autism manifested itself when she was younger. Christopher thinks he must be a violent person and takes the blame for problems he has had with others. He describes hitting a boy who kicked an injured pigeon. He used the story to illustrate his aggression, whereas I would see it as a demonstration of his compassion and sense of justice. KatyLou and Tracy describe their performance as mothers in negative terms, and the mums in the church felt harshly judged.

A sense of being different, with no idea of what to do about it, is a problem for several of the authors. Christopher, Thomas and Samuel have tried to fit in but have had limited success. Thomas feels rejected as a human being. He was traumatised by the experience of not being accepted as a member of the university social group.

Samuel believes that others think he is not as good as them. Andy knew that he was seen as different, and believed that getting his driver's licence would solve the problem. He was upset at being picked on and thought it happened because he was not in 'their type of group'. This suggests a real sense of separation and of being different. He was also aware that having support in class marked him out. Neither of the Julias knew 'what was wrong with them' in early life and were relieved to find out what the problem was. Some of the authors described a fragmented sense of self. Cornish felt as if he was disintegrating. Samuel excluded himself from the 'getting to know you' session because he assumed he would offend someone without knowing what he had done. He described feeling inferior to the rest of the group.

Amber Leigh felt like an afterthought. As a daughter, she felt very low in the pecking order and that her needs were not a significant part of the family agenda.

The profound nature of the barriers people face

Luke Beardon, an established author and activist in the field of autism, suggested to me an interesting definition of the triad of impairments. The triad is the basic bit of knowledge about autism for diagnosis. It suggests that the impairment is located in the person – in terms of flexibility of thought, language and communications and social and emotional competence. Beardon suggested that the true triad of impairment is education, social services and health. The problem is therefore located outside (rather than inside) the person. In other words, it is the statutory services that disable the person. Whilst intended as a tongue-in-cheek device for teaching, this definition has something critical to say about the true location of the problems faced by people with autism. The barriers people face are external, not only in the statutory services (as suggested by Beardon) but in most situations in which the person with autism interacts with the neurotypical world. Readers familiar with the social model of disability will probably recognise this idea; disability is a result of external factors, not a quality in the person.

There are many examples of such barriers in these accounts. Caroline describes how the church was designed to make people feel unworthy; there was a barrier that was meant to undermine the sense of self of individuals in the congregation. Support services also present significant barriers – such as daytime meetings for parents who have children; the dependence on 'experts' for diagnosis; and the autism label being applied, whether you like it or not. Schools, workplaces and social security systems appear to be unable to accommodate differences in most of the accounts in this book. Archita suggests that the curriculum itself is a barrier to children with autism. Julia Clifford had problems with the way exam questions were worded, which led to her significantly under-achieving at school.

Another barrier faced by people with autism is the reaction from other people. Caroline reported that Salvador's mum was being watched throughout the services. Every other author describes reactions from others, which range from mocking to abuse and bullying. As children and young people, Christopher, Cornish, Thomas and Samuel experienced physical abuse and assault.

222

Another common experience is that the agenda is usually set by neurotypicals. Archita, Thomas, Cornish and Samuel describe how the school curriculum is a problem for people with autism. Caroline describes the order of service and church layout as not being autism-friendly. On the other hand Amber Leigh, a neurotypical, described how the family agenda was dictated by her autistic siblings.

What we do as professionals

Do we over-technicalise autism? There is a plethora of formal approaches to working with autism, some of them trademarked and sold. These all have their place and can demonstrate great success. However, a theme that has emerged for me after marking so many accounts of successful professional practice is that the solutions can be elegantly simple. The successful outcome in the 'Spiderman' story, described in the first chapter, rested on the manager's ability to be consciously empathic.

Andy's progress appeared to be helped by having someone to listen to his story properly, although that came about by accident. This accident changed the course of his life but it is unlikely that services would have come up with this solution. Another key part of his support was having a helper to learn to socialise; in other words, a 'mate'. Samuel thinks the best support he could have is someone to help him socially at university. KatyLou wants support that is simply 'human to human'. Thomas wants Christian acceptance for who he is. Cornish wants proper recognition of the advantages that come with autism. Julia Clifford knows she needs simple prompts with daily routines. Richard needed simple guidance at work.

Professionals not listening was a key problem for KatyLou, Lois, both Julias, Tracy, Kate and Gay. Austin acknowledged that, as a professional, he had not always listened. I realised that my listening was not deep enough with Cornish. It is worth remembering the thoughts of Christine Mayer, which were quoted in the Introduction:

If you are going to work with me, you have to
listen to me.

And you can't just listen with your ears,
because it will go to your head too fast.
If you listen slow, with your whole body,
some of what I say will enter your heart.

I think this is a key message to take from these stories. Are we truly listening and hearing? Do we have the skill to hear, through our neurotypical perspective and filter? I guess we would all claim to be non-discriminatory and yet so many of the authors feel discriminated against, and a depressing number of times they feel discriminated against by health and social care professionals. We should afford the same cultural sensitivity to people with autism as we might to someone of a different ethnicity, country of origin or sexuality. After all, Temple Grandin, a woman with autism, describes herself as 'an anthropologist on Mars'. That really sums up how alien she finds the neurotypical world; it is as if we are from a different planet to her. Cornish has expressed a similar opinion.

To cross this divide of perspective requires extraordinary sensitivity. Yet, rather than being sensitive to this difference, the act of diagnosing individuals runs the risk of pathologising autism. Julia identifies the sexism in diagnosis, something we can all be aware of. Despite the fact that this issue has been known of for a number of years, the old figures of male preponderance persist. Finally, we should be careful how we describe people in assessment. Being described as 'having absolute lack of warmth' was a very damaging experience for Gay.

A theme that emerges from several of these accounts is the level of detail in the sameness required to get through the day. My view is that much of the detail I have seen in care plans and routines is at neurotypical level and really not sufficient for a person with autism. The problem, yet again, could be the apparent impairment of imagination suffered by the neurotypical.

Amber Leigh, KatyLou, Richard, Samuel, Tracy, Lois and both Julias described professionals who simply did not listen. The account that cannot be included for legal reasons will probably prove to be a case of criminal lack of listening.

People should have control of their own narratives. Andy's story was a good example of how powerful this sense of ownership could be. However, it is probably the case that very few services would pay for the time required to do this well. One interesting aspect was that Andy actually took over the interview. He was not addressing the questions raised by the research; he was saying what *he* wanted to say. In a typical assessment, the professional will have perhaps half an hour to go through a list of assessment questions (or person-centred guidelines, depending on the agency). Thus, the service controls the agenda.

The final point for me is the individuality expressed throughout these stories. The fact that each person's experience and manifestation of autism is individual is perhaps a truism. On the other hand, this chapter has listed some common themes that have

224

emerged for me. We are all faced with the challenge of balancing the common themes against each individual's uniqueness. Good luck to all who try.

Postscript

There were two stories I was not able to include in this book. Both were stories of extreme problems and one will probably become subject to legal proceedings. A feature of the writing process for some was that old anxieties, traumas and fears were brought to the surface. Another feature for some was a sense that things are getting worse in the current climate. Benefits being cut or removed, services being taken away and jobs being scarce all contribute to a bad situation looking significantly worse for some of the writers. As professionals supporting people with autism, we have limited power to do much about this. We can act as advocates for the people we support, rather than be simple officers of an agency. We can also carefully use our voting power and ask ourselves which party will cause least harm to those in our society who are most vulnerable and least powerful.

Resources

Bibliography

ASPECT Consultancy Report Executive Summary (2007). A National Report on the Needs of Adults with Asperger Syndrome, compiled by Luke Beardon and Genevieve Edmonds.

Attwood, T. (1998). *Aspergers Syndrome: A Guide for Parents and Professionals.* London: Jessica Kingsley

Attwood, T. (2009). The Pattern of Abilities and Development of Girls with Asperger Syndrome.
http://www.tonyattwood.com.au/
http://www.aspergerfoundation.org.uk/infosheets/ta_girls.pdf

Baron-Cohen, S. & Bolton, P. (1993). *Autism: The Facts.* Oxford: Open University Press.

Bogdashina, O. (2004). *Sensory Perceptual Issues in Autism and Asperger's Syndrome.* London: Jessica Kingsley

Bogdashina, O. (2006). *Theory of Mind and the Triad of Perspectives on Autism and Asperger Syndrome.* London: Jessica Kingsley.

Brown, J. (2010). *Writers on the Spectrum: How Autism and Asperger Syndrome Have Influenced Literary Writing.* London: Jessica Kingsley.

Dahl, R. (1995). *Lamb to the Slaughter and other Stories.* London: Penguin Books.

Department of Health (2006). 'Better Services for People with an Autistic Spectrum Disorder: A Note Clarifying Current Government Policy and Describing Good Practice'. London: HMSO.

Eastoe, G. (2005). *Asperger Syndrome:* My Puzzle. AuthorHouse UK.

Faherty, C. (July/August 2002). 'Asperger Syndrome in Women: A Different Set of Challenges'. *Autism Aspergers Digest.*

Frank, A.W. (1995). *The Wounded Storyteller.* Chicago: The University of Chicago Press.

Frith, U. (2003). *Autism: Explaining the Enigma.* Oxford: Wiley Blackwell.

Gerland, G. (2003). *A Real Person: Life on the Outside.* London: Souvenir Press.

Hagland, C. (2009). *Getting to Grips with Asperger Syndrome: Understanding Adults on the Autism Spectrum.* London: Jessica Kingsley.

Hawkes, H. (2009). *Asperger's Syndrome: The Essential Guide.* Peterborough: Need2Know.

Marshall, F. (2004). *Living with Autism.* London: Sheldon Press.

Mee, S. (2012). *Valuing People with a Learning Disability.* Keswick: M&K Update.

Moorehead, J. (4 June 2008). 'It's not just boys who are autistic'. *Guardian* newspaper.
http://www.theguardian.com/lifeandstyle/2008/jun/04/women.familyandrelationships

Nichols, S. (2009). *Girls Growing Up on the Autism Spectrum.* London: Jessica Kingsley.

O'Brien, J., O'Brien, C.L., & Jacob, G. (1998). *Celebrating the Ordinary: The Emergence of Options in Community Living as a Thoughtful Organization.* Toronto: Inclusion Press.

Vermeulen, P. (2001). *Autistic Thinking – This is the Title.* London: Jessica Kingsley

Williams, D. (1996). *Autism: An Inside-Out Approach.* London: Jessica Kingsley.

Wing, L. (2002). *The Autistic Spectrum.* New updated edition. London: Robinson.

Suggested further reading

This book mainly focuses on first-hand accounts by people with autism. The following are other first-hand accounts that offer opportunities to develop a deeper understanding of the lived experience of autism.

Attwood, T., Evans, C.R. & Lesko, A. eds. (2014). *Been There Done That Try This. An Aspie's Guide to Life on Earth*. London: Jessica Kingsley.

Flora, C. (1 November 2006). An Aspie in the City. *Psychology Today*, p.2.
http://www.psychologytoday.com/articles/200611/aspie-in-the-city

Gerland, G. (1997). *A Real Person: Life on the Outside* (trans J.Tate). London: Souvenir.

Grandin, T. (2006). *Thinking in Pictures*. London: Bloomsbury Publishing.

Higashida, Naoki (2013). *The Reason I Jump: One boy's voice from the silence of autism*. London: Sceptre.

Jackson, L. (2002). *Freaks, Geeks and Asperger Syndrome*. London: Jessica Kingsley.

Jansen, H. & Rombout, B. (2013). *AutiPower! Successful Living and Working with an Autistic Spectrum Disorder*. (trans K. Lemmon). London: Jessica Kingsley.

Lawson, W. (2000). *Life Behind Glass: A Personal Account of Autism Spectrum Disorder*. France: Lavoisier.

Lawson, W. (2001). *Understanding and Working with the Spectrum of Autism: An Insider's View*. London: Jessica Kingsley.

Milton, D., Mills, R. & Pellicano, E. (2012). Ethics and autism: where is the autistic voice? Commentary on Post *et al*. *Journal of Autism and Developmental Disorders*. [Epub ahead of print].

Perner, L. ed. (2012). *Scholars with Autism Achieving Dreams*. Sedona, Arizona: Auricle Books.

Santomauro, J. (2011). *Autism All Stars. How We Use Our Autism and Asperger Traits to Shine in Life*. London: Jessica Kingsley.

Sinclair, J. (1993). Don't mourn for us, *Our Voice*. Volume 1 (3). [online] Available from
http://www.autreat.com/dont_mourn.html

Williams, D. (1996). *Autism: An Inside-Out Approach*. London: Jessica Kingsley.

Useful websites

National Autistic Society (NAS):
http://www.autism.org.uk

NAS Webinars:
http://www.autism.org.uk/webinars
(Key topics include Women and Girls, PEERS, PDA, Positive Behaviour Support)

Personal perspectives from people with autism from Health Talk Online:
http://healthtalkonline.org/peoples-experiences/autism

Personal perspective from Dean Beadle:
http://youtube.com/deanbeadleuk

Research Autism:
http://www.researchautism.net

Network Autism:
http://www.networkautism.org.uk

This website was created by a social worker who has a child with autism:
http://www.autism-help.org

A family share their experiences and their son's progress:
http://www.thepeacefamily.force9.co.uk

Links to autism resources:
http://www.autism-resources.com

Tony Attwood's website:
http://www.TonyAttwood.com

Patient voices in online podcasts:
http://www.patientvoices.org.uk

> Filling the void: Martin Lawrence:
> http://www.patientvoices.org.uk/flv/0177pv384.htm

> Just Jack: Liz Askew
> http://www.patientvoices.org.uk/flv/0080pv384.htm

DVDs

Nottingham City Asperger Service (NCAS) with Nottinghamshire Healthcare NHS Trust. (2011). *Being Different: Living Life with Aspergers Syndrome*. £14.99 + VAT.